PRAISE FOR EDWARD LEE

Buttermilk Graffiti

Named a Best Food Book of the Year by *Smithsonian* and Book Riot

"Part adventure tale, part memoir . . . Don't hit the beach without this remarkable book in your bag." **—Fine Cooking**

"Beautifully written." **—NPR**

"Captures what the nation's melting-pot cuisine is today."
—*Food & Wine*, **Staff Favorite**

"Conjures writers as diverse and compelling as Alexis de Tocqueville, M.F.K. Fisher and Anthony Bourdain . . . powerful, poignant, and timely."
—*The Atlanta Journal-Constitution*

"Lee peels open the layers of what it means to be American today. . . . [*Buttermilk Graffiti*] contains a level of awareness that's often missing from chef memoirs. . . . Lee is just as well-read and reflective as master of the genre Anthony Bourdain, but he brings a fresh take to the food travelogue."
—Eater

"Raw, gritty . . . Each chapter in *Buttermilk Graffiti* presents a new adventure."
—*Richmond Times-Dispatch*

"A tapestry of American cuisine . . . Lee's elevation of the often anonymous people behind the food we eat speaks to his concern with not just style, but substance." **—Los Angeles Times**

"Lee is consistently willing to dive into unfamiliar places and challenging conversations to get stories that haven't yet been told, and the reader emerges from Buttermilk Graffiti richer for his efforts."
—*The Christian Science Monitor*

"Excellent . . . a sweet and heady mélange . . . Lee celebrates unexpected confluences of cuisines while refusing to be limited by definitions of 'authenticity.'" —*Publishers Weekly* **(starred review)**

"[Lee] points out the essential role that both immigrants and longtime settlers play in the food we eat. . . . A heartfelt and forward-thinking book."
—*Kirkus Reviews*

"At a time when America's melting-pot culture frightens so many citizens, Lee finds hope and joy in visiting ethnic communities all across the nation's breadth." —*Booklist*

"Altogether eye-popping . . . *Buttermilk Graffiti* is a timely and important work that reminds readers that America's melting pot is alive and well in the most unexpected places. And, that we *all* belong." —*New York Journal of Books*

"A great romp of a read with humor and poignancy and—for people who love food—a page turner." —*Edible DC*

Smoke & Pickles

Named a Best Cookbook of the Year by the *Washington Post*, the *News & Observer* (Raleigh), *Time Out New York*, and more

"Compelling." —*The Washington Post*

"Inventive . . . bold." —*The New York Times Book Review*

"Fascinating. If you're a bedtime cookbook reader, this one will have you up past midnight." —**TheKitchn**

"Inspired, sophisticated . . . This book is likely to leave you feeling very hungry and never bored." —**New York** *Daily News*

"A mix tape of Southern and Asian ingredients . . . Between the strength of [Lee's] recipes and his natural knack for storytelling, we've dog-eared the bejeezus out of this book." —**SouthernLiving.com**

"Comforting soul food massaged with Korean spice and garlic . . . a very tasty blend of cultures." —*The Austin Chronicle*

"Deep, soulful, and utterly honest." —*Charleston City Paper*

"Inventive and exciting . . . an irresistible collection for any adventurous home cook." —*Publishers Weekly* **(starred review)**

Edward Lee

Buttermilk Graffiti

A CHEF'S JOURNEY TO DISCOVER
AMERICA'S NEW MELTING-POT CUISINE

ARTISAN | NEW YORK

The Library of Congress has cataloged the hardcover edition as follows:

Names: Lee, Edward, 1972– author.
Title: Buttermilk graffiti / Edward Lee.
Description: New York : Artisan, a division of Workman Publishing Co., Inc. [2018]
Identifiers: LCCN 2017051428 | ISBN 9781579657383 (hardcover : alk. paper)
Subjects: LCSH: International cooking. | Lee, Edward, 1972—Friends and associates. | Cooks—United States—Biography. | LCGFT: Cookbooks.
Classification: LCC TX725.A1 L346 2018 | DDC 641.59—dc23
LC record available at https://lccn.loc.gov/2017051428

ISBN 978-1-57965-900-4 (paperback)

Cover and interior design by Raphael Geroni
Cover photograph by Ken Goodman

Artisan books are available at special discounts when purchased in bulk for premiums and sales promotions as well as for fund-raising or educational use. Special editions or book excerpts also can be created to specification. For details, contact the Special Sales Director at the address below, or send an e-mail to specialmarkets@workman.com.

For speaking engagements, contact speakersbureau@workman.com.

Published by Artisan
A division of Workman Publishing Co., Inc.
225 Varick Street
New York, NY 10014-4381
artisanbooks.com

Artisan is a registered trademark of Workman Publishing Co., Inc.

Published simultaneously in Canada by Thomas Allen & Son, Limited

Maps appear courtesy of the following individuals and institutions. pp. vi, 45, 156, 192: New York Public Library Digital Collections; p. viii: U.S. Geological Survey; pp. 10, 84, 120: Shutterstock; p. 26: Lowell Historical Society; p. 64: City of Dearborn Heights Archive, c/o Dearborn Heights Libraries; pp. 101, 174, 270, 292: David Rumsey Map Collection (davidrumsey.com); p. 139: Alabama Department of Archives and History; p. 211: Geography and Map Division, Library of Congress; p. 229: Houston-Galveston Area Council; p. 249: University of Wisconsin-Milwaukee Libraries

Printed in the United States
First paperback edition, February 2019

10 9 8 7 6 5 4 3 2 1

> *These are the blazing days*
> *and you are asked to love*
>
> —Rebecca Gayle Howell,
> from "A Calendar of Blazing Days"

TO DIANNE, who is my strength,
my heartbeat, my magic

TO ARDEN, who whispers to me the best stories ever

And to anyone who has ever crossed an ocean
to plant a seed

CONTENTS

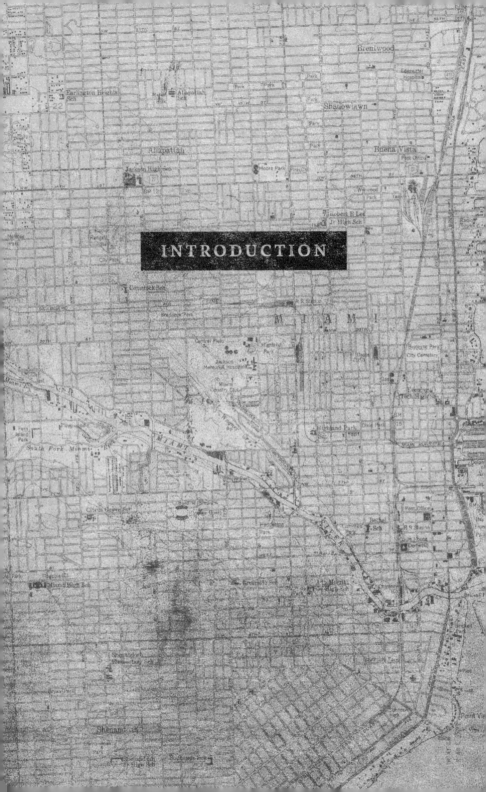

INTRODUCTION

ONE OF THE MOST FASCINATING COOKBOOKS I OWN is a small spiral-bound booklet called *Favorite Southern Recipes*, published in 1937 in Lexington, Virginia. It is a collection of recipes with no introduction or headings; no author's name is given. The recipes appear in paragraph form, are sparsely worded, and are written in a mechanical tone that assumes the reader has a working knowledge of the kitchen. The booklet includes recipes for everything from Crumb Pudding to Welsh Rabbit to an odd but delicious breakfast dish of eggs poached in milk. At the bottom of the table of contents is a sentence that reads, "Some of the recipes in this book were copied from Mrs. Robert E. Lee's book of recipes in her own handwriting."

Though I don't doubt that Mary Anna Custis Lee was a competent cook, I'm also pretty sure she had a good deal of help in her kitchen. *Favorite Southern Recipes*, having been produced after her death, does not give credit to anyone else. The only indication of who might have been responsible for the recipes is the small black-and-white cover photo depicting an elderly African American woman in a servant's outfit: a dark collared shirt, white waist apron, and mobcap. She is standing stiffly in front of a white picket fence. The look on her face is empty, haunting. She is not smiling. Nowhere in the booklet is it explained who she was or why she is on the cover.

I've thought a lot about this nameless woman. I've thought about the stories she could have told us. What if the cookbook had been written in her voice? What if she had been allowed to tell her story through the recipes that were most likely her inventions? It would have made this booklet more than just a collection of recipes; it would have given us a rare window into the life of a slave. Sometimes, when I read the recipes, I get a glimpse of what her life might have been like. When a recipe for corn pone tells me to mix water-ground cornmeal and cold water into a mixture that can be worked through the fingers, I see *her* hands working the batter, not the hands of Mary Anna Custis Lee. I hear *her* voice telling me to fry the oblong bits of corn pone—she would have been too busy to bother with measurements—a little at a time in a skillet with hot oil or lard. I see pots of collard greens and okra tomato stew simmering on the stovetop. I imagine pies cooling in a cupboard and pickles being preserved in jars. I wonder if she had children, and if they helped her in the kitchen. I see her imagined life, both tragic and uplifting, told through nuggets of the corn pone as they fry in the skillet.

Today's cookbooks are much different from that slim booklet from the past. They not only give the name of the author but tend to focus on his or her narrative. This says a lot about who we are as a culture now; we care about the person behind the recipes. For us, it is important to know as much about the cook as we do about his or her dishes. Cookbooks are living traditions. They reflect back to us who we are, as individuals, as a culture. It was the French gastronome Jean Anthelme Brillat-Savarin who first wrote, "Tell me what you eat and I shall tell you what you are." I can modify that to fit our modern times: show me your *recipes* and I can tell you who you are.

When I wrote my first cookbook, *Smoke & Pickles*, back in 2013, I reflected on this idea a lot. It was a two-year process, writing that book. To research it, I read hundreds of cookbooks—everything from Apicius to *Mrs. Beeton's Book of Household Management* to Edna Lewis's *The Taste of Country Cooking*. For that book, I wanted to create recipes for the home cook, but I also knew I had to tell the story of how I had gone from being the child of Korean immigrants in Brooklyn to a Southern chef in Kentucky. It's an unconventional story, and I knew it would be an important one to explain why I cooked the food I cooked. You see, I would not be the chef I am today without the influence of both my heritages: my Korean childhood in Brooklyn and the traditions of Southern food I've learned to love. Because my life has been an improbable journey from Canarsie to Kentucky, an unlikely coupling of Korean and Southern cuisine, I am fascinated by other unlikely couplings that make up the narrative of life in America.

The title of this book, *Buttermilk Graffiti*, is poetic shorthand for my life. Buttermilk is the iconic ingredient of the American South, one that I not only learned to cook with but grew to love. Graffiti is the art form that first inspired my identity, the thing that connects me to the memories of my youth in Brooklyn in the 1980s. Each word by itself is important but one-dimensional. When they come together, though, they become the full story of who I am. If my food were just one or the other, it would be fine, but it wouldn't be as uniquely layered.

While I was on tour for *Smoke & Pickles*, I visited a lot of places. It was the first time I got to experience this country on a rigorous schedule, visiting city after city, day in and day out. I could be in Milwaukee one day and then New Orleans the next, and with each new town, I saw the culture of America unfolding before my eyes. The experience gave me a perspective I'd never had before. There were many lonely nights spent in airport bars or walking unfamiliar streets, and it was during that tour that the seeds of this book germinated. I ate great food everywhere I went, but more than that, I listened to beautiful, unlikely stories told by people from many walks of life, stories that were not necessarily about food but that helped me put what I was eating into a greater cultural context. I think about the town of Lowell, Massachusetts, and the Cambodian immigrants who are creating a lasting influence on the city's cultural and culinary landscape. It is a fascinating example of the American dream and a new American cuisine that is cropping up all over small towns everywhere. But that story of Cambodian immigrants is incomplete without the tale of an Irish boxer who fought his way out of the poor tenement housing projects to become a local legend and owner of the best bar in Lowell. On the surface, the two stories have nothing to do with each other; but to me, they are inseparable. They give texture to a time and place in America where we are witnessing one culture give way to another. Just as my life has been an unlikely progression from graffiti to buttermilk, I see the soul of a city like Lowell linked by a boxer and a chef of Cambodian cuisine. The connection may not seem evident at first, but it exists and will forever shape the history of Lowell.

I cannot eat a dish without wondering who cooked it and what her story is. For me, the discovery of a great dish is not the pinnacle; it is just the beginning. The fun part is figuring out how a cook creates a dish, and why. Was she out of the ingredient called for in a recipe and improvised? Did he embellish a dish plucked from a childhood memory? There is always more to the story than the ingredients on the cutting board. These stories, I believe, are the building blocks of a new American cuisine, one taking root all over the country.

I love food made by immigrants. Not only is it delicious, but it often has all the elements I look for in a recipe: simplicity, resourcefulness, frugality. More important to me, though: it is often made by those whose voices have been overlooked. I've met a lot of immigrants along my journey through the food world, and they all had a story to tell. Some were new to this country; some could trace their American lineage back hundreds of years. All of them, however, have contributed to the evolving story of American cuisine.

THIS BOOK IS THE STORY of American food. It is a recollection of people and places that help paint an image of where we came from and where we're heading. So much of what we think of as "traditional" American cuisine is being challenged. We are witnessing a reshaping of the food landscape, and it is thrilling to some, obscene to others. And that is when it becomes interesting to me—when that tension between two vastly different cultures creates something new.

The story of American food is one of transformation. Any international cuisine changes once it lands on the shores of America. I am reminded of my own family's journey to the United States from South Korea and how important it was for my parents to protect their culinary identity in a world that was foreign and often bewildering. But they also had to improvise with unfamiliar ingredients that were readily available to them: tomatoes, eggplants, and new varieties of cabbage and spices. I'm fascinated by this raw instinct to preserve. I'm less interested in what my parents' food looked like back in the mother country than I am in what happened to it once they'd brought it to Brooklyn and it had to coexist with that of other cultures, when their kimchi had to be made with Jamaican chili powder instead of Korean chile flakes.

The intersection of food and culture happens in strange and beautiful ways. In the book, I travel to places such as Clarksdale, Mississippi, where I meet a pair of Lebanese sisters who sell wigs and make cabbage rolls, and a nightclub owner who sells contraband whiskey. I would never have thought that these two worlds could collide, but in this Mississippi Delta town, they do.

In Paterson, New Jersey, I learn about the multilayered melting pot of Peruvian food while chasing the ghosts of retired soccer players. In Montgomery, Alabama, I challenge a pair of sisters who run a soul food restaurant to a Korean food–eating challenge.

THE WORDS *AUTHENTICITY* AND *TRADITION* are bandied about a lot in the food world. *Authenticity*, which we often use when defending our narrow culinary views, can be a hindrance, a means of exclusion, a distortion of history. Whenever a cookbook exhibits the tagline "Authentic recipes from the American South," I always ask myself, What South are you talking about? Pre-colonial South? Plantation South? Post-colonial? Post–civil rights movement? Paula Deen's South? The immigrant South? All are part of the complicated history of the South. None can claim a true authenticity. *Authenticity* is a word I rarely use, and one I never give credence to. *Tradition*, though, is used to describe nostalgia. It is a sister to *authenticity*, and yet wholly different. We are nothing without our traditions. Our identities are formed from them. I have never been conflicted about the beauty of the traditions my family follows. I still eat Korean rice cake soup on New Year's Day, as was the tradition in my house when I was growing up, and I also love Thanksgiving dinner with all the trimmings. I cherish the importance of passing along both these rituals to my daughter.

The danger with tradition is when it is given authority, when it demands "authenticity." Words such as *true*, *genuine*, and *real* will then quickly enter the discussion. These words reek of a sanctimoniousness I've never thought belonged in the food community. My kimchi bologna sandwich is just as tasty as your mortadella muffuletta, and your tofu cacciatore is just as good as your mother-in-law's version from Tuscany. In the short but incredibly rich history of American food, we are all writing our own encyclopedia entries. Yes, we naturally gravitate toward what is popular, what dominates culture, but I want to fill the voids in between. I want to help tell the stories that have rarely been told.

ONE UNTOLD STORY from my childhood is not about food but it shaped me as a person and, eventually, as a chef. It is about a forgotten graffiti artist named Smith, who eluded the law for a decade in New York City. He started out as part of a duo with his brother, David Smith, who went by Sane. Together, they were Sane Smith. The two were ubiquitous in

New York City in the 1980s. Before there was Banksy or Shepard Fairey, there was Sane Smith. The brothers covered the city like a plague. At first, they were unspectacular, just two writers among thousands of derelict kids throwing up paint on the city's walls. But these two were competitive with each other. What started out as a hobby soon became an arms race between the brothers. Sane became more artistic and complicated in his tags, while Smith turned his "art" into a relentless mission to tag his name on every surface across the five boroughs. Rumors began to swirl that Smith was not one person but an army of minions—it seemed impossible that he could be in so many places at once. The average New Yorker on his way to work probably did not notice Smith tagged up on every corner of the city, but the tags were everywhere: on park benches, subway tunnels, tenement roofs, scaffolding high above the Brooklyn Bridge. His message was clear: graffiti was never about being the best; it was about dominating in a way that made others throw their Krylons in the air with a sigh of defeat.

As a young, aimless teenager, I followed Smith pretty obsessively, while I tried my hand at tagging. I admired his relentlessness. I wanted him to explain to me how his world worked. But I never found him. I never ran into him on a cold, damp night, tagging a pristine wall. Sane died in a mysterious subway accident. The city cracked down on graffiti and Smith drifted off into obscurity. I exchanged my own Krylons for a set of kitchen knives. They were the same thing to me. The kitchen was just another place to paint anonymously. After all, throwing up a tag that hid one's identity was not so very different from being a nameless, faceless line cook pouring sauce onto pretty plates of food in the kitchens of trendy restaurants. And maybe nameless, faceless line cooks are not so different from the nameless maid gracing the cover of that booklet of Southern cooking that sits on my shelf. Yes, she was anonymous, but that does not mean she loved her food any less.

This connection between graffiti artists and that Southern cook brings me all the way back to my present-day life, in Louisville, Kentucky, where I continue to ask myself where I belong in this long, winding narrative of Southern food.

RECIPES COME TO US from all parts of a culture, not just its cuisine. This is why your Polish grandmother's cabbage rolls are the best—because they come with a story that often has nothing to do with the rolls themselves. Perhaps she got the recipe from *her* grandmother, so when you make them, you feel a connection going back five generations. It's why my grandmother's *kalbi jjim* recipe reminds me of how she used to darn the

A NOTE ABOUT THE RECIPES

You will quickly notice that the recipes in this book are not accompanied by photos.* This was done on purpose. I want you, the reader, to trust your instincts and cook the way I know you are capable of. Having a recipe published with an accompanying photo is a pretty modern invention. We have been following recipes without photos for centuries. When we don't know what the end result is supposed to look like, the imagination is allowed to roam free and we come up with our own conclusions. Pictures are excellent guides, and can give you a goal to aspire to, but they can also have a negative effect. If you make a dish and it doesn't look exactly like the photo, you might feel a sense of failure. I don't want that. None of these recipes are restaurant-style dishes, so the accuracy of plating is less important than the taste of the food. I want you to pay attention to the aromas, flavors, textures, to the feel of the food in your mouth. Don't worry if what you make doesn't look good enough to be on the cover of a magazine. If it tastes good, you've succeeded.

---

*Having said that, if you really want to see what the dishes look like, you can find pictures of them at chefedwardlee.com or on Instagram @chefedwardlee.

holes in my old socks while her stew, slowly braising on the stove, filled the house with a sweet and salty aroma. Ingredients are finite but recipes go on forever. And every recipe is linked to a story. Beneath the surface of any recipe is a complex tale of history and family, of time and place.

Take out a piece of paper and write down your current favorite foods. Maybe you can rattle off five or six. Now close your eyes and remember the dishes you ate long ago, when you were a child. Now think about the foods you love that were introduced to you by your spouse, your friends, your colleagues, or even your travels. The list gets longer. Now go back and attach a story to each one. Perhaps bruschetta reminds you of your first trip to Rome. Or a hot dog reminds you of being with your dad at a baseball stadium.

It is in those stories that you will find the flavors and textures of who you are, and where you will find your story. *If you really want to know someone, you have to eat what he has eaten.* The story of your favorite foods is your culinary memoir, not a nameless collection of recipes. And that story will be part of the bigger story we all tell every time we turn on the gas and put on a pot to boil. It is the story of American food.

CHAPTER 1

PILGRIMAGE FOR A BEIGNET

WHILE THE REST OF MODERN SOCIETY BUCKLES under the weight of its morality, we'll look to New Orleans to teach us how to live with equal parts temptation, sin, and redemption. Here, excess is a ritual. Indulgence, like the humidity, fills your lungs.

New Orleans is a port city, founded by the French, ruled by the Spanish, bought by the Americans, and culturally impacted by West Africa, Afro-Caribbean descendants, Germans, Sicilians, and Irish. It is the most racially and culturally evolved polyglot city in America, a flawed but seductive utopia. If I lived in New Orleans, I probably wouldn't last long. There is too much temptation for me. Even today, it seduces the young, from tourists to professional derelicts, all of whom wind up on the banks of the Mississippi searching for their idea of hedonistic abandon. For all the French Quarter's predictable, groomed debauchery, there is still a dark underbelly that awakens in the wee hours, when the college kids have vomited up their Hurricanes and gone home for the evening. This is the New Orleans I know well. A tawdry hangout on Bienville Street is where I often end up. If Jezebel is behind the bar, she'll fix you right up.

There are still places in New Orleans that don't exist on any map. These are the places where you can feel the tensions of being in a harlot's town.

I go to New Orleans once or twice a year, mostly for charitable events. It is one of my favorite cities, and I've watched in amazement as it has continued to flourish after Katrina, when many doubted its survival. There are definitely parts of the French Quarter I avoid because they get so congested with tourists, but the lovely thing about New Orleans is that even the tourist traps are great. Galatoire's and Antoine's are delectable places to have lunch. And I don't care how many tourists I have to fend off to get to Acme Oyster House; it is one of the liveliest joints in town. People who don't know me don't realize how rare this is: for me to seek out the most touristic spot in town. For example, I wouldn't be caught dead eating in Times Square, and most deep-dish pizza places in Chicago are just not that good, but I'll proudly stand in line for a beignet at Café du Monde, which is possibly the biggest tourist attraction in NOLA.

If you haven't been to Café du Monde, it is a sprawling operation with an indoor café on one side and a large outdoor patio that buzzes under a large green-and-white canopy. It is busy all day. The line starts at the window for beignets and stretches around the patio to the street. You have to get there right when it opens to avoid a long line. I've been there over a dozen times, but I can't tell you what's on the menu because I always order the same thing: a plate of beignets and a cup of chicory coffee. If it's too noisy inside the café, I'll take a walk around Jackson Square. I usually end up by the Mississippi River, where I'll just gaze out at the water.

Less than a five-minute walk from Café du Monde, you can find a historic home where William Faulkner spent a brief period when he was young. He was here only about a year and half, but it had a lifelong effect on him. He would go on to write some of the most praised Southern Gothic novels of the twentieth century, centered on the rural culture of his Mississippi roots, but it was here in New Orleans where he met his literary mentor, Sherwood Anderson. Faulkner lived at 624 Pirate's

Alley, writing what would become his first novel, *Soldiers' Pay*. In one of his later books, he remembered New Orleans as "a courtesan whose hold is strong upon the mature, to whose charm the young must respond." New Orleans is a city you must visit when you're young and foolish but return to when you're wiser and still searching for dreams.

For all Faulkner's timeless stories, his lasting contribution to literature was not his descriptions of rural Southern life but how he could bend the concept of time. His novels blend memory and desire in ways that defy the rules of chronology or logic. You're so busy trying to follow the plot that you forget to lose yourself in the beauty of the rambling words spitting across the page like watermelon seeds strewn about a dirt porch after a feast. It is a powerful way to tell a story, even if it confuses the reader on the first go 'round. Some stories are so tragic, so burdened with generations of shame and history and lies, that it's impossible to tell them in a conventional way.

Some recipes are like that, too. Ask any aging matron for a Creole recipe, and you'll get a circuitous answer—that is, if she even gives you the time of day. I have been foraging around for a good beignet recipe for years, only to get meager crumbs of anecdotes here and there. Recipes for beignets involve, by and large, the same ingredients: flour, fat, leavening, and a deep fryer. It's the technique that differs. Every person I ask has a personal technique he swears by. It's not that one is better than another. I've tried half a dozen techniques, and all the recipes pretty much come out tasting the same. The recipe is easy. I can tell you how to make beignets in sixty seconds. But like any good tale, the point of it is not what happens at the end; it's how you get there. Every time I hear a story about the beignet, it's a little bit different. And it's that narrative that makes the taste more satisfying. It's memory and love with a pinch of hyperbole.

The story of my beignet is tied to Faulkner. I was a senior at NYU, taking a class on Hemingway and Faulkner. As part of my thesis paper, I made a trip to New Orleans. Conveniently, Mardi Gras was right around the corner. It was the first time I'd traveled south of Virginia and the first long road trip of my youth. I convinced a friend to join me on my pilgrimage to Pirate's Alley, where I found an uninspired exhibit: a typewriter sitting on the desk where Faulkner apparently got drunk and disturbed the neighbors. The clerk gave me a souvenir bookmark. And that was it. My friend and I arrived on a Saturday, met two girls (on whom we'd spent all our money by Sunday), and come Monday, we were broke. We would be leaving on the morning of Fat Tuesday, with just enough gas money to get home, but before we left, I had my first beignet ever, at Café du Monde. I stood in line with the other tourists, sweating alcohol. My friend was in the car leaning on the horn. He'd had enough of New Orleans. He blamed me for the girls who'd cost us all our money; he wasn't in the mood to talk. I got back in the car, and he pulled away. Slowly, I chewed through a bag of beignets while powdered sugar gathered on my chest. We didn't start talking again until we were almost to Atlanta. It didn't matter to me: I was thinking about Brandi the whole time.

I MET BRANDI in New York City in 1992. To pay for my college tuition at NYU, I worked at the Big Apple Diner, on the corner of Twenty-Eighth and Madison. I knew my way around a kitchen, so a diner gig was easy money for me. The breakfast shift was all I had time for. After all, I had classes to attend. Every morning, I'd arrive at work around 4:30 and light the ovens' pilot lights. I'd mix the pancake batter and muffin mixes. Next I'd drain the sliced potatoes from the night before and start chopping vegetables for the home fries. I'd receive the bread and bagel deliveries, and bring stacks of eggs to room temperature in preparation for the breakfast rush that started at 6:15 a.m. on the dot. Later, I'd show up for my Latin class wearing a T-shirt stained with margarine and blueberry muffin mix. Everyone else in the course came from private high schools and were on their way to law school. I had to recite my conjugations while enduring what I was sure were their glances of pity and revulsion. I started to bring a clean oxford shirt to change into before class.

The Big Apple Diner could never keep a breakfast cook. I soon understood why. Yes, I did most of the prep work alone, but the work wasn't so bad. It was the neighborhood I hated. Today it's called NoMad, and the blocks are lined with high-end restaurants and boutique hotels, but there was a time when those streets were so bad that even the police stopped patrolling them. For decades, the neighborhood between Greeley Square and Madison Square Park was a large swath of no-man's-land littered with defunct luxury hotels. If you listened closely, you could hear the ghost of the last proud bellman dropping a shiny coin in the pocket of his frayed uniform. In the early twentieth century, this was the opulent Theater District, and these lavish hotels were the toast of the town. When the Theater District moved farther north, the hotels floundered, and by the 1970s, they were mostly bankrupt and evacuated. The city had the brilliant idea of converting them into low-income housing for the homeless and mentally ill, and they became known as welfare hotels. The Martinique, which once boasted Circassian walnut wainscoting and gold tapestry panels, became an incubator of drug selling and prostitution, its walls teeming with rats and roaches. Homeless families lived in squalor and fear as drug dealers, pimps, and gangs took over the neighborhood. There were other hotels, places with lofty names such as the Prince George, the Latham, the Carter. If you lived in New York City at the time, you avoided this pit of human travesty. For decades, the city turned its gaze away from the problems there, while its downtrodden residents suffered like animals.

The neighborhood wasn't so bad during the day. There were enough office workers walking about to give the streets a sense of normalcy. But in the hours before dawn, it was a lawless place, dangerous and unpredictable. In just a few weeks of working at the diner, I had gotten mugged, threatened with death, spat on, and accosted with a prosthetic leg while walking to work. Inside the restaurant, things were better, except when vandals threw bricks at the windows or tried to steal my bread delivery.

I got to know a lot of the prostitutes who ate there; we called them
hookers back then. They came into the diner at around 5:00 a.m., looking
for an egg sandwich or a hot cup of coffee with a fistful of sugar in it.
We used to open early, but stopped because of all the trouble the women
brought. Some were strung out, some were just thieves, and a few even
tried to turn tricks in the bathroom. So we kept the front door locked
until 6:00 a.m., when the first orange light of dawn sent the girls home.
Still, a few of them were nice. They were usually young mothers just
trying to make enough cash to get to a better place. If it was a slow night,
I would buy their coffee or throw some bacon into their sandwiches
without anyone knowing. The kitchen was open to the dining room, so
I could see who was at the front door. If I knew the girl, I'd let her in.
The owners never came in until about 7:00 a.m., so I was really the only
one calling the shots until then.

Brandi was a cool girl. She always paid her tab and never made a fuss.
She smelled like plastic carnations and bubble gum. When she spoke, her
accent was *Gone with the Wind* meets *New Jack City*. She always braided
her hair off to one side, which made her look young, about twenty-one,
which was my age at the time. I found it unfair that I was in college
while she was trying to raise a kid.

Brandi always left the diner before the office workers came in for
the morning rush. She always ordered an egg sandwich, and I'd bump it
up to a deluxe, with two eggs, cheese, and bacon. Sometimes, I'd even
throw a cheese Danish into her bag. The morning waitress would catch
me giving away food, but I didn't care. They couldn't fire me: there was
no one else who wanted to work the morning shift.

Brandi would sit at the counter while I prepped for breakfast. We
had little in common, so we talked about trivial things, such as movie
stars and the weather. One day, while I was wrapping up her egg sandwich, she asked me if I was a virgin. I wasn't, but I found her question
so aggressive that I blushed. "I knew you was a virgin," she said. After
that, she called me the Virgin. It was condescending but playful. Every

time she said it, there was an unspoken invitation. After all, I knew what she did for a living.

BRANDI ALWAYS checked the bag of food I handed to her before she left, to see what was in it. She'd wink at me and wave good-bye. I liked when she did that. I let her use that nickname, too. Sometimes, when she said it, I forgot what she did for a living and she was just another girl being silly, flirting with me. And that broke my heart every time.

Around that time, I started trying new things in the kitchen, nothing too advanced, but enough to keep my mind from going numb. I stopped using the diner's instant pancake mix and made the batter from scratch. I made lemon–poppy seed bread and banana-walnut bread. The things I made were selling nicely, and that encouraged me to expand the diner's breakfast offerings. One morning, while I was trying my hand at fresh doughnuts, Brandi happened to be around. I gave her a warm, odd-shaped doughnut just out of the deep fryer. Her eyes lit up.

"This is good. Reminds me of New Orleans," she said.

"Is that where you're from?"

"Yeah. You ain't lived till you been dere and had a beignet."

"A what?" I asked her.

"A beignet."

"What's that?"

"It's like this," she said, holding up the doughnut I'd made her, "but sweeter and warmer and better."

"And they only have them in New Orleans?"

"Only."

"I'll make one for you next time."

"You don't know how, Virgin. It's only dere. It tastes so good. You have to go to Café du Monde and have the real one."

"And what's it called again?"

"A beignet."

"How do you spell it?"

"I don't know. You the college boy."

"Say it again?"

"A beignet."

"A ben-what?"

"A bayn-YAY, mutherfucker. Something wrong wit yo ears?"

One day, Brandi stopped coming to the diner—no good-bye. This was typical: the working girls never stuck around too long. It was 1993, the serial killer Joel Rifkin had finally been arrested, and the city was under pressure to clean up the streets. Even the welfare hotels were shutting down. Still, I thought that Brandi and I had had enough of an acquaintance that she would at least have said good-bye. Maybe I wasn't that important to her. I knew in my heart that nothing bad had happened to her; she was too smart for that. I figured she'd moved on to a better situation. But it would have been nice for her to have let me know, so I wouldn't worry. Then again, what if she had come to say good-bye? Would we have exchanged numbers and kept in touch? Maybe she had been nice to me all that time just because of the free food. Still, I missed her—and I promised myself that I would take her advice and go to New Orleans one day and have a real beignet.

I THINK ABOUT BRANDI every time I go to Café du Monde. I have this crazy notion that I might even run into her one of these times. I like sitting outdoors even when it is deathly humid. I'll walk from my hotel to the French Quarter, under the banana trees, enjoying the smell of piss being sprayed off the streets. Most of the locals tell me to go to Morning Call for coffee, but I like coming to the French Quarter early in the morning, when it isn't overrun with tourists. On this particular day, I'm running a little late. When I get there, it's 9:00 a.m., and the line is already stretching out onto the street. My head feels as if a small pea were bouncing around in my empty skull, and the river smells fetid. All I want is a good beignet.

There are many other places that sell beignets in the French Quarter but none as good as Café du Monde. A good beignet should have a pillow of hot air inside that is released when you take a bite; it should not be hollow, or dense with holes. The powdered sugar should get all over your upper lip and float into your nose such that if you make the mistake of inhaling while taking a bite, you'll wind up coughing up powdered sugar. I like foods that punish the uninitiated.

The history of the beignet varies depending on whom you ask. When you research it, it is impossible not to come across its once more famous cousin, *calas*. The roots of the *calas* (sometimes referred to as a *beignet de riz*) can be traced back to Africa, where the *calas* is called *togbei* in Ghana, *puff puff* in Nigeria, and *mikate* in Congo, and where it is made, again depending on whom you ask, from some form of rice or cassava. Over time, the *calas* made its way to New Orleans, to become the dominant pastry served on the streets by Creole women. New Orleans food writer and radio host Poppy Tooker tells the story of how early twentieth-century prostitutes would dress up for Carnival and go from door to door to be served *calas*. Over time, refined wheat flour and the French influence mutated the *calas* into the popular beignet we know and love today.

Almost all the waitstaff at Café du Monde are from Vietnam. It is one of those unexpected intersections of history and culture that you find everywhere in New Orleans. The Vietnamese have been in New Orleans a long time, ever since the end of the Vietnam War. I watch them hustle around the tables, taking orders and making coffee. They've been working here for as long as most locals can remember. Rumor has it that their predominance at Café du Monde began with one waitress almost forty years ago. She still works here, one of the younger waitresses tells me, pointing out a tiny woman with white hair and pink lipstick. The older woman's white uniform is too large on her. She is too busy to talk to me, and her English isn't so good anyway, the younger waitress tells me. I ask her what the older waitress's name is. She tells me "Annie," but somehow I don't believe her. She asks me if I'm waiting for beignets.

"Yes. I'd rather not wait on line."

"Okay. Wait here for one minute." After two minutes, the young woman returns with a large bag of beignets. I ask her how much. She doesn't answer; just gives me a wink. I hand her a twenty-dollar bill, and she thanks me and darts off back inside. She doesn't return. I walk down Decatur Street shoving warm fried dough into my mouth.

There is only one place in New Orleans that I know of that makes *calas*, and they are dense and uncompromising. I go there after I'm done with my delicate beignets, to see if the *calas* have changed. I sit down in a small, dark grotto, and my waitress brings me a plate of dark, heavy fried dough balls. Their *calas* are made from cooked rice, not rice flour, and they're not very appetizing.

I think about the history of Asian desserts, where rice flour was the backbone of all sweets before the introduction of wheat flour in Asia. The Korean *hoedduck* is basically a rice flour doughnut, a denser version of a beignet, but still delicious. It is topped with granulated sugar and eaten hot. You can find *hoedduck* in street markets all over Seoul. They are as unrefined as they are delicious.

I can't finish the *calas* on my plate. I wonder if the historic *calas* has more in common with the Korean *hoedduck* than it does with this ill-conceived ball of fried rice pudding.

Modern Korean desserts have followed the Japanese love for cakes and pastries made in the European tradition. All over Korea and Japan, you can find tiramisu, cheesecake, Swiss rolls, and sweet custards. These desserts are all made with refined wheat flour and superfine sugar, two ingredients not native to these cultures. But then, in a curious culinary twist, in both Japan and Korea, bakers will dust green tea powder over everything sweet. Also known as matcha, the powder is the most highly prized expression of green tea. Ancient and mystical, the process of making matcha involves picking the best tea leaves grown in shade. The leaves are steamed to preserve their color and flavor, then dried out under the sun and ground into a fine powder. The powder is ritualistically whisked with hot water that never quite reaches its boiling point. In the eleventh century, the Zen priest Esai wrote an entire book devoted to tea, and since then, Japan has cultivated a modern tea culture that borders on fetishism.

I don't remember when I fell in love with matcha, but it was always a treat for me as a kid. It started with green tea ice cream, then green tea *mochi*, green tea cakes and custards. I dust matcha on everything, from chess pie to Nutter Butter cookies. (If you haven't tried this before, you don't know what you're missing.) And over the years, I've watched green tea powder go from obscure Japanese ingredient to trendy must-have item for chefs and home cooks. I love what it does to sweet desserts, especially when the delicate matcha powder is dusted over something as humble and imperfect as a beignet.

AFTER COLLEGE, I quit the job at the diner. I was living on Avenue C, in New York City's East Village, and my girlfriend at the time was a society girl from Japan. She taught me a lot about Japanese food. It seems so puerile to say that I could learn an entire culture's cuisine because I lived with a Japanese girl, but there's a lot to be said for spending a year with someone who loves food as much as you do. She introduced me to all the Japanese pastry shops in Manhattan. She taught me how to make a cup of matcha tea the proper way.

We lived together in a railroad apartment with a small garden, and we were happy for a while. Then one day, she confessed to me that she wanted to get married so she could stay in America. I didn't marry her. Instead, with some credit cards and a loan from a friend, I opened my own restaurant. After that, our relationship devolved into a flurry of negative Post-it notes left on the refrigerator door. I started coming home at 3:00 a.m. smelling of pork and beer and someone else's perfume. I was the unrefined one in the relationship.

I already knew that her father was a famous writer in Japan, and that she was well off. Then I found out that she wasn't just wealthy;

her family was worth a fortune. In other words, she was matcha, and I was a piece of shapeless dough. This made me pull away from her even more. We were too different. She ate her instant ramen with nori and shiitake mushrooms and salmon roe. I ate mine with saltine crackers and mayonnaise. I always found her naïve for thinking we could work things out. I'm sure Brandi must have thought the same about me years before. What would saying good-bye to me have accomplished? We would never have remained friends. Some worlds are just too far apart.

Not so with food. Food can be a bridge, and the best, most thrilling dishes can result from joining two different worlds. I have been making some version of this beignet for as long as I can remember. My version is light and fluffy and savory. I always add fruit to it. In winter, it can be Anjou pears; in summer, try ripe apricots or peaches. I drizzle the beignets with a little sweetened condensed milk thinned out with yuzu (a sour, tart citrus fruit). You might think I'm overdoing it, but sometimes, on a rare occasion, I'll even put a little Nutella on the plate first. And of course, the beignet is always dusted with matcha.

This dessert is elegance colliding with simplicity. Unlike my relationship with that Japanese woman, its various, disparate ingredients work beautifully together on the plate. It works in a way that rarely works between me and the women I have known.

KOREAN DOUGHNUTS
(HOEDDUCK)

The Korean doughnut and the New Orleans beignet are distant cousins with the same purpose—to put a smile on your face. The dough for these doughnuts contains a lot of rice flour, which gives them a crispier crust than the typical American doughnut. The filling is different, too. The cashew nuts are savory, and the sesame seeds add a bitterness to the semisweet filling. In Seoul, you can walk through neighborhoods on a brisk autumn night and see street vendors selling *hoedduck*. These are panfried, and they are best eaten right out of the pan while still warm and crisp.

MAKES 12 DOUGHNUTS

DOUGH	FILLING
2 cups warm water (about 112°F)	1 cup chopped cashews
¼ cup plus 3 tablespoons granulated sugar	5 tablespoons dark brown sugar
4 teaspoons active dry yeast	¼ cup black sesame seeds
2 teaspoons kosher salt	½ teaspoon freshly ground black pepper
2 tablespoons vegetable oil	1 teaspoon ground cinnamon
3¼ cups all-purpose flour, plus more for kneading the dough	5 tablespoons unsalted butter, softened
1¼ cups rice flour	6 tablespoons vegetable oil
	¼ cup honey

TO MAKE THE DOUGH: In a medium bowl, combine the water, ¼ cup of the granulated sugar, the yeast, salt, and vegetable oil and stir well. Let stand for 10 minutes, or until foamy.

Sift together both flours and the remaining 3 tablespoons granulated sugar into a large bowl. Add the yeast mixture and mix with a rubber spatula or wooden spoon until well combined. Cover the bowl with plastic wrap and let the dough rise in a warm place for 1 hour, or until doubled in size.

Transfer the dough to a floured work surface. The dough will be very wet, and that is okay. Dust it with just enough flour so that you can handle it without it sticking to your fingers. Divide the dough into 12 equal pieces and shape them into balls. Transfer to a baking sheet lightly dusted with flour. Set aside while you make the filling.

TO MAKE THE FILLING: In a medium bowl, combine the cashews, brown sugar, sesame seeds, pepper, and cinnamon and mix well. Add the butter and work it gently into the mixture with a fork until incorporated.

(CONTINUED)

Flour your hands, take one ball of dough, and flatten it gently with your hand. Place about 2 tablespoons of the filling in the center of the dough and fold the edges over to enclose the filling. Seal the seams by gently pressing on them with your fingers and set the doughnut seam-side down on the baking sheet. Repeat with the remaining dough and filling, reflouring your hands as necessary so the dough doesn't stick to them.

Line a wire rack with paper towels. Heat a large nonstick skillet over medium heat, then add 1 tablespoon of the vegetable oil and heat until hot. Put one doughnut into the pan and cook for 2 minutes, or until nicely browned. Flip with a spatula and cook on the other side for 2 minutes, gently flattening the doughnut with the back of your spatula. Flip once more and cook for another minute or so, until the top is nicely browned. Remove from the pan and place on the paper towel–lined rack. Repeat with the remaining doughnuts, adding more oil to the pan as necessary. Drizzle lightly with the honey and serve warm.

GREEN TEA BEIGNETS

Typically beignets are garnished with nothing more than powdered sugar, but I add a little green tea powder to the sugar for a refined bitterness and put some matcha in the dough as well. These beignets are pillowy and light, and I love how the bitter green tea powder cuts through the sweetness of the dough. Matcha comes in many different grades. You need only a little powder for the recipe, so make sure to use a high-quality one.

This recipe makes a lot of beignets. It *is* possible to cut it in half, but I don't recommend it. The rise seems to suffer in a smaller batch of dough. Instead, make the full recipe and invite a bunch of friends over to enjoy the beignets with you.

⅓ cup warm whole milk
(about 112°F)

¾ cup buttermilk

3 tablespoons sugar

4 teaspoons instant yeast

5 cups bread flour

½ teaspoon baking soda

¾ teaspoon kosher salt

1½ teaspoons matcha
(green tea powder)

About 4 cups canola oil,
for deep-frying

GARNISH

1 ripe pear, peeled, cored, and
thinly sliced

1⅙ cups slivered almonds

2 tablespoons sweetened
condensed milk

2 teaspoons matcha
(green tea powder)

1 tablespoon confectioners'
sugar

In a small bowl, combine the warm milk, buttermilk, and sugar. Add the yeast, stir, and let stand for 10 minutes, or until foamy.

In a large bowl, combine the flour, baking soda, salt, and matcha.

Add the yeast mixture to the flour mixture and mix until a smooth dough forms. Transfer to a lightly oiled large bowl, cover with plastic wrap, and let rise in a warm place for 2 to 3 hours, or until doubled in size.

Transfer the dough to a lightly floured work surface. Use a rolling pin to roll it out to about a ½-inch thickness. Cut the dough into rectangles about 1 inch by 2 inches. Transfer the pieces to two baking sheets, spacing them 1 inch apart, and refrigerate for 30 minutes.

Heat the oil to 350°F in a small pot. Fry the beignets a few at a time until golden brown on all sides and puffed up in the middle, 2 to 3 minutes. Drain on a paper towel–lined plate.

Arrange the beignets on a large plate and scatter the plate with the sliced pears and slivered almonds. Drizzle with the condensed milk. Finish by dusting the matcha and confectioners' sugar over the beignets. Use more confectioners' sugar than matcha. Serve while they are still warm.

CHAPTER 2

THE PUGILIST
AND THE COOK

THE FIRST CLUE A BOXER IS GOING DOWN IS IN HIS legs. He gets flat-footed, and his feet start to drag. His balance is off. He isn't quick enough to evade a punch that shouldn't even have gotten close. He is vulnerable but tries to hide it. He throws out a few halfhearted jabs to show he's still in this fight. Boxing is as much about bluffing as it is about technique. When a boxer loses the vigor to execute his footwork, you can bet his brain is turning to soup. His hands are not far behind. He forgets to protect his chin. In his torpor, he lowers his guard. A punch lands square in the jaw, and the fight is over. Boxing may be a sport of fists, but it's the footwork that telegraphs a fighter's skill, conditioning, and state of mind. But who wants to write a story about footwork? It's not epic. It's not sexy. Just keep telling us about a boxer's deadly right hook.

Understanding boxing is the first step toward knowing Lowell, Massachusetts. The last time I was here, I spent an evening at Irish Jack Brady's bar, the Gaelic Club, listening to Brady relive his days in the ring. One of the many great fighters Lowell has produced, Jack Brady is revered here as a local legend. Every bar patron bids him good night as he or she leaves. While I was there, more than a few people went out of their way to tell me that he was the best in Lowell.

The best at what? I asked.

Just the best man you'll ever meet.

I'm hoping to meet up with Jack again tonight. I've left several messages at the bar to tell him I'm on the way, but there's been no return call. I hop into my rented Chevy and beeline it out of Boston before the end-of-day traffic jams. I go to Lowell every time I'm in the area. It's about an hour northwest of Boston, if the traffic isn't too bad. There isn't much to see once you arrive. It's telling that when you meet the locals, their first question is "Whaddaya doing in town?," said in a tone not menacing but bewildered. Lowell is the fourth-largest city in Massachusetts, an old mill town, with lots of factories, lots of sturdy brick buildings. It's a town that is proudly Irish and Italian and Polish, a town of tough old men and even tougher old women. Lowell is where they filmed *The Fighter*, a movie about the lives of two Irish American half brothers and professional boxers, Micky Ward and Dicky Eklund, the latter known affectionately as "the Pride of Lowell."

Ramalho's West End Gym, where the real-life brothers trained (and where part of the movie was filmed), is still there. It is an old-school gym with creaky wooden floors and, taped to the office walls, black-and-white photos telling the story of Lowell's rich boxing history. I'm a hopeless romantic for places like this.

I live in Louisville, Kentucky, the city that produced Muhammad Ali, though I am too young to have ever watched him fight. Still, I grew up during a golden age of showmanship boxing: Sugar Ray Leonard, Thomas Hearns, and the Marvelous Marvin Hagler. I remember a time when Gleason's Gym in Brooklyn was the center of the boxing world. When I stand inside Ramalho's, it reminds me of that time. I drink in the sound of punching bags in vibration and the sharp squeak of footwork on a mat. I breathe in the aroma of bruised leather and decades of sweat. The nostalgia in here is contagious, even if it isn't mine. It gives me the chills. A massive Irish flag hangs on one wall, but the kids training here these days are mostly African American and Latino. Boxing is a blood sport that calls to the most desperate young men. Most of the Irish American kids have moved on or moved out of Lowell, but the old-timers are still here, still running the gym, still watching over their town.

Most nights, you can find Jack Brady at the Gaelic Club. I ring the doorbell and wait for a buzzer to let me in. Jack is at the bar wearing a clean white button-down shirt and a green cap with an Irish flag embroidered on it. For five dollars, you can join the Gaelic Club, a privilege that comes complete with a membership card on green cardstock. Because the Gaelic is a private club, you can do whatever you want in here. You can smoke, you can be bawdy, you can play whatever the fuck Irish music you want, and no one's gonna say shit. Just don't break any of Jack Brady's rules. He presides over his bar, whose back wall is lined with black-and-white photos of him as a fighter. "That's my daughter who put up these pictures," he insists. "Me? I couldn't give a fuck about 'em. I haven't watched a fight since I quit the ring."

Jack Brady wasn't the greatest that Lowell ever produced, but he was pretty damn good. At eight years old, he fought in the Silver Mittens. He grew up in the Acre, a rough Lowell neighborhood of working-class immigrants, mostly Irish, who did the worst jobs and tried to make a good life for themselves. He came from a family of fighters; his uncle and grandfather were both fighters. At fifteen, he lied about his age so he could fight in the Golden Gloves. He tells me a story of one of his early fights. He was a young kid, small for his age and fighting men a decade older than he. One evening, as he was lacing up his boots before a fight, Dickey Gauthier, his opponent, approached him and, with a tone of disrespect, told him how he was gonna beat the holy shit out of him. Jack had only one boot on, so he took the other one and smacked Dickey across the face again and again with it until some men stepped in to separate the two. That story impressed the hell out of me.

"How'd the fight go?" I asked.

"I knocked the fucker out in the second round," Jack says with a laugh.

He didn't lose a fight until he was twenty-four. And when he did, it wasn't because he was hungover. It was because he had lost the heart (pronounced *baht*) to fight. "I was done with fightin'," he tells me. "I still had the skills, but my *baht* wasn't in it no more."

As the evening goes on, I pick up on that word a lot. *Heart*. It means something to him when he sees a kid who's got it.

"Bell rings, there's only two of yous in the ring," Jack says. "No one's gonna come to your aid. You're all alone. You either fight like hell or you get your ass kicked. First time a kid gets his head knocked in, you see if he's got any *baht*. The ones that don't, they go down and they stay down. You see a kid get back up and fight, that's *baht*. In all my years, no one ever knocked me out. I had a chin made of cement. And I had *baht*."

He's sixty-eight now, and I can hardly believe that the handsome man with the chiseled body in the photos is the same arthritic person sitting next to me on a barstool. But he talks like any man who has used his fists his whole life. His voice is a soft whisper with traces of menace, as if he might turn on me at any moment. When he wants to make a point, he pinches my shoulder just below the back of my neck, and I actually cringe. What time has taken away from his posture has remained in his enormous hands. His fingers retain the muscle memory of violence; his hand clamps with the force of a man decades younger. If not for his bum shoulder, he could still throw a hell of a punch.

The ice in my whiskey is melting fast, but I don't mind. I hang on every word he says while his hand sits on my neck. Bono is blaring away on the jukebox, and the Red Sox game is on the TV. I light Jack's cigarette, and as he exhales, the last sunlight of the afternoon coming in through the tinted window catches the plumes of smoke like a scene from an old black-and-white movie. I resist the urge to take his picture.

I DIDN'T COME TO LOWELL just for the boxing stories or to write a wistful history of the city's glorious past. I came here to have one of the best Cambodian dinners of my life. America has never glorified Cambodian food, and it is not likely it ever will. Flanked by Vietnam to the east and Thailand to the west, Cambodia (and its cuisine) has long been overshadowed in Americans' minds by these other, more dominant cultures. As Americans, we demand a good helping of Hollywood romance to wash down our ethnic cuisines. Yet for most of us, there is nothing romantic or cheerful about Cambodia. What little we know about it has mostly to do with the 1970s genocide and famine brought on there by Pol Pot's Khmer Rouge. A generation was murdered. The country was burned to the ground. It has yet to recover. Almost all the Cambodians in America today are refugees from that period. All of them still grieve. Sam and Denise are just two of them. They run the restaurant Simply Khmer in Lowell. I fell in love with them right away.

Here in Lowell, a city that has never been on anyone's culinary radar, you can witness the melding of cultures through immigration. Cambodians now make up about 40 percent of the population of Lowell, which is about fifty thousand people. There are more Cambodian restaurants in Lowell than in all of New York City, and they are all really good. Some, such as Senmonorom, cater to a wider audience that wants a hybrid version of Chinese and Vietnamese food. But Sam, of Simply Khmer, stands alone in Lowell as a Cambodian chef whose dishes straddle three worlds, offering flavor combinations that reflect his experiences growing up in Cambodia, Thailand, and the northeastern United States.

Sam has a gleeful, boyish face despite being in his midfifties. "I am Khmer," Sam says, "but my life in Cambodia was so fast, I was so young when I left, I feel like my time here in Lowell has really made me who I am as a chef."

We talk briefly before he heads back into the kitchen for the busy dinner service. This is my third visit to his restaurant, and I sit with a notebook in hand. I have so many questions I want to ask him, so many

details about his life I want to know before we even begin to talk about
the food.

Most restaurants fall into one of two categories: either the identity
of the person cooking your food is incidental or that person is a lauded
chef whose narrative is known to you before you even peruse the menu.
Places like Sam's are unique because you get to unravel the chef's story
yourself, with each steaming bowl of soup that comes out of the kitchen.
It is impossible to write about Sam's food without knowing the narrative
of his life. This is where I disagree with food critics whose mission is to
judge only what is on the plate. The story such critics tell is about *them*,
their preferences, *their* expectations, not the chef's. What they write may
be necessary and relevant to dining culture, but it disconnects the food
from its origins, its narrative, its roots. The plate of food has never been
the be-all and end-all for me. Quite the opposite: for me, good food is
just the beginning of a trail that leads back to a person whose story is
usually worth telling.

After Sam disappears into the kitchen, I sit with his wife, Denise.
She is the outgoing one, with the kind of beauty that dares you to imagine what she looked like in her youth. Now in her late forties, she left
Cambodia in 1983 and settled into a predominantly white American
neighborhood in Wichita, Kansas, where she had a pretty typical
American upbringing—until a marriage was arranged between her older
sister and a Cambodian man who lived in Lowell. That meant the family
would move as well. Denise was just sixteen at the time.

She is a grandmother now, but you would never guess. She speaks
with a youthful smile and moves around the restaurant with the exuber-
ance of someone a generation younger. She is easy to talk to and eager to
explain things on the menu that I don't know—names such as *baw-baw*,
som-law, and *pro-hok* (which is also spelled *praw-hok* on the same menu,
though apparently the two are the same thing; Denise tells me that the
spelling varies depending on whom you ask).

Navigating a menu so unfamiliar is like trying to learn a new language in the time it takes for a waiter to bring you water. My eyes scan the menu looking for patterns, or any recognizable hint to help me decipher the language. Novices will order straight from the pictures, but I know enough to steer clear of that pitfall. I want the dishes that are unique, evocative. I didn't drive all the way to Lowell for a spring roll; I don't care how good they are. I want that one item on the menu that prompts the waiter, when I order it, to look incredulously at me and say, "You sure you want that?" Yes, that's exactly what I want, that and the three other items that make you doubt me.

While Denise is guiding me through the menu, I tell her I want something really different. I don't get what I'm asking for on the first go 'round. (I never do.) I have to politely decline the chicken wings and the spicy shrimp. (Yes, I'm sure everyone loves them, but I'm not everyone, and I want to get down to the nitty-gritty.) Denise suggests the obligatory sautéed beef and pork stir-fry that every Asian country makes in one form or another. Again, thanks but no thanks. Then I see an item on the menu that has a noticeably long name, the combination of consonants hard to pronounce. It stands by itself on the page, awkward and lonely: Som-law Ma-Ju Kroung Sach Ko. Why is it here? It doesn't fit the patterns of the other dishes. It must be good if they bothered to list it. I point to it and study Denise's reaction. She nods halfheartedly, but in a way that is trained, not emotional. It's fishy, she says. I look down at the description written in English, a nonsequential list of ingredients, and I see "tripe." Fishy and tripey? I want this. Smiling broadly, she asks, "You sure?" Double sure.

We also agree on smoked ground fish in mud fish sauce; cow intestines with *tuk pro hok*, a fermented fish paste; and *amok trey*, fish steamed in banana leaves with coconut milk, lemongrass, lime, and shallots. When the food arrives, I can tell just from the aroma that this is different. I have eaten in Cambodian restaurants before, in Houston and Los Angeles, but both times I left feeling as if I had eaten something more reminiscent of Vietnamese food. Before eating at Simply Khmer, I paced uneasily through my life with the opinion that either I didn't really like Cambodian food or it wasn't anything special. In my gut, I knew that neither was true, but I had nothing else to go on. Because the ingredients in Cambodian food are so similar to those of its neighboring countries, it's difficult to detect a distinct, staunchly Cambodian identity. Coconut milk, lemongrass, ginger, basil, and chile are common threads throughout Southeast Asia, which makes it hard to say where Thai food ends and Cambodian food begins, but one noticeable difference is the pungent fermented fish paste at the heart of every delicious dish that comes out of Sam's kitchen. He calls it *pra-hak*, and it is basically fermented fish and guts beaten into a paste with spices and roots until it becomes a magical elixir. It is *pra-hak* that gives Sam's dishes structure and depth.

Ingredients such as coconut, ginger, and lemongrass have become so much a part of the American vernacular that we forget how exotic and aromatic they are. It is one thing to enjoy a lemongrass panna cotta. It is another thing entirely to be confronted with a fistful of lemongrass alongside a slew of other aggressive ingredients. Sam's food makes me hungrier as I eat it. I move into an altered state of mind, the flavors and aromas floating through me at levels I'm not used to. Instead of being sated, I become addicted. Even the mud fish sauce (which at first is so overpowering that I have a mild gag reflex) becomes a dip I can't stop putting my finger in. A lot of the reason is the salt: this is sodium-heavy food, and I crave it. The aromatics not only mask the salt but perfume it, so I mindlessly go back for more and more, until my blood pressure screams for me to stop. I sit there for a good forty-five minutes, and my spoon never hits the table. Denise drops by every few minutes to check on me, and each time, I have sauce dribbling down my chin.

When I finally stop eating, I'm exhausted. The world has gone quiet. As in those brief few minutes after sex, when all you hear is the sound of your lungs working, I sit there just breathing, without a single rational thought in my head. I look down at my notebook, and the page is blank. I have failed to make any notes. Fortunately, Denise is nice enough to go through each menu item again, listing the ingredients.

I will spare you the recipe for the intestines, but I do want you to try making *amok trey* (page 40). I've replaced the tilapia with catfish, but any firm-fleshed fish will work. I've also adjusted Sam's recipe slightly for efficiency, but his ingredients are all there. (In case you're wondering: Sam is open to sharing his recipes—except for his *pra-hak*, which of course is the one recipe I really want.)

At the end of the meal, I wait around for Sam to finish up in the kitchen. My belly is swollen with food, and at one point I actually nod off. When customers eventually thin out, Sam joins me at the table. He is a gentle human being, nervous, beguiling, and utterly polite. Now fifty-five, he arrived in Lowell in 1974, when he was twelve. Everything before that is a horrendous blur for him. He was raised on a farm in a small village near the Thai border. When the Khmer Rouge marched into his village, his life took a violent course, one from which it would never recover. The idyllic farm became a labor camp. One night, the men of his village were accused of plotting to escape across the border. The next day, soldiers arrived and took away almost every male, including Sam's father. None of them were ever seen again. Sam thinks they were all murdered, but nobody knows for sure. He was eight at the time, and does not remember the details. He does remember being sent to a remote labor camp, where life was endless work from sunup to sundown, the only break being a meal of rice porridge in large bowls placed randomly on tables, so the hungry families would have to fight one another for their share. Sam stole food from the soldiers; he hid from work and caught fish. He trapped frogs in barrels and captured grasshoppers, roasting both over fire pits at night. He spent two years in that camp, and when the Vietnamese army invaded, he and his remaining family members were finally able to cross the border to Thailand. He spent two years in Thailand, working in markets and cooking simple meals with his mother to feed the other refugees. His aunt and uncle had managed to get to the United States, and they told Sam and his family of a wonderful place full of Cambodians called Lowell. There was work in the textile factories there.

Sam spoke no English when he arrived in Lowell. He washed dishes at a Chinese restaurant after school. When he finished high school, he started working on cars. In his twenties, he ran an auto body shop. He met Denise through his mother, the seamstress working on Denise's sister's wedding dress. The two married, worked hard, and sent their kids away to college and a better life. And that's it. That should have been the end of a happy immigrant story.

But Sam had a secret desire: he wanted to cook. He had opened a restaurant/nightclub in the 1990s, but it failed. He took this hard, and never forgot it. So, at the age of fifty, he tried again, with Simply Khmer, this time cooking the food of his youth. And with nothing more than a faint memory of the dishes he had eaten as a child, he set about to create a menu of Cambodian cuisine with a new identity.

How do you trust a memory from when you were ten? I ask him. He shrugs and says that maybe it's not exactly the same, but it's close enough, and that he can feel it when it tastes right. That is what being Khmer must mean. I think back to when I was ten, to the things I ate then, and I wonder if I could re-create from memory what my grand-mother cooked. I doubt I could.

Sam sits in front of me with his paper cook's hat in hand, his face weathered and smiling, his expression humble. He probably does not realize that he is doing something most chefs cannot. He doesn't con-sider himself remarkable. I've been cooking professionally and learning continuously since I was twenty. Sam lived an entire life of slow struggle before even walking into a restaurant kitchen. His story is not supposed to work. A person does not just start cooking at age fifty and create food this amazing. He tells me about a lobster dish he is working on because—well, he *is* in Massachusetts, and everyone here loves lobster. He talks about wanting to do frog legs, and liver-and-blood soup, and on and on.

THE NEXT NIGHT, Sam invites me to hang out with him in his kitchen. It is just he and three older Cambodian women who dash around the kitchen with ingredients in plastic bags. I watch one of them hammer away at green papaya ribbons with a large mortar and pestle until the air is filled with a sweet-and-sour aroma. Sam spends most of the evening shuffling his wok back and forth to the rhythms of the fire as it licks up around his hands. During slow moments, we walk back to the small courtyard behind his kitchen and share a cigarette. There are potted plants strewn across the concrete floor, herbs he can't always find fresh at the market. He shows me all the smokers and ovens he is repairing. He is a borderline hoarder. His refrigerators and pantry exist in a state of disarray.

The first thing I learned in a professional kitchen was an uncompromising system of labeling and organization. It hurts my head, therefore, to see Sam's ingredients in opaque bags, nothing labeled, with no discernible system in place. The women who work here are randomly stationed around the kitchen doing jobs that seem to have no direct correlation to the tickets piling up on the expo station. There is no brigade; no regimented line of chefs with clearly defined duties. There is only Sam. He thunders back in front of his wok and starts calling for ingredients, and his dutiful assistants bring him things: holy basil, bamboo shoots, preportioned pork in Ziploc bags. He works alone and furiously. Flames spit up to the ceiling. His voice grows steadily louder, until he is barking orders.

This dance, for all its chaos, now seems choreographed. Dishes come together at a rapid pace. A dented pot that looks like it came from my grandmother's cupboard magically produces a soup of layered textures and colors; it is delivered to the dining room in large melamine bowls. The wok never cools down. As soon as one dish is plated, the wok is rinsed, and another chorus of ingredients gets sizzled.

Who is to say Sam's system is flawed? Most professional cooks create a unified, seamless production line, but do we lose something in the process? In all his chaos, maybe Sam's been able to retain some cryptic connection to his food.

And then, just like that, the rush is over. The ladies return to their random tasks, and the kitchen makes no sense again. While a waiter plates a dish of papaya salad, Sam and I resume our conversation. I stop short of giving him suggestions for how to better organize his pantry. Isn't the food already delicious? Besides, we have much to learn from the foreign-born cook who has not been disciplined by the Western brigade system.

For most of my life, I have always looked to "ethnic" restaurants for the raw materials for my inspiration. I mine their ingredients and ideas and then "reinterpret" them on my menus, which is a nice way of saying that I make their dishes more palatable to an audience that is not used to foods that are too aggressive or spicy. My system, in many ways, is exploitative. I take ideas from another culture and smooth out the edges for a more refined (some might say bland) palate. As chefs of a modern age, many of my peers do the same thing. Even Sam, in his search for a better dish, is refining his food, taking the things he ate at the refugee camp and turning them into something more delicate, polished. I am sure some Cambodians who eat at his restaurant tell him his food is not authentic, not like that from the village where they originated. But in order for any cuisine to evolve, it has to be passed on to people who have not lived the authentic life from which it germinated. Still, if a dish becomes completely unrecognizable, what has become of the cuisine and the tradition from which it was born? There are no easy answers, but when I experience what Sam does, eat what he cooks, I understand that his process is much more complex than I originally thought. When I stand next to him in his kitchen, I do so as a student, not a collector.

Sam has found his voice in Lowell. Denise watches from the expo line as orders stream in. She is proud of him; you can see it in her eyes. I can't name the specific rules for what makes a great restaurant, but I know I am standing in one. I'm in an unspectacular kitchen in the middle of a town that most food writers would never visit, and I'm watching magic being made. I can see the strength of love between husband and wife toiling away, erasing the tragedy of their upbringing by creating something celebratory—and I don't want to let go of this energy. I'm envious.

I stay until the end of service. We talk a little more, until it gets too late to talk anymore. When I walk out into the night, I am reminded that I'm in Lowell, and that there's not much happening here. The city is miserably quiet. Sam and Denise drive away, and I look back at the restaurant, dark and unassuming now. It looks like any other place built on a budget. If you didn't know what was behind the doors, you would never dream of interrupting your travels to stop here.

I WALK TO THE GAELIC CLUB, where I find Jack Brady. I ask him what he thinks of the Cambodians. His answer surprises me. He elaborates for a while about growing up in the Acre. He tells me about all the abuse and oppression he had to deal with from the English and the fucks who wanted to control all the money. He and every Irishman in Lowell had to fight tooth and nail for every piece of their America. He witnessed the same thing with the Italians, the Greeks, the Portuguese, the Lithuanians, the Poles, and on and on. The Gaelic Club was the first private Irish club in Lowell. He is very proud of that. He is unsentimental about boxing. Lowell, he says, will probably never produce another great Irish boxer. If you were Irish and at all smart, well, you got yourself a good job or you got yourself out of Lowell. He knows that the black-and-white photos that line the wall behind his bar represent the glory days of Lowell, but he also remembers the pain and violence of those days.

Jack refuses to watch a fight ever again. He seems torn between the history he loves, tales of fighters such as Phinney Boyle and Larry Carney and Micky Ward, and not wanting to be a sentimental ghost. The Cambodians? They are just the next immigrant group coming down the pipeline. They go to school. They work hard. They come to his bar, and they are respectful. They will leave their mark on Lowell, too, just not in the ring.

I ask Jack if he liked the movie *The Fighter*. Yes, he did. It was accurate, he says. It had heart. All over town, if you go into Irish bars, there are photos of Mark Wahlberg and Amy Adams posing with the locals.

I don't know what it means to be Irish American, but as I listen to Jack Brady talk, I get lost, and for a moment, I feel the struggle of Irish Americans, their tenacity, their love for Van Morrison, their passion, their fight. Jack Brady's eyes sparkle with it. When he passes, we will lose a great spirit and a respected man. We will lose a rare and real piece of American history.

He and I talk some more, and then I notice a young Cambodian girl in her twenties downing a shot of Bushmills with a bunch of young Irish American men. She is swaying her hips to U2's "Bullet the Blue Sky" on the jukebox. When she talks, she has the accent of a Lowell native; it is hard around the edges. It is baritone. It doesn't have the lightness of Denise's sentences. Sam has never seen *The Fighter*.

AMOK TREY

This is a creamy and aromatic fish curry wrapped in a banana leaf. It is surprisingly easy to make at home. Wait until your guests are seated and open the banana leaf packets right in front of them; it's impressive. The sauce is mild yet perfumed with flavor. I use catfish here, but another firm-fleshed fish such as halibut or cod would work equally well.

Serve with steamed rice and Asian-style pickles.

SERVES 4 AS A MAIN COURSE

Four 12-inch squares banana leaf

SPICE PASTE

12 kaffir lime leaves, chopped very fine
1 shallot, minced
2 lemongrass stalks, tough outer leaves removed
5 garlic cloves
1 lime

1 tablespoon grated fresh ginger
2½ tablespoons fish sauce
2 teaspoons pure chile powder
2 teaspoons shrimp paste
2 teaspoons dark brown sugar
1 teaspoon ground turmeric
1 teaspoon kosher salt

1½ cups coconut milk
Four 4-ounce catfish fillets
Kosher salt

Bring a large pot of water to a boil. Add one or two of the banana leaves, and cook for 5 minutes, or until softened and pliable. Remove and drain on a paper towel. Repeat with the remaining leaves.

Pour off most of the water and set a steamer basket in the pot; the water should come to just below the steamer basket.

TO MAKE THE SPICE PASTE: Put the lime leaves and shallot in a small bowl. Using a Microplane, grate the lemongrass and garlic into the bowl. Grate the zest of the lime into the bowl, then halve the lime and squeeze in the juice. Add the grated ginger, then add the fish sauce, chile powder, shrimp paste, brown sugar, turmeric, and salt. Transfer the mixture to a large mortar and pound it to a paste with the pestle. (If you don't have a mortar and pestle, you can also do this by smashing the ingredients with the side of your knife against a cutting board.)

Transfer the paste to a medium saucepan, add the coconut milk, and bring to a simmer over low heat, then simmer for 3 minutes. Remove from the heat.

Season the catfish generously with salt. Place one banana leaf on a cutting board and scoop ⅓ cup of the coconut sauce onto the middle of the leaf. Place a catfish fillet on top and add another ⅓ cup of the sauce. Wrap the fish in the banana leaf, folding over the top and bottom and then the sides, and thread a wooden skewer through the leaf to keep the packet closed. Repeat with the remaining fillets and sauce.

Bring the water in the steamer to a low simmer. Transfer the fish packets to the steamer basket, cover the pot, and steam for 30 minutes.

Remove the packets from the steamer and carefully transfer to serving plates. Set the plates in front of your guests and allow them to open the packets themselves.

PORK LAB WITH FRIED EGG
ON POPCORN BREAD

Cambodian *lab* is made with meat that is cooked, then marinated with spices and chilled. Similar dishes are found in Thailand and Indonesia. Cambodian *lab* (sometimes spelled *laab* or *larb* or *lahb*) is typically made with pork or beef, or sometimes duck, and eaten as lettuce wraps. This one is like a Southeast Asian version of hash on toast: basically an open-faced sandwich with the *lab* piled up on popcorn bread and a fried egg on top. The popcorn bread, which I came up with because I love the tiny bits of detritus at the bottom of a bag of popcorn, reminds me of Irish soda bread, with a slightly nuttier flavor.

SERVES 4 AS A MAIN COURSE

PORK LAB

2 teaspoons canola oil

1 pound ground pork

4 garlic cloves, grated
  (use a Microplane)

¼ cup water

2 tablespoons soy sauce

½ cup minced shallots

2 tablespoons minced seeded
  jalapeño pepper

2 tablespoons grated
  lemongrass
  (white part only)

1 tablespoon grated fresh
  ginger

¼ cup grated cucumber

Grated zest and juice of
  4 limes

1½ tablespoons fish sauce

1 teaspoon sugar

½ teaspoon ground cumin

¼ teaspoon sea salt, or to taste

¼ cup chopped scallion greens

¼ cup chopped fresh cilantro

2 tablespoons chopped fresh
  mint

4 tablespoons unsalted butter

4 large eggs

Kosher salt and freshly
  ground black pepper

Four ½-inch-thick slices
  Popcorn Bread
  (recipe follows)

TO MAKE THE LAB: In a large skillet, heat the canola oil over medium heat. Add the ground pork and cook for 3 to 4 minutes, stirring vigorously to break up the meat; do not let it brown. Add the garlic, water, and soy sauce and simmer until the pork is cooked through, about 5 minutes. Transfer the pork to a large bowl and let cool.

Add the shallots, jalapeño, lemongrass, and ginger to the pork and mix gently. Wrap the grated cucumber in a paper towel and squeeze out the excess liquid, then add the cucumber to the bowl. Add the lime zest, lime juice, fish sauce, sugar, cumin, and sea salt and mix well. Add the scallions, cilantro, and mint and mix again, then taste and adjust the salt to your liking. Cover and refrigerate for at least 1 hour, or as long as overnight.

When ready to serve, in a large skillet, melt the butter over high heat. Crack the eggs into the foaming butter. Cook for 1 minute. Put a lid on the pan and cook for another minute. Lift the eggs out of the pan with a spatula and set them on a plate. Season with salt and pepper.

Heat another large skillet over high heat. Butter the slices of popcorn bread on both sides and toast in the hot skillet, turning once, until lightly browned on both sides, about 1 minute per side. Arrange on individual plates.

Add the pork lab to the hot skillet and stir just until warmed through. Top the toast with the lab and then the fried eggs. Serve immediately.

POPCORN BREAD | Makes 2 loaves

½ cup water	2 large eggs
½ cup milk	5⅓ tablespoons unsalted butter, melted and cooled
1 tablespoon active dry yeast	
2 tablespoons sugar	1 tablespoon melted bacon fat or pork fat
2 cups popped popcorn	
2 teaspoons kosher salt	3 cups all-purpose flour

In a small saucepan, combine the water and milk and heat gently to 112°F. Transfer to a small bowl and stir in the yeast and sugar. Let stand for 10 minutes, or until foamy.

Pulse the popcorn in a food processor until broken down to the consistency of cornmeal. Transfer to a large bowl.

(CONTINUED)

Add the yeast mixture and salt to the ground popcorn. Stir in the eggs, melted butter, and bacon fat. While stirring with a rubber spatula, gradually add the flour until a rough, shaggy dough forms.

Transfer the dough to a lightly floured work surface and knead for 5 minutes, until a loose wet dough forms. Transfer to a lightly greased large bowl, cover with plastic wrap, and let rise in a warm spot for 30 minutes. It will almost double in size.

Punch down the dough and let it rise once more, about 30 minutes.

Grease two 8½-by-4½-inch bread pans. Turn the dough out onto an unfloured work surface and divide it into 2 equal pieces. Shape each piece into a loaf and place in the prepared pans. Let rise for about 1 hour, until doubled in size.

Preheat the oven to 350°F.

Bake the loaves for 35 to 40 minutes, until golden brown. Let the bread cool in the pans for 10 minutes, then remove from the pans and cool to room temperature on a wire rack.

CHAPTER 3

THE
UNFAMILIAR
NOODLE

TAKE A DISH YOU KNOW WELL, A DISH YOU'VE EATEN a hundred times. Now change just one ingredient. Would you still recognize the dish? What if that one ingredient changed everything you thought was familiar? What if the new taste blew your mind? Our bond with our favorite foods is an unsteady balancing act, and even the slightest change can trigger a deep uneasiness. It is like when a coworker you have known for years walks in with a totally new hairdo and you don't recognize her. Her voice is the same, her clothes, her demeanor, but as you listen to her speak, you can't help but think, Do I really know this person? It makes you question yourself. For me, it is one thing when this happens to a person, but quite another when it happens to a beloved plate of food. I become unhinged. It rattles the foundation of my universe. People, you see, are fickle. Food, we hope, is reliable, predictable. But on a frosty fall evening at Kashkar Café in Brighton Beach, Brooklyn, I am faced with the paralyzing fear of the unknown. It happens over a bowl of noodles.

Kashkar Café serves Uyghur cuisine. If you don't know what that it is, don't worry; neither do most of the people on the planet. The Uyghur are descended from a small tribal population in the northwesternmost edge of mainland China, residing primarily in the area known as Xinjiang Uyghur Autonomous Region, a vast nomadic land that borders Russia, Kazakhstan, Kyrgyzstan, Afghanistan, Pakistan, and India. Though the Uyghur are a part of China, they are not really Chinese in the way a person from Shanghai or Guangzhou is. They fall into a demographic known as "Central Asian," a name that refers to a place locked in time and shrouded in mystery. The Uyghur people are Muslim. They have their own language and their own customs, some of which are depicted in a large tapestry that hangs on the wall of this unassuming little eight-table café. The restaurant sits at the end of a small stretch of Brighton Beach Avenue that is crowded with Russian markets, delicatessens, and fruit stands. If you happened to walk by without paying attention, Kashkar Café would not stand out as anything unique, save perhaps for the small star-and-crescent icon above the name, symbolizing the Muslim faith.

Inside, the chef and patriarch of the family, Yousef Umidjon, sits at a table near the kitchen wearing the traditional *taqiyah* on his graying head as he silently eats dinner, his fingers roaming gently over a plate of lamb and cabbage. I can tell from the way he motions with his hands that he does not speak English. His eyes are opaque; they do not wander, they are not inquisitive. His son and daughter, both in their twenties, bounce around the restaurant, taking orders and lighting fires in the kitchen. But Yousef does not move. He is as still as a bear in winter. I sit down at a table by the window, my eyes trained on him, in case he looks up.

Brighton Beach has been many things to many people over the years. Jews, Poles, Italians, Hispanics, and Russians have all called this place home, and now it is the same with the new immigrants from Central Asia, mostly Uzbekistan but also the surrounding countries.

I grew up in Canarsie, just north of here. My neighbors were Indians and Jamaicans and Italians and Jews. Later, I would go to a "smart" high school in the Bronx, and during my sophomore year, we read Neil Simon's play *Brighton Beach Memoirs*, the coming-of-age story of Eugene Jerome and his Polish-Jewish family during the Great Depression. I argued with my English teacher about how I had lived nearby and had never met anyone like Eugene. I was lectured mercilessly on the meaning of the word *memoir*.

In the late 1970s, Brighton Beach was rife with crime and drugs, a ramshackle neighborhood as colorful as it was hostile. Every summer, my family would take day trips to Coney Island, walking the length of the boardwalk to Brighton Beach. I remember eating Nathan's hot dogs with yellow mustard, which always got sand in it no matter how much I tried to block the wind with my back. It was on this beach, more cluttered with soda cans than seashells, that we would have our loud, awkward family fights in Korean. My sister always managed to roam away and make friends with complete strangers. I loved watching her and the other shrieking teenagers on the Luna Park rides I was never allowed to get near. I loved the aroma of hot dogs simmering in a toxic bath of their own pollution, the coconut-scented Coppertone suntan lotion, the empty Budweiser cans, and the melting clouds of cotton candy picking up the salty air of a gray-blue ocean whose only purpose seemed to be to make children laugh. Looking back on it now, I'm pretty sure the place was a poor man's idea of a beach getaway, but to me it was paradise. We would stay until sundown. My sister and I would run as fast as we could, hoping to chase away the fading sun and make summer last just a few more minutes. For me, it was the prettiest place in the world. I think we stopped going there when I was nine.

I can remember the early influx of Russians, who were just settling into Brighton Beach in the 1980s. They were new but unafraid, aggressive, proud. They wore sweat suits and leather. They were flashy and drove nice cars. They were different from the Italian and Polish immigrants already there, and without knowing the details, we knew to avoid them. The "Russian Mafia" was something we'd been warned about.

We moved to Manhattan when I was ten, and I stayed away from that part of Brooklyn for the rest of my teen years. We were lucky to leave Brooklyn, my parents told me. Many families couldn't. My parents' lives there had been a week-to-week struggle, never getting ahead, just barely getting by. So a nostalgia for Brooklyn was never instilled in me. It had simply been a stop on the road to middle-class prosperity.

THIS IS MY FIRST TRIP BACK to the old neighborhood. I'm sitting on the B train. By the second stop in Brooklyn, all the hipsters have gotten off. What are left are the working-class immigrants making the long commute to East Brooklyn. They are from everywhere: Colombia, Haiti, Jamaica, Pakistan, Puerto Rico. They are Jews and Christians and Muslims. As the subway train emerges from the pitch-black tunnel, I see the rooftops of warehouses streaming by, building façades painted with graffiti. The subway cars are modern and clean now, but the view from the windows hasn't changed: low-income housing, junkyards, billboards. The expressionless faces of the subway riders are familiar. Showing no expression is a way to be invisible, to get through the ride without incident. No one makes eye contact, and the ones who do have a stare so empty that they may as well be blind. So much here is still the same.

But Brighton Beach has changed, a lot. As soon as I get off the subway, I'm thrust into a world of Russian dialects. The markets are bursting with smoked fish and cured meats, pancakes and myriad potato concoctions, tins of every kind of pickle your imagination can dream up, walls of caviar and cream cheeses. Russian food never makes the lists of top cuisines in the world, but to wander through these markets, you quickly see that those lists are wrong. This is ridiculously good stuff: everything from *pelmenli* to *vaereniki*, *blini* to *coulibiac*, from different-colored borschts to jellied fish and meats. And the pickles! Oh my lord, the pickles and slaws and relishes of every color and variety. To truly understand the breadth of Russian food, I recommend going to any of the many markets in Brighton Beach that have steam table lunches set out daily. Gourmanoff, in the

Master Theater, is a ritzy upscale market that has everything from Slavic specialties to American favorites, but don't miss the array of foods laid out on the steam table at Gastronom Arkadia, where they have the best chicken *bitochkis* and slaws.

The best restaurant in Brighton Beach for my money is Ocean View Café, which, ironically, does not have an ocean view. The green borscht will instantly become your favorite comfort food of all time, and the café's platter of smoked fish is so oily and decadent that your hair will shine for weeks. The stuffed cabbage is the best I've ever had, but the one dish that makes me blush with excitement is the pickled watermelon. Living where I do, in the American South, I'm accustomed to eating pickled watermelon rinds all summer long, but I never thought to pickle the entire watermelon, flesh and all. The plate comes out with red triangles of watermelon that have been brined for so long, the color and texture turn into something very similar to ahi tuna. It is rosy red and dense, completely limp, and whatever word is the opposite of *refreshing*. The watermelon is redolent of dill, garlic, and chile, and packs a punch of sourness so strong it makes your nose hairs curl. But if you are a lover of pickles, this is the best thing you will ever eat. I consume an entire plate of it with nothing more than a buttered dinner roll for relief.

For all the tasty discoveries of Russian food, though, nothing could have prepared me for my awakening at Kashkar. As I walk through the streets of Brighton Beach, I'm startled by how many Asian people I see: straight black hair, dark narrow eyes, olive skin on Mongoloid faces similar to mine, but speaking Russian, and acting Russian. One forgets how far and pervasive was the reach of the Soviet Empire. It engulfed many cultures across a span of geography that covered half of Europe and all of Asia. Russian is the common language here, but it is spoken by people who may look Chinese or distantly Arabic or as Nordic as Vikings. They are all Russian here in Brighton Beach. As the customers start filing into Kashkar, I notice that they're speaking both Russian and an unfamiliar language I later find out is Uzbek.

In English, I order the Samsa Parmuda, which is like the best White Castle slider. It is a feathery layered dough stuffed with lamb, onion, tomato, and peppers. I could survive on only this for about a year before getting bored. Then I order something called Korean Cabbage Salad, which, to my surprise, is a bowl of kimchi. There is not a trace of irony or hipster cuisine in here—this is literally a bowl of red napa kimchi staring me in the face. Next, I order Kovurga Say, a fried lamb rib dish with tomatoes, garlic, peppers, soy sauce, and cheese, another hybrid dish that feels Middle Eastern but tastes more like something from an Asian pantry.

Finally, I order the café's Lagman Soup. It has broad flour noodles in a rich meat broth with garlic, red bell pepper, celery, tomatoes, cabbage, and long beans. When it arrives, I get a strong star anise aroma wafting from the bowl. The vegetables float in a dark, impenetrable broth. The noodles are tight and glistening. The first spoonful hits me as something wrong. I don't like it—not because it isn't delicious, but because my mind can't reconcile the flavors. After a few more bites, I realize that this is not pork or chicken broth, but lamb. Noodles in lamb broth—a combination I've never tasted before. The aggressive flavor of wet earth and blood paralyzes me. The broth from a typical Chinese cook is viscous but masked with spices and medicine. His hands work fast and light, like that of a piano player, and you can taste that fast work in his broth. This broth, however, is heavy and slow. There is more than just lamb in here. I can taste the ancient cutting board, the hammered tin pot, the heat, the bleating animal, the veined, arthritic hands of a cook moving with pain and tension.

This dish rocks my world. That simple change, that one cultural difference, makes this noodle bowl into a dish I can't quite explain. I've never thought to replace the pork broth in my noodles with lamb broth. As I sit here over this steaming bowl, I realize I have to relearn everything. My instincts tell me that this combination is incorrect, that the gaminess of the broth does not work with the texture of the noodles, the soft cabbage, and the bite of the long beans. And stewed tomatoes? What are they even doing here? I grew up having noodles in pork or beef broth, and that arrangement was so heavily ingrained in me that I cannot think about noodles in any other broth. With other cuisines that are not a part of my DNA, I feel free to roam around the traditions and experiment. But for some reason, I have a mental seizure when it comes to noodles. To like this dish makes me feel as if I am betraying some part of my childhood. And what if this bowl is good? Not just good, but *really* good? What if it is better than anything I had as a kid growing up?

After that first spoonful, the next thing I do is push aside the connection of lamb to Middle Eastern flavors. I repress any inclinations to want yogurt or cumin or unleavened bread. I have to taste lamb as something new. I have to understand that descriptors such as *gamy* are not accurate. Lamb can taste gamy to someone who has not grown up with it. I take a few more sips of the broth and try to isolate the flavor of the lamb. It is the taste of a wet forest, it is a perfume made from mushroom stems (not the caps, just the stems), it is creamy and tangy, it is a flavor that starts in the nostrils and slides down like heavy rain. The broth is strengthened by garlic, cloves, cumin, and star anise. The spices are harmonious in a way that never felt congruous in a duck or chicken dish. It hits me that the origin of Chinese five-spice powder is *here*, in this remote cuisine that straddles the worlds of the Far East and the Levant. The spices and the broth coat the weighty noodles in a thin but pungent film. In a small glass jar on the table is a side condiment of vinegar marinating in ginger, peppers, and spices. I sprinkle a few dashes of it into the soup, and the meal becomes perfect.

At the end of dinner, I sit down with the owner's son, Danik, and a patron acting as interpreter, and we talk through our broken languages. His father, Yousef, Danik says, has been a cook his whole life. In 1961, he left China and settled in Uzbekistan, where he opened a restaurant. When his restaurant there failed, about fourteen years ago, he moved to Brighton Beach. He knew people who had come over and that there was a foundation community of Russians who were friendly to any Russian-speaking people. The same tensions that existed over rival cultures in the Soviet Union did not exist in Brooklyn. It was like the best of Russia, with the mob but not the KGB. I ask Danik where the rest of his people are. Some live in D.C. and Virginia, but as far as he knows, this is the only Uyghur restaurant in America. I ask if this is Russian food. He shrugs, as if to say, What is Russian food? Yousef is reading a newspaper this whole time and barely looks up when I ask this question. He gives his son a look, and everyone gets up to go back to work. Yousef smiles gently at me, as if to tell me good night.

I walk out into the evening with more questions than answers. Why did this soup have such a gut-wrenching effect on me? Who are the people who yearn for this food? Why can't I get drunk in the middle of Brighton Beach? I am told to go to the boardwalk. The cafés there have plenty of vodka and lively Russian entertainment, and they look out over the beach. I walk toward the sound of the ocean. The sky is dark, and the streets are quieter and emptier now. I pass by women in hooded parkas pushing strollers of crying babies as they return home from an evening walk. I get to the boardwalk; it is still jumping with people. Kids screech and zigzag along the wooden planks of the walkway. Girls giggle into their cell phones under dim streetlamps. An old woman pushing a metal cart sells umbrellas on a cold but otherwise clear evening. I don't go near the beach, but I can feel the grit of sand beneath my shoes. It makes my soles roll along the surface of the boardwalk. I can't tell you exactly how many grains there are, but I can tell you exactly whom I had a crush on in the third grade and who bullied me and made me cry. I can tell you exactly what time of day it was when we packed all our stuff into a moving van and unceremoniously hurried out of Canarsie for the last time, no one in my family but me looking back to wave good-bye to our neighborhood.

There's a festive crowd at Tatiana's, so I settle myself on a patio chair made out of green plastic. I get vodka on ice and gaze out onto the boardwalk. I can't see the ocean anymore, but I can smell it. I can hear the waves drowning out the laughter of the old men sitting nearby. I try to strike up a conversation with the waitress, but she doesn't say much. I ask her a bunch of personal questions that are probably dumb and intrusive. I order another vodka, and this time a different waitress brings it out to me. She slams the glass down on the table and immediately turns her back to me. I turn toward an older couple; they are willing to talk to me. Boris and Ludmila—he is from Siberia, a poet and a musician; she is a professor of Russian literature. They are both affable and gray-haired and slightly drunk. I question them about Russia, and Boris is quick to tell me he is Siberian, not Russian. He paints a picture of an untouched, isolated home blanketed in snow—according to him, the most beautiful place on earth. I say I want to visit, though I doubt I will ever even try. I buy them a round of drinks, and he sings me a song from his native town. Vodka is a lovely and terrible thing. I don't know if it was responsible for the demise of the Soviet Empire, but it can't have helped. After a few more shots and a mediocre plate of chicken Kiev, I end up at a bar called the Velvet Rope. The waitress from Tatiana's told me to go there, most likely in the hope that I would leave her section.

Any place called the Velvet Rope promises to be a hard-core, thumping nightclub, but when I walk in, there are only two elderly Russian men sitting on patio chairs, asleep, mouths agape. Slow night. I order a vodka and soda, and talk to a woman next to me who could be a supermodel. She answers all my questions with one-word answers until I get the hint. At the other end of the bar is a well-groomed man in a tight leather jacket smoking a hookah with two beautiful women. The women are dressed in what I can only describe as throwback 1980s glam glitter with a hint of prostitute extravagance. On anyone else, the look would be tawdry, but on them, it's classy. He, on the other hand, is Baryshnikov meets Wolverine. I buy them a drink, and we talk for a bit. Just small talk. The music is getting too loud for us to have a thoughtful conversation. There is karaoke here. There is karaoke everywhere. Smoke and vodka and a cheap microphone. The old men start singing ballads, loud and sad. Someone asks me if I want to sing Sinatra, and I decline. One of the pretty girls gets up to the mic and sings a hard-nosed semi-punk song in Russian. I ask my new friend at the bar to translate, and he starts gesticulating wildly. I can't hear all the words, but I think the lyrics go like this:

She hides her jewelry in her purse
Past the boys on the boulevard, but I've seen worse
Hanging out in the bathroom of Rasputin Inn
It's amazing how a little bill can buy you so much sin

There was a note by the pillow in the script of a child
It was left unfinished but what it said was pretty wild

It said, we are girls and boys for sale
Girls and boys for sale
You might think that we're angels
But you never can tell
'Cause we are girls and boys for sale

The rest of the song gets lost in the noise of the bar, but the refrain stays in my head while I order another vodka and soda. What I get instead is a shot of vodka pulled from the freezer. I don't shoot it in one gulp. I sip it like tea, which makes the bartender look at me suspiciously. The music is getting louder, and the vodka is impairing my hearing. I try to talk, but my voice becomes as thin as the smoke from the hookah pipes. The guy sitting next to me loses interest in what I'm trying to say. Truth be told, I've lost my train of thought, too.

It is late when I leave the bar. I don't say good-bye, just slip out clumsily. I don't know what time it is, but the streets are quiet. Everything is bathed in the soft yellow light of the streetlamps. A train erupts overhead, and for a moment, a few people emerge from the subway platform and skitter away. My eyes are blurry. This street looks like the place where I grew up: elevated subway cars, colorless brick buildings. I get into a cab and ask the driver to drive around until I can find a cheap hotel nearby. He is a young man from Kazakhstan, and we strike up a pleasant conversation. He's here to study. He works the night shift so he can take classes during the day, and he doesn't drink. He came here because his brother came first and liked it. I probe him for some deeper explanation, but that's all he gives me. He has a girlfriend who works at a hair salon. I ask him if he's going to marry her. Perhaps, he says, but he wants to get his degree first.

"She'll wait for you?" I ask.

"Yes," he says.

"Then get three degrees," I reply.

We laugh because it is a stupid joke and because it is something we have in common.

"When you get your degree and you get married, will you stay here in Brooklyn or will you leave?"

He doesn't answer right away. "Maybe," he says in an unconvincing tone.

He drops me off at a Best Western, and as he's pulling away, I realize I forgot to ask him his name.

What did they do to my childhood Brooklyn? When did this part of Brooklyn become Little Odessa? It was gradual, I know, and no one took notice of it until recently. But this is what immigrants do, no? We come here to an inhospitable land, as if under cover of night, find a place that time has forgotten, and make it our own. We find comfort in whatever is handed to us. Koreatown, Little India, Ironbound, Little Odessa—we will take it. We will triumph. The question is: For how long? And for how long do we get to preserve any culture imported from our homeland in a sealed bubble before it becomes watered down, thinned out to a milky semblance of the tradition of our motherland? How do we measure that loss? In months, in years, in generations? How long will it be before the children of Yousef decide that the Lagman Soup needs to be more mainstream? Is it when he is too old to see, too old to care; or when he dies and his memory is too faded to matter?

I don't know how long Kashkar Café will stick around. In the end, though, it is not my fight. Kashkar will never make it to the top of a Zagat list, but it is a special place serving a unique cuisine—I hardly ever use the word *unique*, but in this case, it fits—and I am lucky to have eaten there.

What happened to my childhood Brooklyn? I don't know because I left. And the best thing about coming back is learning that it was never mine in the first place.

I WAKE UP TO MY ALARM CLOCK and the sun already shining on Emmons Avenue. I'm late. I've barely slept, but I don't want to miss the fishing boats. I hurry out and jog over to Sheepshead Bay. There is a narrow wharf that is home to a handful of fishing boats that go out daily on the choppy Atlantic waters. Most of the boats have already set sail. The ones that are left are waiting for last-minute passengers. A thin crowd of people holding forlorn fishing rods waits to get going. Most of the rigs employ a guy who stands at the edge of the dock luring customers—cash deal, about forty dollars for a morning ride out to catch porgy and bass and blackfish. The rest of the boats on the wharf are party boats, large semiluxury outfits that take groups of people out to drink and dance until they start vomiting overboard. These have nothing to do with fishing. I walk up to one of the pitch men, a small Italian American about two hundred years old who is wrapped up in several layers of old coats. He can barely stand. "You're guaranteed a good haul," he says. "We go out the whole day. We're the best rig, hands down." When he realizes that I won't be getting on the boat, that I'm there just to ask questions, he says something in Italian I don't understand and turns around to tell the captain to go ahead.

The Brooklyn I remember was very Italian. The funny, sardonic Italian guys spoke their own version of wiseguy, gangster dialect. They lived their lives thick inside an Italian American culture without much need to integrate with the new immigrants surrounding them. There is an old bait and tackle shop in Sheepshead Bay called Stella Maris Fishing Station. If you hang out there long enough, you see the remnants of the old neighborhood, the Italian brothers cracking jokes as if *The Sopranos* was still on the air. This place has been owned by the same family since 1947, and it is an essential part of a fishing industry that is quickly disappearing. Everyone gives a different reason for the decline: the fishing isn't what it used to be, the tourists don't come anymore, the neighborhood has changed, "people just don't wanna fish no more." The underlying message, though, is uncertainty. In a neighborhood where the Russian immigrants are in control of the economy, a niche industry such as charter fishing boats may not have a place. When I was growing up, these fishing boats were a popular weekend diversion. Whether heading to Sheepshead Bay or down the Jersey Shore to Belmar, the boats were packed with people. It wasn't sport fishing—the boats using sonar to position themselves, and twenty people reeling in as much haul as they could for their dinner table. My mom always let me go fishing because she knew I'd come back with thirty pounds of bluefish slung over my shoulder, and that would be dinner for weeks.

There is very little left of that culture here, except for a few restaurants hanging on to the old days. Randazzo's Clam Bar, on Emmons Avenue, is a classic. A neon lobster signals to you from afar. The restaurant's famous red sauce has kept Randazzo's afloat for decades. The sauce is fine, and the calamari are crispy. I'm told that, in the old days, they used to buy the squid right from the docks. I prefer to go to Maria's, on the same street, which has been serving the same menu for eighty years. What you get here are the staples: chicken parm, baked clams, overcooked pasta, nostalgia on a plate. Those industrial-era, unbreakable, inch-thick ceramic plates can make any food look heavy and unappetizing. There is nothing spectacular about the meal, but it satisfies me. It makes me happy to know these places are still around, that when all else fades away, the last bastion of Brooklyn Italian American culture will be a restaurant that features live shows by Sal Casta.

Take a dish and change one ingredient. Is it still the same dish? Take a neighborhood and swap out one culture for another. Is it still the same American dream?

LAGMAN SOUP

This is a simpler version of the soup I had at Kashkar, but it's just as delicious. It is pungent and floral and warms the body from the inside out. I have tasted *lagman* soups that are almost stew-like, but I like this lighter one with noodles. At Kashkar, they serve a small cruet of vinegar on the side that you can add to the soup. I include vinegar in the recipe itself to brighten the hearty stock, but if you prefer, you can omit it when you make the soup and just add a little at the table when you eat it.

SERVES 4 AS A MAIN COURSE

2 lamb shanks (about 1 pound each)

Kosher salt and freshly ground black pepper

3 tablespoons vegetable oil

1 cup diced onion

½ cup sliced garlic

1 celery stalk, diced

3 tablespoons grated fresh ginger

1 serrano pepper, thinly sliced

2 tablespoons ground star anise

1½ tablespoons cumin seeds

1 tablespoon smoked hot paprika

3 tablespoons tomato paste

4 cups water

4 cups chicken stock

¼ cup soy sauce

1½ tablespoons fish sauce

½ pound long beans or green beans

¼ pound Chinese cabbage, coarsely chopped

1 red bell pepper, cored, seeded, and finely diced

3 tablespoons rice vinegar

1 pound fresh thick-cut noodles, such as udon, cooked according to the package directions and drained (see Note)

Chopped fresh dill, for garnish

Season the lamb shanks with a little salt and black pepper. Heat a large pot over high heat. Add 2 tablespoons of the vegetable oil and heat until hot, then add the shanks and brown them on all sides. Remove and set aside.

Add the remaining 1 tablespoon oil, the onion, garlic, celery, ginger, and serrano pepper to the pot and cook, stirring, for 4 minutes, until nicely browned on all sides. Lower the heat to medium and add the star anise, cumin seeds, paprika, and 1 teaspoon black pepper and cook, stirring, for 1 minute, or until fragrant. Add the tomato paste and cook for 1 minute, or until it darkens slightly. Return the lamb shanks to the pot. Pour in the water, chicken stock, soy sauce, and fish sauce and bring to a boil. Lower the heat to maintain a simmer, return the shanks to the pot, cover, and cook for 1 hour 45 minutes, until the meat is tender. Check occasionally, and if the liquid no longer covers the lamb shanks, add a little more water to keep them submerged. Remove the lamb shanks and set aside to cool. Set the soup aside.

Once the shanks are cool, pull the meat from the bones and discard the bones. Add the meat to the soup, along with the green beans, cabbage, and bell pepper, bring to a simmer, and simmer for 10 minutes, until the vegetables have softened. Add the rice vinegar, taste, and add more salt and black pepper as necessary.

Divide the warm noodles among four large bowls and ladle the soup over the top. Garnish with fresh dill.

NOTE: If you're not using the noodles right away, after cooking, toss them with a little neutral oil, such as canola or grapeseed oil, to prevent them from sticking together.

RUSSIAN PICKLED WATERMELON

To learn to make all things Russian, I implore you to get a copy of Darra Goldstein's *A Taste of Russia*. This recipe is inspired by one of hers. You'll be surprised at how delicious pickled watermelon is. You can serve it as an accompaniment to charcuterie or eat it with smoked fish. It is great as a side for any kind of barbecue. Cut it into small cubes and put it in a salad. Or add it to your yogurt in the morning.

Use a watermelon that is not too ripe for this recipe.

MAKES ABOUT 2½ QUARTS

1 baby watermelon
  (2 to 4 pounds), rinsed
8 cups water
1 teaspoon distilled white
  vinegar
¼ cup salt

2 tablespoons sugar
1 tablespoon allspice berries
2 bay leaves
6 garlic cloves
4 celery stalks, thinly sliced
1 bunch dill, coarsely chopped

Cut the watermelon into 1-inch-thick rounds and then cut each round into triangles. Find a large glass jar that will hold the slices, or several smaller jars, and place the watermelon wedges snugly in the jar(s).

In a medium pot, combine the water, vinegar, salt, sugar, allspice berries, bay leaves, garlic, and celery and bring to a low simmer, stirring to dissolve the salt and sugar. Remove from the heat and let the brine cool.

Pour the brine into the jar(s) of watermelon, filling them all the way to the top. Cover the jar(s) with several layers of cheesecloth and secure with a rubber band. Let the pickles sit at room temperature for 24 to 36 hours, checking the jars every 12 hours. As soon as you smell fermentation happening (you will notice a sourness coming from the brine), put the jars in the fridge.

The watermelon should be ready to eat in about 2 days, but you can leave it in the fridge to ferment for longer. I like my watermelon pickle still crispy and fresh, which means just a few days in the fridge, but you can keep it for up to a month; it gets sourer as time goes by.

COFFEE-GLAZED BACON WITH PICKLED WATERMELON AND FRIED PEANUTS

There are many ways to use pickled watermelon, but if you want to get a little fancy with it, try this composed salad with crispy and sweet bacon. It is small in size but layered with lots of flavor and textures.

SERVES 4 AS A FIRST COURSE

GLAZED BACON

¼ cup brewed espresso

3 tablespoons maple syrup

2 tablespoons dark brown sugar

8 slices thick-cut bacon

FRIED PEANUTS

1 cup water

½ cup unsalted raw peanuts

½ cup granulated sugar

1 tablespoon soy sauce

½ cup corn oil

GARNISHES

1 cup Russian Pickled Watermelon (page 61), cut into ½-inch cubes, with its pickling liquid

Handful of small lettuces, such as mâche, baby romaine, or baby arugula

¼ cup torn fresh basil leaves

Extra-virgin olive oil, for drizzling

½ teaspoon pink peppercorns, roughly chopped

TO MAKE THE BACON: Preheat the oven to 350°F. Line a baking sheet with parchment paper.

In a small saucepan, combine the espresso, maple syrup, and brown sugar and bring to a simmer, stirring to dissolve the sugar.

Lay out the bacon evenly on the prepared pan and brush half the espresso glaze over it. Bake for 10 minutes.

Remove the pan from the oven and raise the oven temperature to 400°F. Drain any fat from the pan. Flip the bacon slices and brush the remaining glaze over the bacon. Return to the oven and bake until the bacon is crisp and candied, 3 to 4 minutes. When it is ready, it will have turned a mahogany brown color and started to bubble. Remove and let cool completely on the pan, then break the bacon into large pieces and set aside.

TO MAKE THE FRIED PEANUTS: In a small saucepan, combine the water, peanuts, granulated sugar, and soy sauce and bring to a boil, stirring to dissolve the sugar, then reduce the heat to low and simmer for 5 minutes. Drain the peanuts and spread on a paper towel to dry.

In a small saucepan, heat the corn oil until hot. Add the peanuts and fry until crispy, about 2 minutes. Drain on paper towels. (The peanuts can be fried a day in advance, but do not refrigerate them.)

When ready to serve, gather four small salad plates. Arrange 3 or 4 cubes of pickled watermelon on each plate. Divide the lettuces and basil evenly among the plates. Add some shards of the candied bacon to each plate. Top with the fried peanuts. Spoon a little of the watermelon pickling liquid over each salad, drizzle with just a hint of good olive oil, and sprinkle the pink peppercorns over everything. Enjoy immediately.

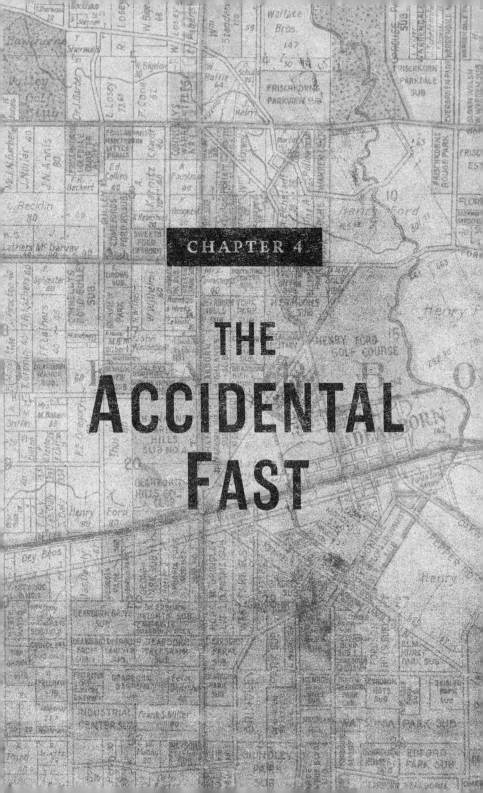

CHAPTER 4

THE
ACCIDENTAL
FAST

'VE COME TO DEARBORN, MICHIGAN, TO EAT. I'VE traveled six hours by car before dawn on nothing more than coffee and Red Bull. It is the middle of summer and my car's air conditioner has died on me, but it isn't reason enough to delay my trip. There is construction along an extended stretch of I-65, and the easiest way to avoid the traffic is to drive during the wee hours of the night. It also gives me time to think about what I'm searching for here in the suburbs of Detroit.

Dearborn is not your typical foodie destination; it is still very much a hidden and misunderstood place. If you search for "Dearborn" on the Internet, you'll find numerous narratives on the rich history of Muslims in the area and their relationship to the Ford Motor plant. But it takes only a quick scroll down to uncover pages of rage and vitriol. "Dearbornistan" is a common nickname, meant to link the American city to its Middle Eastern identity along with a call to arms to "cleanse" the city or "return" it to its rightful owners.

I did a lot of research to prepare for this trip. Many anti-immigrant hate websites mention Dearborn. It is unsettling to discover page after

page of the same vitriol and hate. But when I switched my search to
Dearborn's restaurants, I was pleasantly surprised to find plenty of suggestions for where to dine. Dearborn has dozens of restaurants repre-
senting almost every culture in the Middle East. According to many, I'll
find the best food of the Levant right here, where the Ford plant still
towers over this industrial city. To prep for the trip, I read a lot about
Henry Ford, too. He was a flawed but brilliant figure, and his company
was one of the main reasons that Dearborn is home to the largest Muslim
community in America.

No one knows why the first family from the Levant came to Dearborn.
But it is a well-documented fact that many Muslims worked in the
Ford factory As I near the Dearborn exit in my car, I imagine that first
encounter.

*By 1917, Henry Ford knew that the innovations that had brought the
world the Model T were already obsolete, and he was focused on a much bigger
idea: assembling a flywheel magneto ignition system along the banks of the
River Rouge in Dearborn. This was not merely a factory but a system for all
mankind—eighty thousand men over a thousand acres of factories working for
a common goal: to churn out the most advanced machines ever built by man.
But this ambition came with obstacles. Turnover was hindering production, and
murmurings of union organizing were starting to surface. Human nature, Ford
believed, was defective, and the only salvation was work; the only sanity was a
belief in the system.*

*Along the banks of the River Rouge, iron ore and coal were shipped in daily
on Great Lakes steamers. Mr. Ford could often be found marveling at the great
machines that brought the world's resources to him. It was on those very docks
on a sun-dappled morning that he noticed a young sailor from Yemen. He struck
up a conversation with the merchant marine from Aden. He was curious to know
how far a young man would travel for the prospect of steady factory work.*

*We will travel the world, the sailor replied, but repetition is the curse of the
enslaved.*

Prosperity rewards the industrious, Mr. Ford replied. For five dollars a day, I will earn your loyalty.

The sailor grew excited. For five dollars a day, we will build your automobiles, drive your ships, mine your raw materials. We will bring our families, we will cook our saltah, we will build our mosques.

Mr. Ford could feel the itch of impatience. Then send word to your families, your friends and brethren, he said, until the rumor of prosperity spreads across the entire Levant. I will send ships for them if you promise me the hands of good workers. Send word across the desert until the name of Ford becomes a beacon for all who crave a better life through the sanctity of work.

The Yemeni sailor was already gone, indistinguishable from the dozens of sailors lined up along the mooring. But in his head, the sailor was already composing the letter he would write to his family the first chance he got.

There is no evidence that this exchange ever took place, but it is one of numerous origin stories about how Dearborn, Michigan, became the most heavily populated Muslim city in America. Still, it has a ring of truth to it, and it is convenient, like a dream that ends at the precise moment you wake up. It's probably too good to be true. But there are some histories that can't be explained by green cards or statistics. Sometimes, the closest thing you have to the truth is mythology. Sometimes, you can't experience a city through the Internet. You have to go see it with your own eyes.

CONVENTIONAL WISDOM says that food writing should steer clear of politics and religion, but how do I do this in a place that is defined by its religion and cultural isolation? Isn't cuisine inseparable from the context of the world we live in? Two events happened in the week leading up to my trip. One was the death of Muhammad Ali, easily the most recognizable Muslim celebrity in American history. The city I live in, Louisville, was also his hometown, and the week he died, a week showered with flowers and tears, culminated in a memorial that featured the likes of

Bryant Gumbel, Bill Clinton, and Billy Crystal. The first speaker of the evening was the Rev. Dr. Kevin Crosby. A line from his eulogy struck me: "Ali is the property of all people, but let us never forget that he is the product of black people in their struggle to be free." Those words disturb me for their honesty and brutality. They haunt me for their call to unity in the face of the divide that still exists.

Almost a week after Ali's death, a deranged man walked into a gay nightclub in Orlando, Florida, and committed one of the worst mass shootings in American history. He claimed to be Muslim. All week, the media focused on this, on Muslims, on hatred, on blame. The country was full of rage.

Those two events, Ali's death and the Orlando nightclub shooting, were monumentally different but both impactful: one a celebration, the other a desecration. It is with this frame of mind, in this highly charged national environment, that I am driving to Dearborn, Michigan. When I go to a place like Dearborn, a place I don't know at all, I do it out of a need to understand and connect. Still, I must be willing to accept that the people I meet may not want to connect with me.

Every fifty miles, I think, This is a bad idea. I should turn back. Trucks, lit up like Christmas trees, pass me on the left with a violent force that sucks me toward their rear axles. I steady my steering wheel and slug another mouthful of cold coffee. I drive on at a steady eighty miles per hour. I refuse to pull over for fast food. I don't want to fill up on empty calories. I am going to Dearborn to eat. Little do I know that I will be going there to fast.

The morning in Dearborn is met with distant prayers and empty streets. There is nothing about this place that screams "culinary paradise." It is as somber and dry as a desert. Simple working-class homes unfold into a downtown of two-story buildings that are as dull as they are utilitarian. As I drive down the city's main artery, Warren Avenue, it is evident that I am in a foreign place. The signs are as unforgiving and unreadable as graffiti. The Arabic letters look like art painted on walls, indecipherable to outsiders. There are several eateries on every block, most of them small, with drab awnings that do not seem welcoming. An elderly man smoking a cigarette on a folding chair looks as gray as the asphalt beneath him. The sun provides no color.

I pull into the first restaurant I see that happens to be open at this early hour, Al-Ameer. It is spacious, built for crowds. The staff is hustling despite its being empty, which tells me that the place will soon fill up. My waiter is practiced and concise, perhaps distracted by the thought of the side work yet to be done. I order kibbeh, hummus, chicken *kaftah*, and lamb kebabs. Mint tea comes out fragrant yet dark and heavy, a contradiction I am enjoying. The food arrives in a rhythmic procession, unadorned, delicious, and fast. As more patrons file in, I watch the food come out even faster. There is no romance, no lingering over the last aromatic bites of saffron rice that have folded themselves into the *labneh*. My tea is still warm when the check arrives. I pay and walk over to the counter from where you can see the entire kitchen at work, including a vintage oven where an elderly man is baking round after round of imperfectly puffed flatbreads. I work up the nerve to start a conversation with the old man. I'm usually good at this—I know how to get invited into kitchens; I know how to talk to waiters—but it doesn't work here. There is no tour of the ovens, no talk of family recipes. It is just business as usual. I slink out of the front door and grab a local newspaper. Muhammad Ali is on the cover. I can't read the words, but I don't have to. He was, after all, the Greatest.

The rest of the day is pretty much the same. I walk into restaurants, eat good food, ask questions, and get polite but short answers. Any outsider is first met with suspicion, apprehension. The fact that I'm writing a food story means nothing to the man operating a fifteen-seat eatery catering to clientele who do not need a food guide to tell them what to order. I am at best an oddity, but more than that, I get the feeling that I'm a nuisance. I represent everything this community mistrusts about the outside world. Before I embarked on this trip, I was told to bring along someone who could introduce me to the locals, someone who could speak Arabic—a "fixer," they sometimes call it. I decided against this. I wanted this to be a personal journey, and I wanted to figure things out for myself. Despite the regret I'm starting to feel about this, I march on.

IT IS RAMADAN, the time for fasting, so most of the restaurants I visit are empty during the day. The owners smile and wave, then hide in the back, presumably to avoid any conversation with me. I don't have any way to start up a conversation with them, either. Just before sundown, I drive to a nearby hotel to get some rest, only to be told there are no vacancies. There is a Beyoncé concert in Detroit. I end up at an extended-stay motel, one of those forlorn places with an economy kitchenette that looks more like a meth lab than a place you'd want to cook a meal in. That night, I walk the streets of Dearborn looking for someone to talk to. At sundown, I'm told, the restaurants fill up with people breaking their fast. Everywhere I go, the TVs are tuned to Al Jazeera and the events unfolding in Orlando. The people around me, heavily bearded men dressed as men who work blue-collar jobs do, sternly watch the televisions or are deep in conversation in a language I cannot comprehend. No one is interested in idle chatter, at least not with me. I know they're surveying me, but so practiced are they at this that I never make eye contact with a single person, though I look up from my *ghallaba* every once in a while.

I finish dinner and walk to the most opulent pastry shop in Dearborn, Shatila Bakery, which at first looks more like a casino than a café. The place is buzzing with women wearing the hijab, some with young children waiting in line for their sweets. There is a coffee counter, a glass display about a football field long of pastries, and an ice cream station where every flavor is spiked with neon dye. I patiently wait in line and order as much as I think my stomach will handle: *kashtas*, *katayifs*, and baklavas dripping with syrups redolent of rose water and honey. Aside from the shapes, I almost can't tell them apart. An older man who notices my pen and notepad strikes up a conversation with me.

"You are a writer?" he asks. He is clean shaven and graying, almost professorial but wearing the thin polyester of someone who works in a clerk's office. He speaks with no accent, save the rhythm of a vernacular that is distinct from American English. It almost sounds British, though I know it is not.

"Not really," I say, but I explain why I'm here.

"You are writing about Ramadan?"

"Not necessarily," I respond, and immediately feel his scorn. "I don't know much about it. Where would I learn?"

"You don't *learn* Ramadan. You must *experience* it."

"You telling me I should fast?"

"Why not?"

"I'm not Muslim."

"You think fasting has to do with being Muslim?"

"Doesn't it?"

"Fasting has to do with sympathy for the suffering, for humanity. If you think that is only a Muslim idea, then you are limiting yourself."

Suddenly, I'm in a theological debate. I want to get up and leave, but like the speeding trucks along the dark highway, I'm being pulled toward something, this idea.

"What if I can't do it? I mean, I'm here to eat."

"That is up to you, Mr. Writer. No one will find fault in you. But what are you really trying to discover here?" He wishes me good luck and abruptly leaves. That "Mr. Writer" line seemed a bit condescending, and it stings me, until I realize that he paid for my pastries without my knowing. I dip my fork into the dense baklava, already knowing it will be my last bite of food for a while.

I PLAN ON waking up before sunrise to drink plenty of water and eat a hearty breakfast. Instead, I oversleep. I wake to a blade of sunlight piercing my room. I'm hungry and parched. I get out of bed bleary-eyed, slowly walking on stiff ankles. I walk over to the sink, cup in hand, and fill it with cold tap water to soothe the aridity of my tongue. With my eyes half open, I bring the cup to my lips and then remember the man from last night, his tone, his condescension. I am alone; no one knows or cares about my promise. I can get a late start this morning; no one will know. I'm not Muslim, anyway. Then I hear his ironic voice calling me "Mr. Writer." I put the cup down and lie back in bed, trying to collect enough saliva to coat my tongue. It is 9:00 a.m. I have more than twelve hours to go before sundown. I'm kinda fucked. I decide I'll take this down the road as long as I can.

I start the day at a mosque, the Islamic Center of America. It is the largest and oldest mosque in America. It is a flawless structure of white stone and gold domes surrounded by immaculate lawns in the middle of perhaps the most nondescript city in America. It is a humbling building, like most monuments of prayer, and, as I walk into this vast marbled foyer, spotless, cold, and empty. I can hear the chants of prayers nearby, but otherwise, I'm alone in a hall where even my breathing is an echo. I hear a latch buzz open, and I'm met by a woman in her forties who has emerged from an office wearing the traditional hijab. She asks me if I would like a Koran, and we walk across the grounds. She doesn't question why I'm here. She tells me to respect the book of the Koran. I tell her I have never read the Koran other than a few passages from an art history class in college. She smiles warmly and speaks in a patient voice. She does not lecture me about Islam. She tells me that to fast is to suffer as the poor do. Surprisingly, we talk about things that don't seem like religion. She tells me about her daughter and asks me if I have children. I ask her about the shooter in Orlando.

He is not Muslim, she says. One cannot be Muslim and do those things.

She takes me into the prayer room, a cavernous space of ancient carpets and people kneeling in prayer. I take off my shoes and kneel in one corner. She tells me she must pray and that we can resume our talk later. She moves to the center of the room and kneels while reciting lines from the Koran. After a few minutes, a man taps me on the shoulder and points at me to follow him out of the room.

You are not Muslim, he tells me; you should not be in there. His voice is soft but stern. She will pray for a long time, he adds. You can talk to me.

We walk together toward the parking lot. We sit on a bench, and he tells me about the history of this mosque, the times it has been desecrated, the many times people have traveled to Dearborn only to protest here. He stops there, as if to acknowledge that he has nothing to explain, that he doesn't need to defend himself against a crime he didn't commit. He gives me a list of restaurants to visit and wishes me good luck. I forget to ask him his name. In my effort not to pry too much, I find it difficult even to ask the simplest of questions of the people I meet.

THE NEXT PLACE I VISIT is a tiny Iranian kebab restaurant. There's simmered lamb's head on the menu. I order that and three other plates. I wait patiently for the food. When it arrives, I smell it, make some notes, and take the obligatory cell phone pics. The lamb's head is ungarnished; it is simply a plate of tender meat sliding off the skull of a young sheep. I ask for to-go boxes. The owner looks at me curiously, and I tell her I'm observing Ramadan but want to write about the food, so I'll eat it later tonight. Her hard face instantly warms with a smile. She is a large woman with the wrinkles of a person who has endured much. Her English is made up mostly of nouns. She wants to know where I'm from. She packs up my food lovingly and gives me plastic bags tied up in a knot, so it'll be easy for me to carry. She calls her husband over; he shakes my hand. He is wearing nothing but a T-shirt, slacks, and flip-flops. He welcomes me into his space. He does all the cooking in a kitchen so small that I can't fathom where his *mise en place* is. He doesn't smile much, but I sense that he doesn't smile much for anyone. We talk for some time, and he gives me a few suggestions for places I should try.

I go to a few more lunch spots and do the same thing. I'm so excited to be talking to people that I barely feel hunger. One of the places everyone

keeps telling me about is Al Sultan, on Inkster Road near the outskirts of
Dearborn, a diner-like building wrapped in neon signage depicting a man
on horseback wielding a sword. The airbrushed image is surreal, but the
food is top notch. It's 2:00 p.m., and I have four bags of take-out food
in the backseat of my car fermenting in the summer heat. Then I go to a
place that has live chickens they slaughter to order for you. I don't have
the heart to get a chicken, but I walk out of there with a mango custard
I know will only spoil in my car. I have about six hours to go before I
can have my first taste of food, and so far, aside from being parched,
I'm doing fine.

The day is flying by. I pull into a pastry shop and sidle up to a glass
case filled with pastries. For some reason, the smell of burnt sugar trig-
gers something in me that none of the meats did. It makes me weak. I
start moving noticeably slower, more heavily. My brain sees the sugar,
and I'm irritated. I leave without ordering anything. I jump into my
car and I'm fucking mad. The car smells like a lamb carcass, and my air
conditioner is out. I drive back to my hotel with Young Jeezy playing as
loud as I can stand it.

I organize all the food in my refrigerator and lie down on the floor,
which smells like carpet mites, whatever they're supposed to smell like.
My hunger dissolves again. I don't know for how long, so I start reading
through e-mails I've already read. I fall asleep pretty quickly.

When I wake up, it's around 5:00 p.m. I am only four and a half hours
away from food. The hunger is less painful than my parched mouth. I
know that I shouldn't be in this much discomfort; it is only one day of
fasting, and plenty of people do this for a month without complaint. But
for someone who is accustomed to consuming three thousand calories
a day, this is a shock to the system. *Judge Judy* is on TV, and the sound
of her voice comforts me. I start talking aloud about the specific pains
I'm having.

"Stomach not so bad, actually, but my arms and legs feel heavy and
weak.

"I can feel myself breathing."

I have a headache, not a sharp puncture of pain, but more like the constant noise of weeping without pause. The inside of my ears hurt, which I think is because I'm swallowing every few seconds, hoping for moisture but just pulling more dry air down my trachea. I touch my thumb to the rest of my fingertips, one hand at a time, again and again. I fall back asleep.

I wake up to a dim orange cloud. The sun is finally going down. I have not seen the sun like this in many years, in a way I'm so invested in. I'm sweating; more water is draining from my body. Yet I'm oddly invigorated, as if high. I'm not delirious, but I'm also not well. There is a point where the stomach ceases to growl and you can feel it shrinking. The sound of the TV hurts me. I can't find the remote, so I have to crouch down and find the Power button. The vibration of color rakes across my face. It is 8:30 p.m. An hour to go. I go for a walk. This is less a decision than a way to fight inertia, my body trying to stay awake. Not knowing where to go, I pace the parking lot. The heat is too much. It has never bothered me before, but now it feels like a cloak on my back. I didn't put on socks, and my feet hurt in my shoes. My legs are getting numb. I go back to my room and lie in bed, though this time I can't sleep. My mind is racing, while my arms and legs remain lethargic. I try to write, but I can't find any coherent words. I can feel myself just giving in, but to what? I know I won't die, so what is my body trying to do? It is shutting down. My vision is getting blurry.

This is my twentieth hour without food or water. I'm not sure I can even walk straight, but staying here watching the clock is making me insane. I get in my car and drive. I find a Syrian restaurant that's on my list. I'm looking for company more than food at this point. It's only about fifteen minutes now until *iftar*, or the breaking of the fast. Tables are filling up with men; they seem calm. I talk to the owner and tell him what I'm doing. He's from Syria and does all the cooking, while his wife helps with the service. He has silver hair and a dark tan. I order kebabs and hummus and pastries. He gives me a stare of disappointment.

The purpose of fasting is not to overeat at sundown, he says. You must remain humble, eat meagerly and slowly.

Oh great, I think. I'm about to chew off my arm and I'm supposed to be modest.

You can eat for a long time, he explains, but always in small bites. Start with tea, he suggests. Have a simple soup, some bread and chickpeas. It is in this moment that we can understand what it truly feels like to be one of the unfortunate. Also, if the first thing you eat is a kebab, it will give you a stomachache later.

AT THE PRECISE MOMENT OF SUNDOWN, he places a cup of tea in front of me. I drink it . . . and it is as if I have never tasted mint before. It is so sharp, so singular. I'm actually not even hungry anymore. The tea calms me. I don't devour the food. I have soup, a creamy soup that has only about three ingredients but is so delicious that I can't stop eating it. I eat unleavened bread and chew slowly. I go back to my hotel. It is dark now. I unwrap all the spoils from the day. Twelve Styrofoam trays of food in all. I take a bite from each one and jot down impressions in my notepad.

It is hard to judge a plate of food when you eat it hours after you're supposed to, but the *arayes* from Al Sultan is remarkable, a flatbread-type sandwich stuffed with minced lamb and vegetables. I am sure it was much better hot, right off the grill. Even at room temperature, though, this is easily my new favorite sandwich. You have to make the dough from scratch; it is amazingly easy. It just isn't the same using store-bought pita.

That night, sleep comes easily.

I'M ABLE TO KEEP UP THE FAST for three more days. Each day, I meet more people who allow me into their lives. I feel the suspicion dissolve away. I get invited to *iftar* by a couple who owns a pastry shop. I eat pita with *labneh* and fritters. I'm taken aback by the *labneh* for its simplicity and yet also for how it wakes up my taste buds. Now that my mind is not focused on the pain of fasting, my senses feel heightened, my taste buds sharp. I don't even eat the lamb. I'm transfixed by the flavor of warm pita and *labneh*.

The pita is homemade, the pastry chef says.

Of course it is. I feel like I'm eating something that is not just a family recipe or a tradition back home, but something deeper, more ancient. The sour notes of the *labneh* taste like an ancient flavor bringing relief after a day's abstinence. How much has this cuisine changed over the last fifty, one hundred, two hundred years? Muslims have been in Dearborn for more than a hundred years, yet this city still walks a fine balance between hushed uneasiness and calm, tension and tolerance. Most of the people I meet have been here all their lives. They speak perfect English; they study in universities and drive American cars. But they are also deeply devout and deeply loyal to their religion and to Dearborn.

On my last day, I pack my car with food and drive back home. I invite friends over, and we feast on the delicacies while I tell stories about my fast. It sounds like a dream. No one believes me. I promise to keep the fast going, but I don't last even another day. The next morning, I wake up and stuff a biscuit in my face while getting my daughter dressed for day care. Without the context of Dearborn, the fast becomes impossible. Without the community of people engaged in the same ritual, it seems facile. I look at my notebooks. Usually, I fill pages and pages with notes. Oddly, I didn't write much on this trip. I forgot to get names; I didn't collect menus. I realize that once I took myself out of the role of the observer and became a participant, I didn't have the desire to write. I didn't interview people; I just talked. I met many kinds of people but never thought to ask their names or interview them about their jobs. For a brief few days, I didn't need explanations or testimonies. I just floated among others from a culture I would never truly understand, but I felt I got a little closer to understanding the food. I could taste the devotion, which is everywhere in the culture: the prayers, the fasting, the rituals. I've been eating hummus and tahini and falafel all my life, but for the first time, I understood why these foods feel so deeply enriching. After a day's fast, the flavors and fats cling to your bones like medicine and heal you from the inside out.

FOUR MONTHS after my trip to Dearborn, I'm sitting in the recreation room of a local church on a Friday night. In response to the Orlando tragedy, I made a donation to a local LGBTQ organization that supports young teens discovering their identities. On this night, I talk to the group of kids about what I do, and we snack on some appetizers from my restaurant. They ask me questions, such as what my favorite food is and if I like to yell in my kitchen. We joke and laugh about our failures, and the whole time, we're just talking about food. We don't talk about the Orlando tragedy. I don't ask them what troubles them. A fourteen-year-old girl plays me a song on her ukulele. I answer questions from the kids and from a box of questions written anonymously. We take selfies and trade Facebook accounts. The evening is lighthearted, though the cloud of violence is always nearby for these kids. I'm having a great time.

By most accounts, Henry Ford was a pretty bigoted man, one who believed more in the logic of mechanics than the humanity of people. I've never found any evidence that he was a gourmand. To care about food is to care about people. To understand the food of another culture is to know that there will be limitations. But there can still be a deep satisfaction in trying to understand a culture that will never understand you. I still have not read the entire Koran; I still know very little about Islam and the ancient cultures that gave rise to one of the most important cuisines we have in America. Still, I feel I've learned more about being human from attempting to fast. I learned to eat or not to eat in a city that is trying to preserve a culture that was born thousands of miles away and thousands of years ago. Maybe Dearborn is not your typical American city, and maybe we think the people there should eat more pizza and watch more South Park. Maybe we want them to be so much more assimilated than they want to be. But we love the hummus their culture created, and the falafel and the lamb kebabs and the yogurt sauces and the flatbreads. They give those to us freely, and they don't complain when we make them our own, when we put artichokes in our hummus or fill our pita breads with *char siu* pork.

Does everything have to be assimilated to be American? Can we learn to respect the distinct lines of a culture that does not want to be like us? I hope so, because as much as I love pizza and chanterelle hummus, I also want to know that I can go to a restaurant in Dearborn that will serve me a boiled lamb's head, teeth and all, as if it were the most natural thing to eat for lunch.

LAMB ARAYES
WITH TAHINI DRESSING AND
PICKLED SWEET PEPPERS

I learned about so many new dishes during my trip to Dearborn. I'm including this one because not only was it one of the tastiest dishes I ate, it also translates easily to a home kitchen. No special oven needed or long cooking times. This is basically a lamb sandwich in pita bread, but the lamb filling is aromatic and vibrant. And making the pita from scratch can be a transformative experience. I always make extra pita to enjoy with hummus the next day. Or crisp the leftovers in the oven and cut them into pieces to use in salads for a garnish.

LAMB FILLING

One 1-pound piece lamb loin, finely chopped

1 cup chopped tomatoes

½ onion, finely diced

⅓ cup chopped fresh flat-leaf parsley

½ teaspoon ground allspice

¼ teaspoon ground cinnamon

1 teaspoon salt

½ teaspoon red pepper flakes

½ teaspoon freshly ground black pepper

1 tablespoon pomegranate molasses

4 Rye Pitas (recipe follows)

Olive oil, for brushing

Salt

1 small onion, sliced

½ cup arugula

¼ cup Pickled Sweet Peppers (recipe follows)

½ cup Tahini Dressing (recipe follows)

Preheat the oven to 350°F.

TO MAKE THE LAMB FILLING: In a large bowl, combine the lamb, tomatoes, onion, parsley, allspice, cinnamon, salt, red pepper flakes, black pepper, and molasses and mix well.

Split the pitas in half. Spread a thin layer of one-quarter of the lamb mixture on the bottom half of one pita and replace the top half. Repeat with the remaining pitas and filling. Carefully brush both sides of the pitas with olive oil and sprinkle with a little salt.

Arrange the pitas on a baking sheet and bake for 15 to 20 minutes, until the lamb is cooked through.

Remove the pitas from the oven, lift the top of each one, and layer with the onion, arugula, and pickled peppers. Drizzle a little tahini dressing over the top and put the top back on the sandwich. Serve immediately.

RYE PITAS | MAKES 8 PITAS

1 cup warm water (about 112°F)	1¼ cups all-purpose flour, plus ½ cup for dusting
2 tablespoons active dry yeast	2 teaspoons salt
½ teaspoon sugar	2 tablespoons olive oil
¼ cup rye flour	

In a large bowl, combine the warm water, yeast, sugar, rye flour, and ¼ cup of the all-purpose flour and mix well. Let stand for 10 minutes, or until foamy.

Add the salt, olive oil, and 1 cup of the all-purpose flour and gently stir with a wooden spoon for 1 minute to combine. You may need to add a little of the remaining all-purpose flour; the dough should be wet but pull away easily from the sides of the bowl. Turn the dough out onto a floured work surface and knead until it is smooth and holds its shape, just a few minutes, adding more flour if necessary. Put the kneaded dough in a large oiled bowl and cover with plastic wrap. Let it rest in a warm place for 1 hour, or until doubled in size.

Put a baking sheet on the middle rack of the oven and preheat the oven to 475°F.

Punch down the dough and divide it into 8 pieces. Form each piece into a ball, arrange on a floured work surface, and cover with a damp towel. Let the dough rest for 10 minutes.

Remove one dough ball, leaving the others covered to prevent the dough from developing a skin, and, using a floured rolling pin, roll out the dough on a lightly floured work surface to a ⅛-inch thickness, about 5 inches in diameter. Set aside and roll out the remaining dough balls. You can stack them between sheets of parchment. Carefully remove the preheated baking sheet from the oven and place as many dough pieces on it as you can fit. Return the baking sheet to the oven. Once the pitas puff, after about 2 minutes, flip with a spatula or tongs and cook for an additional minute or so. The pitas should remain pale, with hints of brown spots. Remove from the oven and set aside on a plate.

(CONTINUED)

Repeat with the remaining dough. If not using right away, store the remaining pitas by letting them cool to room temperature, wrapping them individually in plastic wrap, and storing in the freezer for up to a month. When ready to use, place in a 300°F oven for 5 minutes to warm up.

PICKLED SWEET PEPPERS | MAKES ½ QUART

10 small sweet peppers, seeded and thinly sliced, any mix of bell, cherry, or Italian sweets	⅓ cup sugar
	1 teaspoon salt
	1 whole star anise pod
1 cup rice vinegar	½ teaspoon whole black peppercorns
½ cup water	1 large strip lemon peel

Thinly slice the sweet peppers and pack them into a jar. In a small saucepan, combine the vinegar, water, sugar, salt, star anise, and peppercorns and bring to a boil, stirring to dissolve the sugar. Add the lemon peel, remove from the heat, and let cool to room temperature.

Pour the pickling liquid into the jar, close the lid tightly, and refrigerate overnight. Discard any excess liquid. The peppers will keep in the fridge for up to a month.

TAHINI DRESSING | MAKES 1 CUP

½ cup labneh or Greek yogurt	¼ cup water
3 tablespoons tahini	1 tablespoon sherry vinegar
2 tablespoons toasted sesame oil	1 tablespoon fresh lemon juice
	½ teaspoon paprika

In a small bowl, combine the labneh, tahini, sesame oil, water, vinegar, lemon juice, and paprika and whisk to combine. Cover and refrigerate until ready to serve. The dressing will keep in the fridge for up to 2 weeks.

CHANTERELLE HUMMUS

In an age of culinary appropriation, there is a raging debate among chefs and food writers about what you can and can't call hummus. For the most part, I tend to side with the purists. Black bean hummus isn't hummus (it's just gross). But I do call this a hummus, because the chanterelles remind me of chickpeas in flavor and color. Spread the hummus over pita bread (page 81) for a wonderful vegetarian snack. This is also great with Pickled Sweet Peppers (opposite).

Don't make this with other mushrooms, though—it won't taste right. And only use chanterelles when they are at their peak, which may be from early summer into the fall, depending on where you live.

SERVES 4 AS A SNACK

10 garlic cloves	½ cup water
6 tablespoons olive oil	⅓ cup extra-virgin olive oil
1½ pounds chanterelle mushrooms, cleaned	Juice of 3 lemons
	1 tablespoon tahini
3 teaspoons salt	½ teaspoon red pepper flakes

Preheat the oven to 350°F.

Place the garlic cloves in the center of a piece of aluminum foil. Drizzle 3 tablespoons of the olive oil over them and wrap in the foil, sealing the seams tightly. Roast for 30 minutes, or until the garlic is softened.

Meanwhile, in a medium bowl, toss the chanterelles with the remaining 3 tablespoons olive oil and 1 teaspoon of the salt. Spread on a baking sheet and roast for about 15 minutes, until the mushrooms are cooked through.

Transfer the roasted garlic, with all its oil, and the chanterelles to a blender. Add the water, extra-virgin olive oil, lemon juice, tahini, remaining 2 teaspoons salt, and the red pepper flakes and blend on high speed to a smooth puree. If it seems too thick, add a little water a spoonful at a time until you get the desired consistency. The hummus will keep, covered, for 1 week in the refrigerator.

CHAPTER 5

EXILE
AND
CIGARS

THE INSIDE OF AN AIRPORT DURING INCLEMENT weather is the last place on earth I want to be. It is a waiting room of uncertainty, paranoia, and helplessness. The anger of delayed passengers is contagious. I try to meditate by gazing out at the tarmac, at the weary planes lurching toward their gates. The sky is overcast, with muted cloud cover. It is the color of smoke, a dense, unmoving smoke that refuses to let sunlight pierce through. It is not raining yet, but that doesn't stop the plane delays from pouring in. One by one, each destination city is announced. I quickly scan the terminal to see who is throwing up his arms in disgust, as if it were a surprise, as if the heavens were listening. My flight to Miami is over an hour and a half delayed. It is little joy to watch as other people's schedules are equally dismantled, but it is all the comfort I have right now.

I'm hoping to meet up with chef Norman Van Aken. He's been a hero of mine since I was a young cook, and of late, we've become good friends. I text him, and he apologizes but says he has to head to Mount Dora, Florida, where he's opening a new restaurant. He'll catch up with me in a few days, he tells me. I settle back in my seat and follow the drama of a heavyset British man yelling feverishly at an emotionless dark-skinned woman who is typing away robotically on an antiquated keyboard. The sky looks like it will open up at any minute and release a storm of biblical proportions.

As a young chef, the only cuisine that mattered to me was from Europe, mostly French. If you wanted to be a chef, you learned French cuisine; you studied Escoffier, you learned the brigade system, the mother sauces. Jacques Pépin and Julia Child were on TV, André Soltner and Gray Kunz in the newspapers. Jean-Georges was making waves with his Asian style of French food, but it was still a Eurocentric approach to food. Asian food was popular, but the kind I saw marketed in the magazines all smelled of an exoticism that seemed disingenuous to me. Martin Yan was on TV, but he was branded for the home cook. Ming Tsai was taking the world by storm with his East-meets-West cuisine, and though I hung on his every word, there was something about his rugby good looks and Ivy League smile that I knew was an ocean away from who I was. In an ironic twist, I had to look to England to find an Asian cook to identify with. Though he was American, Ken Hom did most of his television work and publishing through the BBC. In fact, for most of my life, I thought he was a British chef. Still, as inspirational as Ken's books were to me, they told a one-sided story. They did not address the conflict of someone like me, who felt about as much a part of the Asian diaspora as I did the American TV dinner generation of my youth. I never understood why the Asian identity and the American identity had to be compartmentalized, the way my Salisbury steak and apple pie were separated in my Swanson's dinner. I wanted them all in one bite.

Then I learned about Norman Van Aken, a person of vaguely Dutch roots but also French and maybe some German as well. Originally from Illinois, he moved to the Florida Keys as a young cook and began a culinary journey that would embrace all of Florida, from the Southern roots of the Panhandle, to the flavors of Cuba, to the spices of the Caribbean, to Asia and beyond. He was doing all this at his restaurant, Norman's, in Miami. In fact, it was Van Aken who coined the term *fusion*, an idea that caught on so wildly that *fusion* became a national catchword for any dish that combined the disparate flavors of two cultures. The term, and the gimmicky cuisine that followed, quickly became a joke, though. Fusion became wasabi-flavored mashed potatoes or roast chicken with a sticky, sweet mango-ginger sauce. What everyone missed was the real impact of Norman's message.

Van Aken's cuisine was one that could have happened only in South Florida, where a world of flavors met at his tablecloth, as he would say. It was his openness, his inclusion of these cultures that made him important to me. He was making a case for a permanent cuisine, one that embraced both one's own ethnicity and that of one's geography. All of a sudden, you didn't have to choose. You didn't have to live in a culinary solipsism of forced borders. To him, cooking Caribbean food was natural if one lived near a market that sold jerk spices, goat meat, and mangoes. Norman's brilliance was in harmonizing "foreign" ingredients with his formal culinary training and understanding that both could coexist in a meaningful way. The term *fusion*, therefore, was not about combining or co-opting disparate cultures, not about spiking shitty mashed potatoes with artificial wasabi powder, but about finding ways to balance the formal structural cuisine of Europe with the home cooking of the immigrant cultures around him. That was the fusion. It was a powerful statement by a chef who, quite by accident, influenced the cuisine of every young chef who came after him. Because the term *fusion* would become so badly misinterpreted, Van Aken would not get the credit for it, and it would take an entire generation of chefs to refute it and the next generation of cooks to embrace its true meaning. It was Van Aken who convinced me that it was okay to study in the French tradition but also to know that I could have a career outside it.

In 1998, I went to Norman's in Miami. I boarded a Greyhound bus from New York City and slept most of the way. At the restaurant, I nervously ordered almost everything on the menu and quietly savored every bite. I didn't ask to meet Norman, though I knew he was in the kitchen that evening. I stole a menu. I had nothing else to do in Miami, so I returned to the bus station and waited for my ride back home to New York. While waiting, I read his menu over and over again. When I moved to Louisville in 2003, to take over the reins at 610 Magnolia, the first thing I did was frame it and hang it on a wall.

AFTER TWO HOURS OF WAITING, I finally board my plane to Miami. I like the quiet isolation of planes. I have in my hand the manuscript for Norman's latest book about Florida. It is an ambitious work. He is trying to define the cuisine of Florida, a place of so many geographic and cultural layers that it seems impossible to touch upon them all. His publisher asked me to write a blurb for the book jacket. It feels strange to be doing this. To write a sentence of encouragement for someone I have looked up to for so long is a daunting task. In many ways, heroes can never be your peers, no matter how much you achieve. I feel they should remain distant and polished, for to know someone intimately is also to observe in him the flaws that make him human, and maybe I don't want to know or accept that in Norman. To me, he is a chef, a writer, and a thoughtful historian. He is also a complex person who has had business failures. He has not gotten the attention bestowed upon some of his peers. At sixty-five, he is rebuilding his empire. We are at a place in the timeline of American cuisine when the gatekeepers are defining its history. It is difficult to see Norman creep back into the American consciousness when I feel he never left. In coming up with a blurb, I'm trying to find the words to pay him homage but not sound like a drooling fan. I want my quote to sound dignified and grateful at the same time, but for now, the words fail me.

It is a windy day in Miami when I arrive. The palm trees are bending at the waist. My first stop is at Versailles, an institution in the Calle Ocho, also known as Little Havana. I get a Cubano, fried plantains, and a beer. Norman had e-mailed a list of places to visit: El Mago de Las Fritas, El Tambo Grill, La Camaronera, Garcia's, Azucar, and many others. I won't have time to visit them all. At Versailles, there is no shortage of people who will tell you the history of the neighborhood. It seems odd to credit Fidel Castro with the economic boom of Little Havana, but if you talk to enough Cubans here, it won't be long before his name comes up. From the moment Castro took power in Cuba, it was clear that the ideological fight over communism would be played out on American soil. Refugees were coming to Miami as early as the late 1950s, and the U.S. government was happy to have them partake in the superiority of the American way of life, to lord it over their communist neighbor. The result was multiple waves of Cubans refugees whose numbers rose and fell with the whims of Castro's policies. From the early refugees of the 1960s after the Cuban Revolution to the Marielitos in the '80s, Cuban immigrants tell a story that is long and manifold. The opinions of the older refugees are not always shared by the younger generations who arrived much later in the saga. Maybe the only thing that unites them is their disdain for Castro, even as he is still revered by many inside Cuba. "We left our families, our friends, our homes to come to the United States," says one older man wearing a straw fedora, whom I met at a juice stand in the Calle Ocho. "Here, we are united against Castro."

The sky threatens rain all night, but it never comes. A swirling wind brings salty grit to the already humid air. I spend the night in my hotel room reading Norman's book cover to cover—so many recipes, collected over a lifetime in the kitchen; so many stories. The crazy thing is that for all his writings and recipes, I feel that the best thing about Norman is listening to him speak. He has a conviction in his voice that is quiet but unstoppable. The words in the book don't do him justice. To hear him speak those same words would make a world of difference, the difference between information and truth. Sometimes, all that is needed to make that leap of faith is the candor of a reassuring voice.

The next day, I head to El Mago de Las Fritas for one of its paprika-spiked pork burgers topped with potato sticks. The meat is bouncy, almost a little too worked over; the spices create a thin crust on the patty that makes me nod in approval. The potato sticks fall all over the place, and the only sensible thing to do is to grab the burger with both hands and flatten it. The bun is cheap, processed, and soft— in other words, perfect. It's not the original way the burger is served, but I get mine with a fried egg on top. I don't look up until I've finished. I order a water and a mamey juice. I have a tamale, too. I look around the restaurant. It is a colorful place, with plastic ferns and old-fashioned menu boards. The waitress looks at me furtively.

Oh, fuck it. "Give me a plate of churros, too," I tell her.

The problem with food exploration is stopping oneself from overeating. When I'm enjoying a meal, I don't know how to stop at one or two bites. I walk out of Las Fritas too full to eat again right away. I walk a few blocks to the Wynwood Art District and find a cozy cigar shop where I can rest and rekindle my appetite. It is dark, hazy, and air-conditioned. The manager takes me to his humidor to peruse his selections. I ask him if there are any locally made cigars, and he guides me to a Canimao. It is robust and balanced, he says. I don't know what that means, but I'm willing to give it a try.

There are two other people in the lounge puffing away: a sinewy woman with deep smoker's lines on her upper lip, sitting in a leather chair much too large for her small frame; and next to her, a young man, broad and clumsy, wearing a T-shirt and jeans, with a short military haircut. He is talking about jazz; she is talking about politics. They are both drinking cocktails. She is holding her cigar so deftly. I imitate her grip. I introduce myself to them and am given a box of matchsticks to light my cigar. The young man is going next door to the bar and offers to bring me back a rum. I gladly accept. Klaus Waldeck is playing over the speakers; it is like ballroom music on a psychedelic acid trip. On a large-screen TV is a black-and-white video of Fred Astaire dancing. I can't tell if the video is random or a part of the music. The mood here is laid-back. No one is in a hurry to go anywhere. The manager tells me that if you stay here long enough, you'll meet everyone from the neighborhood.

What about the person who makes these cigars?

You mean Mel? Yeah, he lives not too far away.

A young Cuban woman stops in, dragging a cooler full of desserts. Her name is Ody, and she sells pastries: two kinds of tarts, guava and coconut, and something she calls *semovita*, a kind of puff pastry square dusted with powdered sugar. The pastry is light, delicate, and crispy in a way that tells me it is made with lard. They are a dollar each. I buy *pastellas* for everyone, and we continue to drink and talk. Four cops come in dressed in full gear, and I tense up. They sit down at a long banquette to smoke cigars. They take exactly twenty minutes to smoke and then politely leave.

They are regulars, the manager says.

I explain that I have to leave, that I don't want to let Norman down when he asks me how I liked his recommendations.

But Mel is on his way, the manager tells me. I gave him a call.

My head is spinning for an excuse to leave, but the cigar smoke has gotten me light-headed. Something tells me I should wait.

I'll finish my drink, but then I'll have to leave, I say.

Mel Gonzalez is tall, fit, bald, and slightly bent over. It is the posture of a man who has spent years working in a hunched position—not unlike the posture of an aging cook. He is in his sixties but looks much younger. He asks me how I liked his cigar. I confess that I don't know very much about them. Aside from the occasional late-evening indulgence, I have never made it a conviction to learn.

You are smoking a Flor de Caño, he tells me, made from Vuelta Abajo.

I nod as if to say, *Well, of course I am.*

He takes me into the humidor and tells me about cigar making. He is a confident man, eager to explain his craft. He picks up one of his boxes, inhales deeply, and gives it a light tap with his finger.

"It starts with the box," he says. Cedar to age the cigars. He shows me the box. It took him a year to come up with the design. It bears an illustration of Matanzas Bay, surrounded by sandy beaches and palm trees. A sun is setting beyond the horizon. Everything about the illustration could easily be a cliché, until you listen to Mel explain it. *Matanzas* means "massacre," as this land was built on bloodshed.

"It is on these lands that the Vegas of Canimao started a culture that would make the best cigars in the world."

Mel comes from a family of cigar rollers. He is third generation.

"Just beyond the hills here, there is a ridge." He points to a place on the cigar box outside the frame. "From there, you can see the entire bay. My dream is to build a house there and retire."

Mel arrived in Miami on September 23, 1992. He remembers the date because it is etched into his identity. He went to school; he did sales for Electrolux and made a good living. In 2006, he started his own cigar company and called it Canimao. Last year, he sold 150,000 cigars.

"So, what makes a good cigar?" I ask him.

He raises an eyebrow as if to say, *That's a dumb question, but I'll tell you anyway.* "A cigar is made from one thing and one thing only: tobacco leaves. It is how you blend them, how you roll them, that creates flavors. A good cigar, you can feel aromas in your mouth, you can taste nuances: *matices.* First thing you must do is smell." He handles the cigar as a chef might a piece of fruit. Eyes closed, he takes deep but controlled breaths to show that something is being communicated between the cigar and his olfactory senses. Then he touches it. He taps the cigar, rolls it between his deft fingers. "It should be dense and tight but not too much, or you won't get a good pull." He lights it. "You light it first and then pull. Good materials mean you will have a good strong ash. This is a Connecticut wrapper, sweet and delicious. There is a sweet spot to every cigar. And that is what you are searching for. The first few puffs will tell you nothing. Wait until you get a good glowing ember. Then pull. Roll the smoke through your mouth, under your tongue. Is it woody? Is it creamy? Taste your lips. Look at the smoke. It is seductive. Look at your ash; it should be sturdy."

I am mimicking his every move.

"Don't ever tap the ash off the end of your cigar. Let it fall away. Take a rest, drink rum or coffee or wine. Don't smoke too fast. Pause. Enjoy." He takes a long pull from his cigar and lets the smoke roll off his puckered lips.

I want to have lips like his.

He is silent for a while, then jumps back into the conversation. "Talk to someone, make a conversation, make the day last longer. Only then do you go back to the cigar."

Suddenly, I am a student fishing for the words to describe my sensations. The first time I tasted food, gourmet food (a *bordelaise* sauce, a rémoulade, a *dacquoise*), I remember liking it but not knowing how to describe it. It was only after I learned the words that were established long before I was born that I was able to articulate my emotions. That was so long ago that I have forgotten what it feels like to be at a loss for words, to be literally choked up and speechless by a sensation happening in my mouth. What do words such as *silky* or *pungent* or *savory* really mean? They fall so short of the actual thing that is happening. Words fail to describe it because we are trying to convey not merely flavor but emotion.

I don't have the words right now to tell Mel what I'm feeling. My eyes are watering from all the smoke in the room, but I feel a fullness in my heart. My senses are tingling with something. My tongue is sandy and bitter; the taste is of the earth and sunlight and heat and age and sweat. I can't say for sure that it is cherry or burnt walnut or licorice. Descriptors like these are imaginative but misleading. What I'm tasting is an aroma so deep that my nostrils burn. The idea of tasting smoke is so savage and yet so damn sexy at the same time that I can't peel my mind away from the primal nature of it. I have a sudden urge to take my shirt off.

We get to the end of the cigar, and my mind is exhausted. Mel is not unlike a winemaker trying to create and layer flavors using only one ingredient. His ingredient just happens to be tobacco leaves. His sensi-tivity to smoke is so measured—the tightness of the roll, the density of the smoke. I try to imagine, if I could focus that intensity on just one ingredient, the depths of flavors I could reach. I'm beginning to under-stand how immensely difficult his craft is.

We try another cigar, a Kentucky Fire Cured, to taste the difference. This one is harsh, hickory flavored, chocolaty. And then it hits me: I can define one thing only after I have tasted its opposite. That is how we learn. We experience one thing, and then we do its opposite, and *that* gives us a spectrum. How do I know if a banana is ripe? Because I have tasted the cruelty of an unripe one. I am getting a lesson in how to taste. It is a lesson I know intuitively, but it has been so long that I've forgotten the rudimentary laws of tasting. I'm starting again from the beginning.

If we were in Cuba right now, Mel says, this is what we would be doing: sitting in a café smoking; talking about music, philosophy, love, drinks; passing the day. What else is there to do?

He talks about the Cuban cigar, that mythical unicorn of perfection. He says he prefers filler from Nicaragua, wrappers from Ecuador. "In Cuba right now, it is hard to get the right ingredients; they have to make do with very little. They have the knowledge but not the right materials. How can you be proud of your craft in that kind of world? Cuba does not allow you to pursue your dreams. You live day by day with patience, nothing else. Because of communism, we had to mix our coffee beans with piss," he says angrily. I'm unsure if this is a euphemism or if he means this literally. He is disturbed by it, so I don't ask him to clarify. "My father is still alive," he says. "He is ninety-nine. I probably will not see him again before he dies."

I feel terrible. I have brought on unpleasant memories. Mel is visibly shaken. I figure this is when we say good-bye. Instead, he asks if I'm hungry. Yes, I am. It is almost dusk. I have more smoke in my belly than calories. "I'll take you to La Fragua," he says. "They make the best chicken."

We get in his car and drive through traffic. The sky is overcast, and the wind gusts are swirling stray newspaper pages across the streets. I have yet to see a drop of rain.

"It will come soon," he says. "We always get a big storm this time of year."

His wife calls. He was supposed to be home hours ago, he says. I hear him talking about me in Spanish, clearly blaming me for his delay. He puts her on speakerphone, and I ready myself to get yelled at by someone I've never met. Instead, a lovely voice comes from the speaker asking me if her husband has been nice to me. The best, I say. She says that next time she will invite me to her home, but right now it's not a good time. I thank her.

Mel drops me off at the restaurant and tells me he can't stay. He orders dinner for me: Pollo Frito Asado con Mojo with a side of yucca and *maduros* (fried plantains). We embrace as though we've been friends for ages. I sit down and devour this salted roasted chicken, which may seem ordinary but for the mojo sauce. Simple in its composition—a concoction of orange, lime, oil, garlic, salt, and pepper—it elevates the chicken, gives it a softness you might not otherwise notice.

I devour my dinner and get up to pay. "No worry," the waiter says. "Mr. Mel has taken care of your dinner." It is at this moment that I understand the depth of Mel's quiet kindness.

THE NEXT MORNING, I get a call from Norman. He asks me to meet him at Enriqueta's. It is a small restaurant that is always busy. I get there just before noon, and it is already packed. Norman and his wife, Janet, are sitting patiently at a small table. We all order the special of the day, Vaca Frita, which is fried and shredded flank steak that is minimally seasoned. It is so emblematic of the Cuban food I love: simple and resourceful, just a few ingredients but made with techniques that most chefs today would not have the patience for, not every day at least. The meat is chewy and tender at the same time, dutifully seasoned and yet bland, as if the cooks do not want the younger generation to forget how simple the food of their elders was. If the meat is a dissertation on simplicity, the black beans and rice are a lesson in how to extract flavor from humble ingredients. It is astounding how much moisture and richness can come from a plate of beans. Mix them together with the beef, and you can feel the harmony in the meal. A few fried plantains round out the dish.

I ask Norman about his favorite haunts in Miami. He rattles off the names of a number of places and then looks to Janet for reassurance. She is a quiet woman, thoughtful and kind. They have been a team for so long that they finish each other's sentences. Norman is excited about his new projects, which include a cooking school in Miami. Janet smiles but seems weary of a life in the kitchen, a life that is relentless and unforgiving.

I admire Norman for so many reasons but mostly for his composure. I have worked for chefs half his age and twice as bitter. There is a serenity to him that puts me at ease. I know how nervous he must be days away from opening a new restaurant, but he took the time to buy me lunch and talk to me. I know he and Janet are busy, and I'm trying to fill every moment with questions, as I don't know when I'll get to see them again. And I know I'll miss them the minute we part ways.

What do we lose when we become Americans? I ask Norman. Do we abandon our forefathers' cultures in favor of an American identity?

"We do," he says, "and then, at some point in our lives, we feel an undercurrent pulling us back, and we rediscover who we are. And what is gained? The future. That is what we gain. And Miami is where the future comes to rehearse."

I can't remember if that was him saying it or if he was quoting someone, but that is Norman. He speaks in grandiose sentences, and then you listen to him expound on his thoughts, and time slows down. The three of us keep talking over coffee and flan.

I give both Norman and Janet a long hug, and I leave the restaurant. Sometimes you meet your heroes, and they are everything. Sometimes they disappoint. Sometimes you discover more about yourself than you do about the person you have idolized for so long. Norman is all those things to me and more. I found in him a kindred soul, and I feel a nagging sense of loneliness as I walk back to South Beach, with all its glitz and glamour. I realize that I forgot to tell Norman about the blurb I'm writing for his book. I forgot to tell him that I could not imagine life without him, that he was the one who set the world in motion for me, that even now, as I assemble the words in my head to write his blurb, I'm being swept up by the early winds of a hurricane picking up speed and hurling me toward the center of an inconsolable storm.

The week after I leave Miami, news of Fidel Castro's death spawns celebrations all over Calle Ocho. The restaurant Versailles drapes a flag of Cuba over its awning as crowds dance, banging on pots and pans. I bought a box of Mel's cigars, and I'm enjoying one in my office, watching the celebrations on the Internet. I go to the kitchen to make something that would go well with a robust cigar, something smoky, earthy, and balanced—a dish for Mel, for Janet, a dish to honor my friend and mentor, Norman Van Aken.

MANGO FRIES WITH JALAPEÑO-MINT AIOLI

All over Calle Ocho, there are mangoes in varying stages of ripeness. I love the way a mango can literally change overnight as it ripens. For this recipe, use slightly underripe mangoes—they should not be green, but they should be firm. Frying mango makes it soft and buttery. The jalapeño-mint aioli brightens the dish. It's great with fried fish, too.

SERVES 2 OR 3 AS A SNACK

3 slightly unripe mangoes

About 6 cups corn oil, for deep-frying

1¼ cups all-purpose flour

2 teaspoons salt, plus more to taste

4 teaspoons freshly ground black pepper

2 teaspoons cayenne pepper

1¼ cups club soda

Sea salt

About 1 cup Jalapeño-Mint Aioli (recipe follows)

Peel and pit the mangoes. Cut them into ⅓-inch-thick slices, then cut the slices into ⅓-inch-thick strips.

Pour about 2 inches of corn oil into a medium pot and heat to 350°F.

In a medium bowl, whisk together 1 cup of the flour, the salt, black pepper, cayenne pepper, and club soda to make a light batter.

Put the remaining ¼ cup flour in a small shallow bowl.

Working in batches, coat the mango fries lightly in the flour, then dip them in the batter, shake off the excess batter, and gently add to the hot oil. Cook, turning them once or twice, until the fries are golden brown on all sides, 1 to 2 minutes. Remove the fries using a slotted spoon and drain on paper towels. Sprinkle with salt while they are still warm.

Serve the fries hot, with the aioli on the side.

JALAPEÑO-MINT AIOLI | MAKES ABOUT 2 CUPS

2 cups mayonnaise, preferably Duke's	2 jalapeño peppers, seeded and minced
¼ cup chopped fresh mint	3 garlic cloves, minced
	Grated zest and juice of 1 lime

In a medium bowl, combine the mayonnaise, mint, jalapeño peppers, garlic, and lime zest and juice. Cover and refrigerate. The aioli is best when just made, but it will keep in the fridge for up to 3 days.

CHICKEN "VACA FRITA" WITH COCONUT RICE AND MOJO SAUCE

This recipe was inspired by the *vaca frita* I enjoyed with Norman. The dish is traditionally made with beef, but I've swapped in chicken legs instead. The meat gets tender, and the lemon gives it a vibrant acidity. I serve it with a sweet coconut rice to complement the chicken. Slices of ripe mango brighten the dish.

SERVES 2 AS A MAIN COURSE

2 whole chicken legs
½ lemon
4 garlic cloves
1 teaspoon chopped fresh oregano
2 teaspoons smoked hot paprika
2 teaspoons ground cumin
1 tablespoon olive oil
¼ cup Mojo Sauce (recipe follows), plus more for serving

COCONUT RICE

3 cups light chicken stock
2 cups coconut milk
1 cup Carolina Gold rice
2 teaspoons fish sauce
1 teaspoon salt
Pinch of sugar

2 tablespoons olive oil
Kosher salt and freshly ground black pepper
Mango slices, for garnish
Fresh cilantro leaves, for garnish

Preheat the oven to 350°F.

Place a large sheet of aluminum foil on your work surface. Put the chicken on the foil, then layer the lemon, garlic, oregano, paprika, and cumin over the chicken. Sprinkle the olive oil over the top. Top with another sheet of aluminum foil. Form the foil into a packet and crimp the edges tightly to seal.

Put the packet on a baking sheet and bake the chicken for 40 minutes, or until the meat is tender and falling off the bone (open the foil packet carefully, avoiding the hot steam, to check it). Open up the packet and let the chicken cool.

(CONTINUED)

Transfer the chicken to a cutting board or plate; strain the liquid in the packet and reserve. Remove and discard the chicken skin. Pull the meat off the bones and put it in a bowl. Add the mojo sauce and toss to coat. Let the chicken marinate at room temperature for 20 minutes.

MEANWHILE, TO MAKE THE RICE: In a large saucepan, combine the chicken stock, coconut milk, rice, fish sauce, salt, and sugar. Bring to a simmer, then lower the heat, cover, and cook, stirring occasionally, until the rice is tender, about 20 minutes. The rice should be creamy and loose; if necessary, add a little water to the rice and stir just before serving.

Drain the chicken and discard the marinade. Heat the olive oil in a large skillet and fry the chicken, turning occasionally, until crispy on all sides, about 4 minutes. Season with salt and black pepper.

Spoon the coconut rice onto a serving plate. Place the chicken on the rice. Garnish with mango slices and cilantro leaves. Pour the reserved chicken juices over the chicken and rice and finish the plate with a little more mojo sauce.

MOJO SAUCE | MAKES ABOUT ¾ CUP

¼ cup fresh orange juice	½ teaspoon chopped fresh oregano
¼ cup fresh lime juice	¼ teaspoon ground cumin
¼ cup olive oil	8 garlic cloves
1 teaspoon salt	

Combine the orange juice, lime juice, olive oil, salt, oregano, cumin, and garlic in a blender and puree until smooth. This is best used right away, but you can store it, covered, in the fridge for a few days.

CHAPTER 6

Slaw Dogs
and
Pepperoni
Rolls

WHEN I FOUND OUT THAT RONNI LUNDY WAS embarking on a series of road trips through Appalachia for her book *Victuals*, I called her up and volunteered myself as a road trip companion. Lundy's book *Shuck Beans, Stack Cakes, and Honest Fried Chicken* was the first cookbook I bought when I moved to Kentucky. It was the first cookbook I read cover to cover, as you would a novel. Until then, I had always thought of cookbooks as references you flipped through to find what you needed: a recipe for a clafoutis, or how much salt one used to brine a chicken. Cookbooks provided measurements and instructions, but I never thought to go to them for a sense of time and place. Though she has published more than ten books, *Victuals* is the one Lundy was destined to write. It is the book that no one but she could have written, and it is why I wanted to follow along while she researched it.

Ronni didn't know me very well at the time. She agreed to let me tag along, I think, out of generosity. She would be the first one to tell you she was nervous about letting me join her. What if we didn't like each other? Five days together in a car with someone you barely know can be a disaster. When she agreed over the phone, I hung up before she could change her mind. This is the story of our trip together.

I MEET RONNI at the Asheville airport. She is a small, sprightly woman in her sixties who glows with energy. The first thing I notice when I jump into her van is an oversize Rand McNally road atlas. It is so big that she is completely hidden behind it, except for her fingers curled around the edges of the cover. Her singsong voice echoes from the driver's seat. I start to laugh involuntarily. I ask her if she wants to use my GPS.

"Mr. Lee, are you making fun of my maps?"

"No, ma'am." I snap back to attention.

And so begins our road trip through Appalachia.

If there ever was a yin to my yang, Ronni is it. She smiles when I pout. She is the vigor to my dullness, the intellect to my instinct. She is honey, and I am treacle. Ronni is a mountain girl from Corbin, Kentucky. She began her career in Louisville, writing about music, mostly blue-grass, and there is no lengthy conversation with Ronni that does not at some point steer toward the music of Bill Monroe. It is because of her that I listen to his music. It is because of her that I don't put sugar in my cornbread.

Ronni's family moved to working-class Louisville when she was a child, but she remembers vividly her father's longing to return to the mountains. "These mountains belong to me, and I have always been drawn back to these parts."

She insists on driving, and driving fast. I'm not sure when they stopped making the Astro van, but hers looks like it came from an early Soviet-era space program. The steering wheel is wider than her torso, but she manages to whip the van around curves with little effort. She won't slow down before taking the curves, and the wind-ing mountain roads bend and weave without mercy. We're listening to Allegheny Mountain Radio. I look over at Ronni. She is smiling as she talks.

"It's a difficult life here, but these lands speak to me. They are more sacred, more holy. The difficulty is part of the appeal. And would ya look at the view."

The van sputters as we crest over a ridge. These steep, verdant hills carved out of prehistoric violence have had an eternity to become smooth. They roll and undulate like fairy-tale landscapes. The homes sit far apart, isolated. A church stands alone on a hill. Through a clearing, we see an abandoned covered bridge spanning a shallow stream flanked by hulking limestone rocks. It is hard not to fall in love with this land. It is hard to look at this place and not believe in God. The roads through the valleys are lined with poplar and ash trees, dense and emerald green. You can drive for miles without feeling sunlight on your cheeks. When we arrive at another vista, Ronni slows the van to a crawl so we can breathe in the view. She points to where the pasture meets the heavens. Her coral green eyes fall on me like sunlight on a dewy morning. Her short white hair hugs the curves of her temples. She starts every new sentence like the lyrics of a love song: "You are never far from death and darkness even when you are standing in the light."

For our first stop, we find a small roadside diner that sells sandwiches and pies. Ronni talks to me about the pickles of this region, about bread and pigs and why pork became the major source of protein—cattle were not a viable industry in the steep landscape of Appalachia. She schools me on J.Q. Dickinson salt and the history of the salt mines in these parts. We talk about coal mines and carbon factories, about religion and crystal meth. The paradox of poverty nestled in an Edenesque forest of abundance is everywhere. When coal was discovered here, it altered the course of paradise. The promise of this "black diamond," as it is called, attracted people from far and wide. Prosperity fraught with peril became the mountain way of life. These days, the mines are closing, and a more insidious practice of mountaintop removal provides plenty of coal with-out the need for as many workers. What remains is a complex story of community that is both distressing and uplifting. My slice of pie is $1.29.

One of the foods I'm most excited about is the West Virginia slaw dog. I have committed to memory the essay Emily Hilliard wrote for the Southern Foodways Alliance in which she recounted her travels on a quest for the famous dog. I have recorded the places she wrote about in the article, hoping to try a few, but I don't bring that up at first. The Appalachia that Ronni is writing about is more historic and culinary. I'm embarrassed to interrupt her discussion of salt-risen bread with a request for a processed hot dog. I sheepishly ask her if we can stop off at a few places if they're not too far out of the way.

"Well, buddy, why didn't you say so earlier? You're talking my language."

My heart nearly explodes.

A West Virginia hot dog is a regional specialty that starts with a soft commercial hot dog bun. Yellow mustard is slathered on first. A boiled beef wiener is placed in the bun next. Ground beef chili without beans is added to that. The kind of chili will differ from place to place, but it is commonly a tomato-rich variety easy on the spice. On top of the chili is placed chopped cabbage slaw held together with mayo and vinegar, creamy and tart. Finally, a light smattering of finely chopped raw onion gets put on top. You can find this dog almost everywhere in the region, from roadside diners to gas stations and local bars. In Virginia, it's called a slaw dog. In West Virginia, it's simply a West Virginia hot dog, though in the northern parts, folks tend to serve it without the coleslaw. At the famous Umberger's in Wytheville, Virginia, they call them Skeeter Dogs and sell them for two bucks apiece, but at most places, you can find them for two dollars for a pair. At first glance, there is nothing about this hot dog that looks special, but once you take a bite, you know you've touched the nirvana of hot dogs. That first bite tells you everything. The structure of the chili is critical, because if it's too tight, it doesn't collapse in your mouth with the other ingredients. Too loose, and the chili dog falls apart after the first bite, dissolving into a sloppy mess in your hands. The same goes for the slaw. When it's done right, there is harmony and balance. I don't think Ronni truly trusted me as a person until she witnessed me take down two slaw dogs with a slug of hot black coffee before 8:00 a.m.

The West Virginia hot dog is a regional celebrity. There are websites devoted to it. Though the wiener and bun are almost always factory made, there is pride in the slaw and enough technique and variation in the chili that a lively debate rages about who makes it best. Skeenies or King Tut? Skeeter's or Buddy B's? No one knows the precise origin of this dog. Ronni traces it back to the chili buns served in the pool halls that littered the railroad towns of the region. Another plausible story tells of the struggling immigrant families, many of whom grew vegetables in their backyards to supplement their humble diets. Cabbage was easy to grow, so families started to make slaw—lots of it. The slaw found its way into many dishes, including the hot dog. The first place to sell the slaw dog was the Stopette Drive-In in the 1920s, but many argue that home cooks in the region started eating their hot dogs with slaw well before that. One thing is for sure: the slaw dog is a celebration and a source of pride.

The slaw dog stands in stark contrast to West Virginia's other regional specialty: the pepperoni roll. A humble food of Italian origin, it was invented by immigrant Italian coal miners who needed a hearty snack that was both portable and easy to eat. D'Annunzio's, a landmark bakery in Clarksburg, has been making it for decades. The preparation couldn't be simpler: pepperoni cut into sticks about four inches long and baked into a soft, sweet roll. Nothing else: just dough and pepperoni baked together.

I arrive at D'Annunzio's at 8:00 a.m., when the rolls are just coming out of the oven. I stand in a line of polite locals, many of whom are buying the rolls by the dozen. I take a bite of mine. The dough is soft and forgiving, the pepperoni lukewarm. All I taste is powdered paprika, dry and unbalanced. It takes a few chews to loosen the fat from the sausage and for flavors to develop in my mouth, but even then, it is bland and monotonous. I am underwhelmed, to say the least.

Ronni tells me that the pepperoni roll is the food of the working class. It is about making connections. When your entire day is spent deep in a coal mine, that little bit of pepperoni may be all that connects you to the sanity of family and your identity and life aboveground.

I buy a dozen rolls and decide to carry them with me for the next few days.

Clarksburg, once a thriving city, is now grappling with a rise in poverty and a decline in population. The downtown is nearly empty. As we drive through the outskirts of town, near the factories, we see abandoned houses in foreclosure and trailer homes in varying states of decline. The only bright lights come from the legal gambling stores, called hot spots. Some are also bars, but mostly they are small spaces, dimly lit and sparsely furnished, with about five or six video slot machines lined up against a wall. The patrons in the hot spots are old. They smoke while spinning the slots, beers snugly protected in plastic cup holders attached to their seats. At one of these places, I meet Alba, the manager. She tells me she is Italian in a West Virginia drawl so thick I can taste the molasses. I order a root beer, and she teaches me how to play Keno. She tells me that most of the people who used to live here have moved to Bridgeport. She tells me to go to Minard's for a good Italian meal. You can get fried chicken and spaghetti there.

Alba's family came generations ago, to work in the factories, and never left. There are a lot of Italians here, she tells me. I tell her I think it's funny that, after so many generations, she would still call herself Italian and not West Virginian. Well, she says, we're all rednecks first.

I give her a pepperoni roll, and she thanks me. D'Annunzio's is the best, she confirms. Then the door buzzer rings, and she lets in an older lady who is alone. They know each other. Alba tells me she has to go make some money and leaves me alone to my gambling.

The old lady isn't interested in talking to me, just playing the slots. She takes a seat at the machine farthest from me. The reflection of the spinning slots bounces off the glasses on her shriveled face. She looks like she might be of Italian heritage as well. Alba whispers to me that the old woman doesn't socialize much but that she used to bake pepperoni rolls and they were the best. She'd sell them from her home, but she is too old to do it anymore. I watch this old lady's hands as she works the touch-screen slots, and I see they are still nimble. I want to learn from her hands, not how to win at slots but how to work the dough for a pepperoni roll.

As modern cooks, we are spoiled. We can take a recipe out of its native environment without the tedium of having to find a person who will teach us. We have removed the culture from the foods we consume and replicate. For most of human history, it has been quite the opposite. I'm sure that for many grandmothers, the idea of learning how to cook from a book was as foreign to them as it is for us to learn a recipe without a book, with nothing more than a matriarch at our side showing us how to knead a fistful of dough.

I offer the old lady a pepperoni roll, but she refuses. She moves her purse to the other side of her chair, away from me. I eat the pepperoni roll myself. They are starting to grow on me. It is dark in the room, save for the digital luminescence of the video slots.

So many of my assumptions about food come from a desire to tell a neatly packaged story, one that has a happy ending of climactic flavors and rewarded chefs. But that tidy story is rarely the case. Along my journey, through Appalachia or any of the small towns I've traveled to in the writing of this book, the most insightful moments have been quiet and unseasoned. This has made me question myself and my expectations. I'm owed nothing by the people and the culture of this place. I have neither the right to judge nor the history to comment on them. If the pepperoni roll seems bland to me, it is a fault in my own palate, which is unable to detect the value of its plainness. I chew another bite and try to think of someone who has been working at a physically grueling job since dawn. This pepperoni roll is the one pleasure he may have been looking forward to all morning long. This pepperoni roll may be all he has to eat until he sits down to supper late in the evening. Slowly, I get it. The darkness of the room is suffocating, and I've been here only twenty minutes. The

pepperoni roll suddenly tastes like the best thing I've ever eaten. I leave
ten dollars' worth of credits in the slot machine and head out the door.

The road from Clarksburg to Staunton is about as scenic a drive as
you'll ever experience. Tiny towns such as Elkin appear out of nowhere,
like apparitions. There are a lot of abandoned homes and buildings along
the way. Many people have left.

"What makes the others stay?" I ask Ronni.

"There is the solitude, the independence. Some folks need it. It calls
to them. The mountains provide that, if nothing else, sometimes."

Staunton is a quaint town that draws tourists from the Shenandoah
Valley. Here, you don't see the economic struggles that plague most
of the region. It is a place where a chef such as Ian Boden can cook a
forward-thinking, Southern-inflected tasting menu. His kitchen is the
size of a broom closet, but he has had glowing articles written about him
in *Esquire*. His place is closed today, so Ronni and I visit an old diner called
the Beverly, where the menu is handwritten on the wall and the daily
pies are displayed on a wooden table against a chest of vintage plates.
We linger over mediocre coffee and fabulous pie.

One of the trends of modern restaurant culture that disturbs me
is the obsessive need for all facets of a meal to be perfect. Not so at the
Beverly, where they focus on pies. My chess pie is delicious. There is a
layer of slightly cracked sugar on top and sweet custard in the middle over
a bottom crust that is thicker than most but that still politely surrenders
to a push from my fork. Ronni's coconut meringue pie is tall and proud,
the meringue is sweet and airy but taut at the same time and perfectly
toasted on top. The Beverly's silverware is plain, and the tablecloths need
to be replaced, but there is a quiet confidence here. The food is good; the
desserts are even better. The coffee may be bitter and watery, but the
owners of the Beverly are okay with that. The place is run by two aging
sisters who don't have time for suggestions. They don't have a craven
need for praise, either. I like places like these, places that aren't perfect.
At the end of the day, the flaws make the Beverly seem more human.

The sisters seem to deflect criticism. It isn't that they don't care about the restaurant; they simply don't feel the need to please everyone. (Sadly, they are also outdated. The Beverly shut down soon after my visit.)

The two sisters who run the Beverly are a part of the rural Appalachia that Ronni champions. They may be set in their ways, but they come from a poor working-class culture that embodies a fighting spirit. The sisters are simple folk, as people around here say, but they are not a part of the stereotypical portrayal of toothless, Mountain Dew–drinking hillbillies that angers people like Ronni. I'm here with her partly because I want to see beyond the stereotypes, but I need a guide to help me. It is too easy to look at the sisters of the Beverly, with their missing teeth, and think, Oh, what a duo of wonderfully authentic hillbillies! There is more to the story than that, though.

I ask Ronni, in earnest, "Who are the people of Appalachia?" Are they the idyllic, fiddle-playing, dungaree-wearing, happy tribe of mountain folks untouched by time and corruption? Are they the poor immigrants who have fought tooth and nail to carve out a small piece of America for themselves in this unforgiving land? Are they a misunderstood people whose desire for isolation has been interpreted as an insular culture formed out of racism? Maybe somewhere in the middle of all the above lies the truth.

Ronni talks to me about immigrant families, about the migration that populated these lands. This is not an impoverished place of desolation. It is full of historical paths, some painful and some angelic. She tells me that the early migrants here were hardworking, mostly white Englishmen, Scots, Italians, and Germans—mostly honest, all scrappy. When immigrants to America were making their way westward, most passed through the Appalachian region without stopping, preferring to settle instead on the flatter, farmable terrains of Ohio, Indiana, and Illinois. It takes a stubborn, thick-skinned person to decide to settle here.

I think about my wife's ancestry. She is a Dürholtz. They come from the Black Forest region of Germany. I imagine they must have crossed through these mountains at one point along their westward journey. They have been in Indiana more than six generations. They are meek, they go to church, and they keep to themselves. Gossiping is the worst of their sins. I see nothing of them in the feisty people I meet here in Appalachia, be they from Germany, Ireland, or Scotland. The people of the mountains are cut from a different cloth.

To prove this point, Ronni takes me deep into the heart of the Appalachian Mountains. We drive along a winding freeway of wild thickets and woodland, without seeing another car for almost an hour. Suddenly, we come to a historic landmark sign telling us we have arrived in Helvetia, an isolated village that painstakingly preserves the way of life of the original Swiss settlers who arrived here via Brooklyn in 1869. The population is purported to be sixty people. Everything about this place should scream "theme park," except for the fact that people actually live here in the middle of the wilderness, embracing this antiquated way of life. There is a church, a small school, a few buildings that store dry goods and another where flour is milled, a pretty stream, and the log cabin–housed Hütte Swiss Restaurant. We dine on schnitzel, applesauce, and sauerkraut. We are the only ones in the dining room.

We must make for an odd sight, Ronni and I, an older white woman and a Korean American man in his forties dining together in the mid-afternoon, licking the last of the applesauce from our plates. After so many hours together in a car, it is impossible for us to keep up any disguises. With every passing hour, we reveal things to each other that don't get said in polite conversation. It therefore seems perfectly normal for us to sit down for lunch and begin a conversation with "So, what is the meaning of authenticity?" or "Who owns the food of the South?" Hours later, along a stretch of unending highway, we are still going back and forth, laying the foundation for an enduring friendship.

Ronni wants the recipe for the applesauce. The owners of the Hütte say it is in their cookbook, which I suspect is not true, but I buy the book anyway. It is a small yellow booklet of typed pages stapled together. The title page reads:

OPPIS GUET'S VO
HELVETIA
Compiled for
THE ALPEN ROSE GARDEN CLUB
Helvetia, W. Va.
by
Eleanor Fahrner Mailloux

In addition to recipes for pretzels and *Rösti*, and regional favorites such as corn relish and apple fritters, there is an oddly titled recipe called Ammonia Cookies. The book gives an applesauce recipe, but I can tell it's not the one served in the restaurant. At the back of the book are tips on how to wash black stockings and what to do in case you're struck by lightning: "For a couple of hours shower in cold water. In case there is still no sign of life, add a cupful of salt and continue for another hour." The book is full of amusing remedies and wisdoms, which I read out loud to Ronni as we drive out of town.

I fall asleep. Too much pork and sausages. It is almost dark when I am roused by the sound of tires on gravel. We are at a gas station in between towns. We have to find a place to get dinner soon or else resign ourselves to highway fast food. While Ronni is pumping gas, I run up the road to investigate a small restaurant. I tell her to meet me there. The sunlight is quickly sinking behind the lush trees. The restaurant is a gabled one-story building with a window obscured by a checkered curtain. There is only one car in the parking lot. I'm breathing hard. I open the door and walk in. There is a young cook in the kitchen cleaning up, a woman at the register, and a young man mopping the floor near the back. There are no customers, but the place is clean and smells good. Without a second thought, I ask, "Do you sell slaw dogs?" I say it louder than I intended, and with an unintentional drawl. After a few days with Ronni, driving through the region, I've started to pick up the accent.

Everyone is staring at me. No one says a word. The silence lasts a long time. Finally, the lady behind the register, who I assume is the mother, tells me politely but stutteringly that they are closed. I thank her and head back to the parking lot. Ronni is just pulling in. I think nothing of the information I've just been given, other than that maybe they want to close up after a slow dinner service. I hop into the van and tell Ronni to pick a fast-food joint. At that very moment, though, a young girl, about fourteen, comes running out of the restaurant and catches up to me. I roll down my window. She is blonde, with blue eyes, pigtails, and a smile as bright as the moon. She says, "C'mon back and have dinner. They din' mean nothing by it." The expression on her face tells me she will not accept no for an answer.

She seats us at the end of a long wooden table and hands us menus. She is talkative and distracted. She brings us water and takes our order. I ask for a plate of slaw dogs.

"We don't call them slaw dogs in these parts," she tells me in a sympathetic voice, and heads for the kitchen.

Ronni asks me in a whisper if I'm bothered by being here. I am not. As someone who has roamed freely through the small communities of America, I am always aware of being the odd person in the room, regardless of the room's complexion, white, black, brown, or other. I was once in a traditional Korean restaurant in New Jersey and *still* felt the sting of suspicious eyes on me because I was not one of them.

We sit there in the dimly lit restaurant, enjoying a pleasant dinner, and one by one, the family comes by the table to say an awkward hello. The sky is now glowing dark. I wonder how often they get someone like me stopping at their restaurant. How odd it must have been for them to see me, a cowboy shirt–wearing Korean American man, crash through their front door breathlessly asking for slaw dogs. It makes me chuckle to think about it. Maybe their shock was less over my not being white and more about my daring to call their West Virginia hot dog a slaw dog. Maybe.

AT THE END OF OUR TRIP, Ronni and I pop into an antiques store, and I'm moved by a piece of artwork that illustrates a two-dimensional image of the currents and overflows of the Mississippi River over time. It reads, "Geological Investigation of the Alluvial Valley of the Lower Mississippi River." The turns and twists of the flowing river patterns are shown in faded colors that remind me of the arterial networks connecting our internal organs. River lines weave and tangle and eventually find their way out to the ocean. Some of the flow patterns don't make sense. They seem to linger and meander in long curves as if they don't want to leave. I see the conflict of Appalachia in this drawing. I see the necessity to flee but the instinct to remain. I see joy and hospitality and warmth and mistrust and fear and isolation. And it is no different from any small town in America, where the values of the old are being challenged by the temerity of youth. I purchase the drawing not knowing where I'll hang it.

"Hey, buddy, you know what you just got, don'tcha?" Ronni lays her hand over mine to comfort me.

"No, what?"

"A map!" And she laughs for what seems like hours.

I return to Appalachia and the Shenandoah Valley as often as I can. Possibly my favorite food—road trip itinerary is Staunton to Roanoke to Wytheville to Bristol. Try Ian Boden at the Shack in Staunton; check out the Homeplace Restaurant in Catawba; go to Roanoke for the River and Rail and then have a bowl of chili at the Texas Parlour just a few blocks away. After that, drive on to Wytheville for the world-famous slaw dog, and end up in Bristol, where Travis Milton is planting a flag for Appalachian cuisine. Tune into Allegheny Mountain Radio as you drive through the mountains and take in some of the most breathtaking views you'll ever see.

When I'm in Appalachia, my heartbeat rests, my breathing slows a little, my blood runs clean. I am smitten by wildflowers and the smell of biscuits. With every trip, I learn a few more things about the simplicity and resourcefulness of the dinner table. I eat humble food when I'm there, and I don't ever feel that I'm missing out. When I get home, I create slow and provocative meals. I cook pork chops and find new ways to cook corn. I say things to my wife like "I'm going to get a house in the Appalachian Mountains one day and live off the land." To which she responds by rolling her eyes. Maybe she's right and I'll never actually do that, but at least for a week after every trip to Appalachia, I recalibrate my priorities and make chili for slaw dogs and bake pies and listen to bluegrass music.

Each time I visit, I come away knowing that the people of Appalachia are not limited to one definition or stereotype. Every few years, a movie or a book comes out, as the memoir *Hillbilly Elegy* did in 2016, that reaffirms the stereotype that Appalachia is a troubled place full of people who can barely take care of themselves. This always sparks a great deal of backlash and anger from people such as Ronni, who see Appalachia as a place of deeply sacred traditions and strong ethics. Still, stereotypes exist for a reason, and nothing about *Hillbilly Elegy* is untrue. For anyone who believes that Appalachia is a godforsaken place, I would invite them to drive up to a mountain ridge north of Staunton at sunset and peer out over the lush treetops and witness the grace and beauty that is God-given in this part of the world.

MY VERSION OF A SLAW DOG

Don't expect me to give you a newfangled "artisan" version of a slaw dog. Some things don't need to be tinkered with. Also, in an age where everything is uber-organic and overscrutinized, it's nice sometimes just to indulge in something that is store-bought and simple. By all means, use organic beef franks and even brioche hot dog buns, if you want. But this version, made with processed ingredients, which I normally don't cook with, is what reminds me of West Virginia in all its faults and glory.

CHILI

1 tablespoon canola oil

1 pound 85% lean ground beef

1 sweet onion, such as Vidalia, finely diced

5 garlic cloves, minced

¼ cup tomato paste

2½ tablespoons chili powder

1½ tablespoons ground cumin

2¼ teaspoons salt

1½ cups lager beer

1 cup water

SLAW

½ head cabbage, cored and finely chopped

3 tablespoons sugar

3 tablespoons mayonnaise, preferably Duke's

1 tablespoon distilled white vinegar

1½ teaspoons salt

8 all-beef hot dogs

8 hot dog buns

3 tablespoons unsalted butter, melted

Yellow mustard

1 sweet onion, such as Vidalia, finely chopped

TO MAKE THE CHILI: In a Dutch oven or other heavy pot, heat the canola oil over medium-high heat. Add the ground beef and onion and cook, stirring, until the beef is browned and the onion has wilted, 6 to 8 minutes. Add the garlic, tomato paste, chili powder, cumin, and salt, stir well, reduce the heat to medium, and cook for 5 minutes, or until the vegetables soften. Add the beer and water, bring to a gentle simmer, and cook for about an hour, until most of the liquid has evaporated and the flavors have merged together. Once the chili is done, turn off the heat and let it rest at room temperature.

MEANWHILE, TO MAKE THE SLAW: Put the cabbage in a bowl, add the sugar, mayonnaise, vinegar, and salt, and stir well. Cover and refrigerate for 1 hour. Stir again just before using.

Bring a medium pot of water to a boil. Drop in the hot dogs and cook for 4 minutes.

Meanwhile, open up the hot dog buns and brush the insides with the melted butter. Add them buttered-side down to a large hot skillet (work in batches, or use two skillets) and cook until warmed and lightly toasted, about 3 minutes.

Reheat the chili until hot. Drain the slaw and stir well. Brush the toasted hot dog buns with a little mustard. Drain the hot dogs and add to the buns. Brush a little more mustard over the hot dogs. Spoon some chili onto each hot dog and top with a little slaw and a light scattering of diced onion. Arrange on plates and serve.

FRIED PORK CHOPS WITH MISO CREAMED CORN AND PICKLE JUICE GRAVY

The foods of Appalachia are robust and satisfying but not flashy. Much like the people I met on my journey, the food is humble. To try to elevate it would be disingenuous; it shouldn't be fussed over too much. There are many wonderful family-run restaurants in the region that serve home-cooked meals like these fried pork chops, or schnitzel, which Ronni and I enjoyed at the Hütte Swiss Restaurant. Instead of the traditional Swiss accompaniments, though, I pair the pork with an earthy, umami-rich creamed corn made with miso. The briny pickle juice livens up the traditional gravy with a surprising but delicate acidity.

SERVES 4 AS A MAIN COURSE

4 rib or center-cut pork chops (about ¾ inch thick and 6 ounces each)

Kosher salt and freshly ground black pepper

½ cup all-purpose flour

2 large eggs

1 cup bread crumbs

3 large fresh sage leaves, minced

Vegetable oil, for panfrying

Pickle Juice Gravy (recipe follows)

Miso Creamed Corn (recipe follows)

Season the pork chops on both sides with salt and pepper. Set out three wide shallow bowls. Put the flour in the first one. Put the eggs in the second one and lightly beat them. Put the bread crumbs in the third bowl, add the sage to the bread crumbs, and stir to combine.

(CONTINUED)

Dip a pork chop in the flour, then gently dip into the egg mixture and finally transfer to the bowl with the bread crumbs and coat evenly. Repeat with the remaining pork chops and set aside.

Pour ¼ inch of vegetable oil into a large skillet and heat over high heat. Lower the chops into the oil and fry, turning once, until browned and crisp on both sides, about 3 minutes per side. Adjust the heat as needed. Transfer the browned chops to a paper towel–lined plate to drain briefly, and season with a little more salt.

Arrange the chops on plates and serve with the gravy and creamed corn.

PICKLE JUICE GRAVY | If you make Pickled Sweet Peppers (page 82), you will have some delicious brine. Most people discard the brine when they finish the pickles, but I never do. It is a great way to add flavor to vinaigrettes, braises, and this simple but addictive gravy. MAKES ABOUT 2 CUPS

5 tablespoons unsalted butter, plus 1 tablespoon cold butter to finish the gravy	½ teaspoon salt
	½ teaspoon freshly ground black pepper
5 tablespoons all-purpose flour	¼ cup pickle juice from Pickled Sweet Peppers (page 82), or to taste
1½ cups chicken stock	

Melt the 5 tablespoons butter in a medium skillet over medium-high heat. Sprinkle the flour over the top and whisk to combine, then cook the roux, whisking constantly, for 1 minute, or until a rough paste forms. While whisking, gradually add the chicken stock.

Bring the gravy to a low boil, then reduce the heat and season with the salt and pepper. Gently simmer until thickened, about 2 minutes.

Stir the pickle juice into the gravy. Finish it by adding the remaining 1 tablespoon cold butter and swirling it in the pan until it just melts. Serve hot.

MISO CREAMED CORN | Creamed corn is a staple dish on family tables all over Appalachia. I love creamed corn, too, but this non-traditional version combines the bracing sweetness of corn with the salty richness of miso. The miso flavor isn't pronounced; there's just enough to add some depth and umami. SERVES 4 AS A SIDE

5 ears fresh corn, husked	3 tablespoons red miso
3 tablespoons unsalted butter	1 teaspoon salt
¼ cup chicken stock	½ teaspoon freshly ground
¼ cup heavy cream	black pepper

Slice the corn kernels from the cobs into a large shallow bowl. Use a large spoon to scrape all the pulp from the cobs into another bowl.

In a medium saucepan, melt the butter over medium heat. Add the corn and cook, stirring, for 2 minutes. Add the corn pulp and chicken stock, bring to a simmer, cover, and cook for 10 minutes. Remove from the heat.

Transfer one-third of the corn mixture to a blender and puree until smooth. Return the mixture to the saucepan, add the cream and miso, and stir well to combine. Bring to a simmer over medium heat and simmer, uncovered, for 5 minutes, until slightly thickened. Season with the salt and pepper.

CHAPTER 7

A KIBBEH IN CLARKSDALE

PULL OFF THE ROAD IN TUNICA, MISSISSIPPI, TO TAKE a break from the monotony of miles and miles of identical farmland and the onslaught of the dusty casino billboards that I seem to pass every seven seconds. The sun is burning my eyes. Along Highway 61, you can behold the dying casinos, like miniature castles in the distance, with names such as Hollywood, Gold Strike, and Isle of Capri. They are far enough away that you can't see the poorly maintained structures, but close enough to be a temptation. This is the Delta. This is the land of cotton fields. This is the land of fertile soil over sandy loam nourished by the historic overflows of the Mississippi River. But this is not Mississippi, as many here will tell you. This is Coahoma County, the land of Parchman Farm prison, aka "a prison without walls" where they used to let prisoners work the nearby farmlands, practically daring them to escape. When the land is this flat and cleared of trees, there is no place for a convict to run and hide. I look around me at the flat earth and conjure up an image of an inmate running as fast as he can, trying to outrun the rifle sights trained on his back. It makes me shiver. I live in a valley of trees and low rolling hills. One can find solace in a creek by a riverbed

in the hills of Bernheim Forest. Here, the land is bare and scalded. Here, I can see the entire sky from horizon to horizon. I am choking on the vastness.

I take a seat at the counter of the Blue and White Restaurant, an old diner beloved in the area. It is 1:00 p.m., and this is my first decent meal of the day. The posters on the wall tell the story of the blues musicians who came from the Delta. It is an astounding list of names, from Lead Belly to Robert Johnson to John Lee Hooker to Muddy Waters and so many more, all of whom came up through this one area of Mississippi. This is a sacred place for musicians, the birthplace of modern rock and roll. But I'm here for the food. I order a catfish sandwich, turnip greens, and coconut pie. I then strike up a conversation with a lady sitting next to me. She's wearing a billowy white cotton dress that reminds me of a pillowcase.

"What you think you gonna find in Clarksdale?" she asks me. She is not menacing, just unimpressed. Her gray afro ripples from her head like a wave crashing against the world behind her. She tells me her name is Mary. She grew up in Clarksdale, lived in Atlanta for twenty years, and recently moved back. She doesn't say why.

"You don't look like one of them blues tourists," she says to me as she finishes her coffee.

"What does that look like?"

"A muthufucka with a camera and a book about Robert Johnson."

We laugh. In my bag, I have book about Sam Cooke that I now can't take out.

She's a seamstress, she tells me. I ask her if she made the dress she's wearing. She makes everything she wears, she says. I tell her my parents used to run a garment factory, so I know a little about sewing. I compliment the featherstitch on her dress. She warms up to me. I ask her where I should go eat. She tells me about Delta tamales; she tells me to eat at Ramon's, at Abe's BBQ. I ask her about soul food.

She shakes her head. "Most black people cook out of their homes. The casino's got a cook making decent food," she says. "Or go to the Chinese buffet—they got soul food o'er there."

She doesn't find it the least bit ironic that she is sending me to a Chinese restaurant to get soul food. I ask her how she likes the food here at the Blue and White. She tells me she drives up here once a week to get a good meal and to get out of Clarksdale for a bit. She never intended to come back to Clarksdale. It just happened. She keeps looking into her empty coffee mug.

The food is good. The catfish is firm and mossy, with tender flakes encrusted in a fried batter that bends before it cracks. The greens are withered and tender, with a potlikker that is cloudy and rich. We've been sitting at the counter with an empty stool between us, but now I move closer to Mary to share my coconut pie with her. The waitress smiles at me and says, "Where'd you come from, you sweet thing?" She doesn't wait for an answer. Everyone here is either white or black, mostly white. The clatter of plates comes nonstop from the kitchen. The scent of strong coffee makes the air smell like dirt.

Mary leans back to look me up and down. "You came all the way down here looking for soul food?"

"I'm not exactly sure why I came here, but yes, food was one reason."

"I'm sure you'll find what you want." She smiles and thanks me for the pie. On my way out, I almost buy a T-shirt, but I don't want Mary to see me doing anything so touristy.

I'm trying to find a blues station on the radio, but all I get are Christian songs. I stop at a song with a gentle male voice full of conflict and falsetto. It takes me a few verses to realize this is gospel. It is Jonathan McReynolds. A young man's pretty voice describes the inner turmoil of wanting to indulge in worldly delights but also to follow the word of God. You can't serve two masters, he says. I'm not a fan of Christian music, but I'm transfixed by McReynolds's voice, his delivery. It's so hypnotic, you don't want him to stop. But he paints a picture of an inflexible world, one that does not allow for a middle ground, for unorthodox interpretations of the Gospel. It is white or black, he says. He sets up an either-or paradigm. You are either in heaven or in hell, either good or evil. This is Clarksdale, and religion is strong here. This is a place of stark opposites: earth or sky, wealth or poverty, power or servitude, white or black. You are either from the Delta or you are not.

I don't believe that the world is a two-sided coin. Living in the American South as I have for more than fifteen years, I've collected so many stories that vibrate in the middle, stories that add to the culinary narrative without diminishing the history of the struggle between binary poles, or black and white. I am also Asian American, so I don't fit inside this convenient dichotomy. To be in Clarksdale, though, is to be reminded that, in some places, the world has yet to be reconciled.

The first time I traveled to Clarksdale, in 2015, I cooked a dinner at Dockery Plantation with the Delta Supper Club, a group of young chefs trying to bring economic and cultural vitality back to the region. We cooked Delta rice and local birds. We ate chess pie with dense local ice cream and drank bourbon until we couldn't see straight. We ended up at Po' Monkey's house, to see if he would open up his juke joint, only to get cussed out. Po' Monkey's is a legendary juke joint in the middle of nowhere, where people gather once a week to drink and dance and get nasty. Anthony Bourdain featured it on an episode of *Parts Unknown* about Mississippi, and it has since gotten attention from all over the world.

Po' Monkey, aka Willie Seaberry, died in 2016. At his funeral, a fight broke out when a woman claimed he owed her money. Everyone is convinced he had a great deal of cash stashed away somewhere inside his club. There is an ongoing debate over whether the club should be kept going without Po' Monkey. For anyone who ever met him—he often wore a pink suit—it is clear that there was only one Willie Seaberry and there will never be another.

One of the participants in that Dockery Plantation dinner is meeting me in town. Tom, a Mississippian from Jackson, is a chef and writer. I agree to meet him for lunch. With some time to kill, I drive around the empty streets of Clarksdale, watching, like a stranger in a postapocalyptic town, the occasional person walk down the street. The downtown is dotted with a few notable blues places for tourists, but the rest is a ghost town of precious yet abandoned buildings. Morgan Freeman owns a popular blues club here. I spot signs for Muddy Waters's cabin, for Dockery Plantation, for the hospital where Bessie Smith died, and I wonder what exactly the tourists are here to experience. A few landmark buildings long abandoned? A blues concert? Nostalgia for something that was never theirs to begin with?

I drive past a small cotton field along the outskirts of Clarksdale. The cotton harvest happened months ago, but a few snowy white puffs cling stubbornly to thorny black stems. At first glance, it is beautiful, until you think about the history of inhumanity underlying this one crop. My mind vacillates between the beauty and the violence. I ask myself what I'm doing here. I may not be one of the blues tourists, but am I not another kind of tourist, a culinary tourist seeking a nostalgic food experience that I am hoping to write about? How many bowls of collard greens will be enough to make me feel included? For me, the conflict is always the tension between nostalgia and the present. If we live in nostalgia, we will strangle the possibility for a future. But without it, we don't have stories; we don't have people preserving a culture before it slips away into an elusive memory, a kind of oblivion.

I was fifteen the first time I went to CBGB in the Bowery. I went with two girls who looked a lot older than I did. The place was dark and sticky, with decals and graffiti covering the walls and beer soaked into the floorboards. The band that night was loud and dissonant, the musicians pale, thin ghosts and high as fuck. I loved every minute of it. I was too young to have seen the Ramones, Patti Smith, or Debbie Harry, so these gaunt musicians would have to do. While I was peeing in the bathroom urinal, someone vomited on my jeans. He didn't apologize. The girls I was with were grossed out, and left without me. I disappeared into a corner, paralyzed by the heat, the energy, and the crazed smell of beer and urine. I couldn't see the band from where I stood, but I could feel the vibrations coming from the speakers. The crowd was going nuts. I remember thinking, This can't be real. If they let someone like me in here, then, really, how authentic can it be? But then I wondered what it must have been like to be here in its heyday, when the real shit was happening. Maybe the answer is that CBGB was just a place where people came to play, and they chose this spot not because it was special but because no one else wanted it. It was just a place where people came to play music before it became a sacred site for the antiestablishment—just as Clarksdale was not the home of the blues when Muddy Waters was living in a dilapidated cabin; it was just a place where life was hard and music was one of the ways people coped.

I suppose that's what I'm looking for in Clarksdale—not a legend, not a signpost, just a place where people come to cook.

AGNES AND TONI are sisters not by blood but by marriage. Their husbands are half brothers, or were. One has been dead almost twenty years, and the other divorced from Toni for nearly as long. Agnes and Toni run a small clothing store in downtown Clarksdale. They have a sign on the curb that advertises "High Fashion," along with magnets, spoons, lapel pins, and cosmetics. A handwritten piece of paper taped to the upper-left-hand corner of their sign reads "Pecans." I'm intrigued. Inside are sequined dresses on hangers, wrapped in heavy protective plastic. There is a section for choir suits next to a small lingerie section. Behind the glass counter is a row of purses and weave wigs. Costume jewelry adorns the glittery, fabric-lined cases. A tall woman in her sixties appears from behind the counter. Agnes has perfect posture; her accent is a strain of Mississippi that is polite and proper, at an octave ever so gently raised. Her coiffed hair does not move as she glides toward me like an apparition.

"Can I help you with something, young man?"

I tell her I'm curious about the sign for pecans, and maybe spoons.

She sells me a pound of pecans for seven dollars. They come in a small brown paper bag. I take one out and pop it in my mouth. It is surprisingly aromatic, nutty and earthy, with an oiliness that you get only from fresh pecans. "Where did you get these?" I ask.

"My son farms them near our house."

I start fishing through my wallet to see how much more cash I have.

Another woman emerges from the back. She is short and perky, and looks at me with suspicion. She is about a decade younger than Agnes. She is brown-skinned, with the features of the Middle East, but she speaks with the common Mississippi drawl.

"Are you Lebanese?" I ask her.

"Well, sure, honey," she replies.

"Do you know where to get good Lebanese food?"

The women chuckle, and Agnes leans in and tells me that Toni makes the best cabbage rolls and kibbeh in Clarksdale. She makes them from her house and advertises them on Facebook whenever she has a bunch to sell. People come from all over.

I ask what makes hers the best.

This starts a roiling debate. "If you put cinnamon in your kibbeh, well, now, you are just wrong. The folks in Vicksburg might do that, but not here," Agnes informs me.

Toni tells me her forefathers were Maronites, Christians fleeing persecution in Lebanon. Most knew they were not going back, so when they landed in Mississippi, it was not to seek temporary refuge. This was to be their new home. They did manual labor, peddled anything they could (soap, lotion, towels) to tenant farmers. They spoke Arabic and French. They were businesspeople. They made and sold food, too.

"We've been here a long time," Agnes tells me. "And kibbeh became our calling card. If you were Lebanese, you came to Clarksdale and walked the dirt streets saying the word *kibbeh* over and over again until a Lebanese family would hear you and take you in. That's how kibbeh became so popular here."

Toni says she is thinking about going to school to learn more about cooking.

"Quite frankly, you have more to teach than to learn," I tell her. This warms her up.

I take a picture with her as I leave, but Agnes refuses to pose.

"It's just not proper," she says as she runs her fingers across the immovable shell of her hair. She tells me to dine at Chamoun's Rest Haven, which is where I'm meeting Tom, the chef from Jackson, for lunch.

Chamoun's Rest Haven is an old diner with low drop ceilings, heavy gray curtains to block out the sun, and a collection of random family photos decorating the wall behind the counter. Paula owns and operates it now, almost single-handedly. Her parents, Louise and Chafik Chamoun, bought it from its original Lebanese owners. The Rest Haven has been open since 1947. Paula wears thick glasses, and her dark hair curls in a hundred different directions. Her hot-pink nail polish matches the pink flower petals on her shirt. She hustles across the restaurant to take an order.

She is the only one on the floor, talking to Tom and me while waiting on three other tables. She doesn't stop talking or moving. Sentences from one conversation trail into a question to another table, all one long, uninterrupted soliloquy. When coffee runs low, one of the customers gets up and refills his cup and those at the table next to his.

The menu is split into three sections: Southern favorites, Lebanese foods, and Italian dishes such as spaghetti and lasagna. I order something from each section. Tom is impressed by my appetite. He has the girth of a chef who likes to eat and a handlebar moustache that he teases with his fingertips when he speaks. Tom and I talk about the history of Clarksdale, about food and authenticity, about what it means to have a culture sewn so tightly into the fabric of everyday life that it is normal for a white blue-collar worker to come here and ask for his kibbeh on a roll as though he were ordering a cheeseburger. This isn't Lebanese food anymore, Tom tells me. This is Delta food and, more specifically, Clarksdale food.

You can order the kibbeh two ways, raw or fried. The raw kibbeh is eaten like steak tartar. It is dense and red, more like an uncooked hamburger patty. It is rich and filling. And then it hits me: this kibbeh is made with beef, not lamb. I have never seen kibbeh that was anything but lamb. I ask Paula about this, and she stops to catch her breath before answering. Lamb is too expensive and hard to find; the beef here is cheap and good, and it is a local favorite. All around us, there are customers eating it. Some have it fried and put in a roll, which makes it really just a hamburger.

Rest Haven's lasagna is a mess of tortured pasta and thick red sauce. The cabbage rolls are tender and fragrant. They are slightly sweet, and I can't tell if this comes from added sugar or the large amount of onion that dominates the beef stuffing. The coconut pie is the best I've ever had. The little coconut bits on top are charred to a charcoal black, a contrast to the shiny mass of white meringue holding a firm texture.

Paula sits with us for just a few minutes. Her parents still come in to make the kibbeh, she says. No one else can make it right. I can feel the restlessness in her bones that only another chef can truly understand.

"I never thought I would end up in Clarksdale all my life, but oh well, here I am. I do it for the customers—they need me." She is happy here, she tells me with a bit of hesitation. She corrects herself: she is needed here.

I don't ask for an explanation. I understand her. For most of us, that is enough to make us stay in the kitchen for a lifetime. Before I get a chance to compliment her on her cabbage rolls, she is already talking to a customer who has just walked in the door. The two talk as if they've known each other their whole lives, and they probably have.

While we're on our way out, Paula mentions that her parents owned a grocery shop in Friars Point before buying Rest Haven. It is where they first started selling Lebanese food. The shop is now run by Chinese, she says, and they have good fried wings, apparently.

I ask Tom to drive me there. It is in a part of town with one museum and nothing but a few stores on a single dilapidated block. The grocery

store is the only place open. The Chinese lady taking our order speaks
no English. The handwritten menu features everything from chicken
gizzards to egg foo yung. We point to the chicken wings. While waiting for the food, I study the place. The shelves of the store are scantily
stocked but offer enough for a family to live on. Jars of pickled pig's feet
sit bemusedly next to packs of instant ramen. A grandmother emerges
from a back room and sits at the only other table in the place. She lifts a
basket cover, and in it I glimpse her lunch: a cloudy soup of pork bones
and scallion, rice, and a side dish of cabbage. I smile at her, and she nods
sternly before turning her back to me and slurping her food.

On our way back to Clarksdale, I ask Tom to take me to the Chinese
restaurant called Hibachi Buffet. Yes, the one that serves up a generic
brand of Chinese food for $7.99 a plate. It sounds like a horrible idea,
so of course we go. The buffet station is split up into categories: sushi,
fried foods, Chinese, salad, and soul food. I make myself a plate of fried
chicken, greens, lima beans, cornbread, mashed potatoes, and a fortune
cookie. It is good, really good. I try the lo mein, and it is horrible. I can't
even look at the sushi. The owner goes by the name Simon. He's from
Hong Kong, via Atlanta. He's been here only a few years. He's got a good
business, he tells me. I ask him if a Chinese person is cooking the soul
food. No, he tells me. His kitchen is run by three people: a Chinese man,
a young Mexican cook, and an African American woman. They split up
the menu, and each prepares his or her station.

"Do they get along?" I ask him.

He hesitates, clearly not ready for a question like this. He shrugs
and smiles. Sometimes, he says, sometimes. I ask him if I can talk to the
cooks. He says no and then gestures for me to move so the next customer
on line can pay for his food.

I step aside but ask him one more question: Why doesn't he serve
more authentic Hong Kong food? It has to be better than this generic
version of Chinese food.

"People not ready for it. Not yet."

I feel at home here. This is America. Maybe not the white-picket-fence version we are used to seeing, but the one that exists in every town just beneath the surface, embodied by the diversity in the labor economy. I'll bet the kitchen here is a fascinating place. I'll bet it is an uneasy collaboration at times, bound together by the necessities of food and culture and commerce. I'm glad to have found some good soul food. I'm even happier that I had to go to a Chinese buffet restaurant to find it.

That night, I go to Red's Lounge to hear some live music. Tom used to be in a band, and we talk about the last days of CBGB. We were both there during the decline. The last time I went was about a year before they announced it was closing. The band onstage was just as angry and pierced, their music just as cacophonous as anything you might have heard a decade before. It was actually good music, but it didn't matter anymore, not there, anyway, in the heart of the most desired piece of real estate on the Bowery. It was no longer Skid Row. Across the street, you could buy a six-hundred-dollar leather handbag. The tanned and wealthy youth were hanging out drinking saketinis in lounges just a few blocks to the north. The first time I went to CBGB, I was fifteen, and it meant a lot to me. By the time it closed, the city had no need for it anymore.

I AM SIPPING FROM MY PLASTIC CUP of Kentucky Gentleman bourbon. Red stands behind the bar. I'm standing next to him. He is an intimidating man with huge shoulders and a uneven beard that is spotted with gray. He has a square jaw, and he chews gum angrily. I ask him about the authenticity of the blues. He is not listening to me. Red's Lounge is a tiny club along the water in Clarksdale where musicians come to play. It is dark, its walls lined with concert posters. Red string lights pierce through the dark. The blues musician Lucious Spiller sits alone on a plastic chair in the middle of the room, spitting out noises that a guitar shouldn't make. Red looks forward even when he talks to me. He has been chewing the same piece of gum for an hour. His raised eyebrows look like two fists hovering above his round sunglasses.

"You can go through yo' life trying to explain every little thing that happens to you, or you can just shut up and listen to the music in my house," he says.

It's a Wednesday night, so it is slow. Lucious is taking a Sting song, one of his sappier ones, and bending it to say things profane. He is not doing blues; he is just bending music. Lucious doesn't live in a binary world; he pushes and pulls through everything. The song isn't recognizable anymore.

It reminds me of the food of Clarksdale. Italian, Lebanese, barbecue, Mexican, soul food, Chinese—some of it authentic, some not; it all bends to serve the community.

I TRY TO TELL RED A STORY. From 1998 to 2002, I had a small restaurant in downtown Manhattan that I built on a budget and ran into the ground. I was young and barely knew what I was doing. After 9/11, I was tired of New York City. I was tired of partying and I was tired of cooking. Around the time I was about to close the restaurant, I had a party for Bob Gruen, who had photographed many of the rock-and-roll legends of the last generation. That evening, I peeked out from behind my kitchen curtain and saw Lou Reed, Jim Jarmusch, and a few other luminaries, but by the time I got done cooking, only a handful of people were left. As was our tradition back then, I locked the doors and hung out with the crew until we were all good and ready to go home. I remember I grabbed a woman's hand and tried to kiss her behind the bar. "I'm with Joe," she said. After a few minutes, I tried with another girl. "I'm with Joe," she replied. Who is this Joe whom every girl seems to be saving herself for? "You don't know Joe Strummer?" she asked me in shock.

I spun around to stare at the slouching man mumbling to himself in the corner booth with a brandy and Coke. In my defense, if you remember Joe Strummer only from the Clash, this was hardly the person I saw sitting in my restaurant that night. After a few more drinks, everyone danced on tables and lit cigarettes from the stove. He piggybacked me across the restaurant, knocking over chairs and glasses. The sky was getting light by the time we got done with the place. Everyone got in a cab, but I walked to a deli to get breakfast in the chill of the autumn morning. I laughed at myself, knowing no one would ever believe that I'd partied with Joe Strummer. But, hell, Joe would remember, and for sure we would run into each other again. You don't easily forget nights like the one we'd just had. He'd even hugged me to say thanks. A few months later, I would see on the news that he'd died while recording a new album in England. Within a few months, I would close my restaurant, and everyone I knew would soon move to Brooklyn or Queens. CBGB would host its last concert in 2006.

I am recalling a swell of memories as I listen to Lucious and his guitar. Red is barely listening to me. I don't know how all this is connected. I don't know what relates the last days of CBGB to Red's Lounge to Joe Strummer to Po' Monkey to Agnes and Toni, but I know that for me, these events are inseparable. The only binary is life and death. Everything in between is a potluck dinner.

TOM HAS A FRIEND who owns a farmhouse nearby, and we spend the night there. I stay up until dawn sipping whiskey and watching the sky turn from pitch black to iridescent pink. I see the sky erupting with color. The weather is clear, and I can see from my window all the way until the earth drops off. I don't take my eyes off the sky. There are infinite progressions that need to happen before night turns to day, yet I can't say exactly when dawn happens. All of a sudden, you realize it is daylight. It's a reminder that the world isn't delineated by night and day. There are so many layers in between—in the same way that Lucious doesn't play one genre or another; he melts them into something uniquely his own.

I want to be Lucious. I want to skip from one idea to the next with the speed of thought. I don't know how to cook just one thing, and I don't know when my food goes from one place to another. I may not have the speed and subtlety Lucious possesses, but I hope to get there.

I am drawn to places like Clarksdale because in them, I see a smaller version of the world at large. Clarksdale gives me the space to contradict without repercussions. Places such as Clarksdale are not stymied by tradition. It's just that their pace runs slower, and like the bends of the Mississippi, it flows in majestic currents of slow change, in revolutions that require a deeper appetite. Maybe it is not Clarksdale that is behind the rest of the world. Maybe it is the world that needs to slow down a little to keep pace with Clarksdale.

CABBAGE ROLLS
WITH NASTURTIUM LEAF KIMCHI

This recipe for Lebanese-style cabbage rolls was given to me by Toni, one of the owners of a clothing store in Clarksdale. Cabbage rolls may seem pedestrian, but these rolls, filled with seasoned ground beef, are hauntingly complex for a dish that is so easy to make. I like to pair them with nasturtium leaf kimchi because of the spice it brings to the dish. After you cook the cabbage rolls, save the delicious broth and use it as a base for chicken noodle soup.

SERVES 6 AS A FIRST COURSE, 3 AS A MAIN COURSE

½ cup long-grain rice

1 head cabbage

4 cups chicken stock, plus more if needed

1½ teaspoons salt

12 ounces ground beef

1 tablespoon plus 2 teaspoons olive oil

½ teaspoon ground cumin

½ teaspoon ground cinnamon

½ teaspoon freshly ground black pepper

¼ cup chopped fresh mint

4 garlic cloves, 2 minced, 2 whole

Grated zest and juice of 3 lemons

½ cup Nasturtium Leaf Kimchi (recipe follows)

1 cup labneh

Extra-virgin olive oil, for drizzling

Pour the rice into a bowl and soak in 2 cups of very hot water for 15 minutes. Stir occasionally.

Meanwhile, peel off 12 leaves from the head of cabbage; reserve the rest of the cabbage for another use.

In a large pot, bring the chicken stock to a boil over high heat and add ½ teaspoon of the salt. Immerse the cabbage leaves in the broth and simmer for 8 to 10 minutes, until tender. Remove from the heat and carefully pick the leaves from the pot and let cool. Set the broth aside.

Drain the rice in a sieve. In a medium bowl, combine the ground beef, rice, 2 teaspoons of the olive oil, cumin, cinnamon, ½ teaspoon of the salt, the pepper, mint, 2 minced garlic cloves, and half the lemon zest.

Trim the cabbage leaves to rectangles about 6 by 3 inches. Place about 2 tablespoons of the meat mixture in the middle of one leaf, fold the sides of the leaf over, and roll up tightly around the meat. Skewer the leaf with toothpicks to secure it. Repeat with the remaining stuffing and cabbage leaves.

Place the stuffed cabbage rolls in the pot of chicken stock, seam-side down, fitting them snugly in the pot. Make sure the broth covers the cabbage rolls; if necessary, add a little more stock or water to the pot. Add the remaining 2 whole garlic cloves and lemon zest and the lemon juice to the pot, drizzle the rolls with the remaining 1 tablespoon olive oil, and sprinkle with the remaining ½ teaspoon salt.

Cover the pot and bring to a gentle simmer over low heat. Cook for 30 to 40 minutes. To check for doneness, remove one of the rolls from the pot and pinch it—it should bounce back when you squeeze it, indicating that the meat is fully cooked. Let the rolls cool in the broth for 10 minutes before removing them to a platter.

Serve the cabbage rolls with the kimchi on the side and a small bowl of the labneh, drizzled with extra-virgin olive oil, for dipping.

NASTURTIUM LEAF KIMCHI | MAKES ABOUT 1 PINT

40 nasturtium leaves	2 garlic cloves, minced
2 tablespoons fish sauce	1 scallion, finely chopped
1 tablespoon red pepper flakes	1 teaspoon sugar
2 tablespoons grated onion	1 teaspoon toasted sesame seeds

Wash the nasturtium leaves and drain on paper towels.

In a small bowl, whisk together the fish sauce, red pepper flakes, onion, garlic, scallion, sugar, and sesame seeds.

In a small jar, start layering the nasturtium leaves, with a small spoonful of the marinade between each layer. Spoon any remaining marinade over the top when you've used all the leaves.

Wrap the jar tightly in plastic wrap, then poke a few holes in the top. Let stand at room temperature for 24 hours, then put in the refrigerator with a tight-fitting lid. The kimchi will be ready to eat in a week and will keep in the fridge for up to 1 month.

BEEF TARTARE–STUFFED DEVILED EGGS WITH CAVIAR

The ground beef mixture in the kibbeh Tom and I had at the Rest Haven got me to thinking about a recipe for deviled eggs stuffed with beef tartare. These look like ordinary deviled eggs, but when you bite into one, you get the surprise of the spiced beef. They make a great canapé for parties. The salty punch from the spoonbill caviar, also known as paddlefish caviar or roe, is a great accompaniment to the earthiness of the raw beef. It's an inexpensive roe made from sustainable farmed paddlefish that is delicious.

MAKES 24 SMALL BITES

BEEF TARTARE

¼ cup bulgur wheat

One 8-ounce boneless
   New York strip steak

1 cup cold water

2 teaspoons mayonnaise

1½ teaspoons grated lemon
   zest

1 teaspoon minced garlic

1 teaspoon grated fresh
   horseradish

1 teaspoon Dijon mustard

1 teaspoon Worcestershire
   sauce

⅛ teaspoon ground cumin

1½ teaspoons salt

½ teaspoon freshly ground
   black pepper

½ teaspoon extra-virgin
   olive oil

DEVILED EGGS

12 large eggs

¼ cup mayonnaise,
   preferably Duke's

2 tablespoons extra-virgin
   olive oil

2 tablespoons water

1 teaspoon Dijon mustard

1 garlic clove, minced

Grated zest and juice of
   1 lemon

½ teaspoon salt

¼ teaspoon freshly ground
   black pepper

1 ounce paddlefish caviar or
   other black caviar

3 or 4 leaves Nasturtium Leaf
   Kimchi (opposite), finely
   chopped (optional)

TO MAKE THE TARTARE: Put the bulgur in a small bowl, add cold water to cover, and soak for 30 minutes.

Meanwhile, put the beef in the freezer for 15 minutes to firm it up. This will make it easier to cut.

Using a sharp chef's knife, mince the beef as fine as you can get it. Think of ground beef, but it is important to cut it with a knife so you don't "smear" the meat and fat, which would happen if you used a food processor. Transfer to a bowl and refrigerate until ready to use.

Drain the bulgur in a cheesecloth-lined sieve, then squeeze out the excess water.

In a large bowl, combine the beef, bulgur, water, mayonnaise, lemon zest, garlic, horseradish, mustard, Worcestershire sauce, cumin, salt, pepper, and olive oil. Mix gently but thoroughly. Cover with plastic wrap and refrigerate until ready to use.

(CONTINUED)

TO MAKE THE DEVILED EGGS: Heat a large pot of water over low heat until the water is just warm to the touch. Gently lower the eggs into the water, turn up the heat to medium-high, and bring to a simmer. Set a timer for 6 minutes. When the timer goes off, turn off the heat under the eggs and set the timer for 4 minutes.

Meanwhile, set up an ice bath. When the timer goes off, carefully remove the eggs from the hot water and plunge them into the ice bath to stop the cooking.

When the eggs have cooled, drain them, peel, and cut each egg lengthwise in half. Transfer the yolks to a blender and set the whites aside on a platter.

Add the mayonnaise, olive oil, water, mustard, garlic, lemon zest and juice, salt, and pepper to the yolks and blend until smooth. Transfer the mixture into a piping bag fitted with a small round tip.

Stuff the reserved egg whites with the beef tartare, about a tablespoon per egg. Pipe the yolk mixture over the beef tartare, covering the tartare completely. Top each egg with small dollop of paddlefish roe and some of the kimchi, if using. Serve immediately.

CHAPTER 8

MATRIARCHS
OF
MONTGOMERY

EVERYTHING I KNOW ABOUT FOOD, I LEARNED FROM a woman. Everything I know about competition, I learned from a man. It started with my grandmother's hands, which touched everything I ate as a child. They were frail, wrinkled, and clenched with the muscle memory of a lifetime of cooking. I remember the times when she touched my face with those same hands. As I got older, there were other women, women such as Clementine, who taught me the delicacy of salt, sometimes on a ripe tomato, sometimes a saline kiss on a bare shoulder in summer. She taught me that dinner wasn't something to scarf down with a cold beer, but rather a slow meandering of discoveries as the wine in my glass warmed and released layers of molecules, each with a different perfume.

Every chef I ever worked under was a man, and from them, I learned structure, technique, urgency, and how to make people cringe, but none of them ever pointed out the precise moment to cut into a tomato bursting with juice under its skin. Clementine taught me that. I never really ate tomatoes until I lived with Clementine. They had always smelled like the inside of a refrigerator and tasted of water and astringency. It was Clementine who taught me to ripen them in a wooden bowl on the counter next to a vase of fresh-picked herbs. She taught me the profane joy of biting into one as you would an apple. I was already a cook when I met her, but she took the lessons I'd learned in the restaurant kitchen and made them real for me. She taught me the nuance of French butter left out by an open window, so it would pick up the scent of the blossoming trees on West Thirteenth Street. She taught me how much better pasta tasted when we ate it in large bowls standing up in the kitchen instead of sitting at the dinner table. That last summer before we broke up, we fought a lot, and I remember the musty smell of overripe tomatoes wafting into my face every time she slammed a door or walked by me without saying a word. In one summer, Clementine taught me more about the pains of love and the joy of tomatoes than all the rest of my years combined. I could fill a book with the things she taught me, but this story is not about her. I still have a hard time eating a ripe, raw tomato.

ON THIS TRIP, I am meeting Sarah Reynolds in Montgomery, Alabama. She is a respected producer and journalist. She writes about poverty, immigrants, and everyday people who have meaningful stories to tell. She is working on a podcast for the Southern Foodways Alliance about Korean food in Montgomery and how the Korean immigrant population has blossomed in this small Southern city where she spent some of her youth. Nearly a decade ago, the Korean automotive manufacturer Hyundai opened its first plant in the United States, employing about eight thousand people and basically making Montgomery a second home. Koreans have been coming here ever since. In a city of about four hundred thousand people, there are roughly fifteen Korean-owned restaurants. Per capita, that's more than in Manhattan.

Sarah suggests we meet at Davis Café, an established soul food restaurant minutes from downtown. The outside of the restaurant is painted an unappealing shade of army green. A rusty sign is all that signifies its location. It is 2:00 p.m. when I arrive, and Sarah is already at a table fiddling with her recording device. Like her stories, she is lean and sparse in her mannerisms, but with a youthful intensity that flows from the gray-blue eyes behind the square frame of her glasses. We are the last table to order. They are out of okra, potatoes, liver, and sweet potato pie. We order what's left on the menu with "Wednesday" printed across the top.

I've met many talented folks through the Southern Foodways Alliance, so when I heard about the story Sarah was working on about Korean food in Montgomery, I volunteered to help out as an interpreter. I may have let on that I know more Korean than I actually do.

The food at Davis tastes like home cooking. That may sound like a cliché, but the flavor of home cooking is actually a difficult impression to achieve in a restaurant: fried chicken that is freshly salted; toothsome pork chops smothered in a rich, sweet gravy; long-cooked turnip greens that disintegrate in your mouth; and a bean salad that is both chewy and forgiving at the same time. I can tell this food was cooked by a woman. It has a flavor that announces itself proudly. It is food made out of patience and intimacy, without shortcuts. Still, I am careful to keep my prejudices to myself. I don't want Sarah to think I'm a man who sees gender in food.

Like any good journalist, Sarah has an easiness to her that makes me want to talk. We skip the awkward process of getting to know each other, and our conversation finds a rhythm right away. Maybe it's because we share the language of food, or maybe it's because I feel a kindred spirit in her. Or maybe I'm part of her story, and she's guiding me to a safe place so I may ramble on about my childhood growing up as a child of Korean immigrants.

"Koreans are stubbornly shy, but it's mostly an act," I tell her. "The real obstacle is that they don't trust anyone."

"How so?" she asks quietly.

"Anyone who remembers the poverty after the Korean War also remembers how families were pitted against each other for what little there was to be had. Koreans saw a lot of awful things, and they never forgot them, though they won't talk about them, either."

"Did your parents talk to you about it?"

"No, but I believe sadness can be passed on through DNA. It takes generations to wipe the slate clean."

The staff is cleaning the last tables. We could sit here talking all day, but the restaurant is closing up. Cynthia Davis, one of the owners and the chef, is resting by the cash register as I walk up to pay. Her grandparents George and Josie started this restaurant thirty years ago in 1988. Her niece, Sheila, runs the cash register and works the phones. Her sister Shauna waits tables and helps package the take-out orders. Together, they are a force of nature. I ask Cynthia if she always runs out of food. Every day, she tells me. We talk about Montgomery. We talk about the history of her restaurant. I ask her how the okra was cooked, as I didn't get to try it. She tells me to come back tomorrow. I say I will, if she'll save me some sweet potato pie. I tell her I'm here to research Korean restaurants. None of these women have ever tried Korean food. Why not? I ask. Cynthia tells me she's suspicious of what they serve.

"Yeah," I tease. "It's hard to read the menu in Korean."

"No, I mean the meat. People sayin' they serve all kinds of animals." She winks and nods. I know where this is going.

"It's usually beef or pork," I say.

"Is it really, though?"

"If I bring you some, will you try it?"

"If *you* bring it, yes, I'll try it." She says this with the confidence of someone who believes I'll never return.

Food is trust, and trust is intimacy. The hardest part of trying something unfamiliar is not the fear of the unknown, but rather the mistrust of the person cooking the food. When we read about a celebrity chef in a glossy magazine, we feel we're getting to know that chef as a person. It makes us comfortable enough to eat whatever the chef puts in front of us. I'm always amazed at the level of intimacy that perfect strangers display when they come up to me on the street. They feel they know me because of an article they've read. A lady once asked me to pose for a picture while holding her newborn baby. But with immigrant restaurants, we talk only about the food; rarely do we profile the chef behind it. The food may be delicious, but the cook is invisible. The trust is never quite fully formed. In a town like Montgomery, with such deep-rooted traditions, the recent wave of Korean immigrants naturally brings with it skepticism and mistrust, from both sides. The Korean culture has yet to hold hands with the Old Guard of Montgomery. It may take another generation to do so, but one day, Korean food may become as familiar to the locals here in Montgomery, Alabama, as kibbeh is to residents of Clarksdale, Mississippi. Only time will tell.

Sarah drives me around Montgomery's pretty neighborhoods. The trees along the parks are covered in Spanish moss, and the warm air glistens with humidity. She shows me the city of her youth, the F. Scott and Zelda Fitzgerald Museum, and the Southern Poverty Law Center, where she worked. This is a picturesque city, full of history and stories. I wish we could stay here, but our story takes place along the wide traffic lanes of Eastern Boulevard, which is choked with exhaust fumes and big chain stores. There is not a tree for miles.

The first place we visit is a Korean grocery store that makes its own kimchi and *banchan*, small side plates of mostly pickled vegetables, which they sell in clean, well-organized refrigerated cases. The store's shelves are stocked with colorful bags of rice, dried noodles, spices, and at least six different kinds of seaweed. There is an entire aisle dedicated to soap, washcloths, loofahs, and Korean body scrub towels. In the back is a small makeshift kitchen lit by bright fluorescent bulbs. Two elderly ladies are silently chopping daikon radish. I make small talk, but they aren't responsive. Sarah is recording from behind me. I ask the women what they're doing. They tell me they're making *kakdugi*, a cubed radish kimchi. My Korean is not that good, which makes the women even more skeptical of us. The older one is Mrs. Park. She married an American soldier many years ago in Seoul. She has been in Montgomery for more than twenty years. She won't tell me if she owns the place. I want her to tell me about her family, so I start to describe my life growing up in Brooklyn.

Just when I think she's warmed to me a bit, she notices the microphone being pointed in her direction. She asks Sarah in broken English what she's doing. The moment goes from awkward to belligerent so quickly that I can't come up with the words fast enough to defuse the situation. Before we know it, Mrs. Park is throwing a fit and demanding that Sarah erase everything on her device. Two more ladies come out of nowhere to reprimand us. Mrs. Park looks at me with piercing eyes of betrayal. I feel terrible. It was my idea to start recording without asking. Sarah is backing away confused, but stalwart in her mission to get the story. I understand every nasty thing the ladies are saying. There is a long, unsettling pause, and Sarah and I assume the women have calmed down. We ask for their forgiveness and inquire if we can start over. But Koreans are not quick to forgive. I tell Sarah I know this from experience. We slink out of the store defeated and stunned.

I have a flashback from my youth. I grew up inside this immigrant culture, with hardened grandmothers and secretive whispers. My parents, my aunts and uncles, and all their friends harbored a mistrust of American institutions. They always kept cash hidden in mattresses. They talked only to people they knew. They rarely let outsiders into their home. They told me that if a stranger took your picture, he was stealing a bit of your soul. I explain this to Sarah in the car. The ladies have a name for people like me: *jemi-gyopo*, a person who is Korean by blood but raised in America. It isn't a slur exactly, but it carries with it a complex set of prejudices about someone who has traded in his Korean soul for a set of American values, who is to be regarded as a foreigner.

The rest of the day is more productive, and we hit two other good Korean restaurants. I let Sarah do most of the talking, interpreting when necessary. At Shilla Restaurant, we eat *bulgogi*, thinly sliced marinated beef; scallion pancakes; and octopus stir-fry. The restaurant is eerily empty. The food tastes like that from the Korean restaurants I grew up with: a menu of popular dishes executed well but without pushing the envelope. Shilla is run by the Kim sisters, who agree to let us into their kitchen the next morning as they prepare box lunches for the executives at the Hyundai offices. They make these lunches every weekday for about two hundred people. They start at 6:00 a.m.

THAT NIGHT, Sarah and I wind up at a Japanese restaurant run by Koreans. The place is cavernous, with private rooms behind curtains and a bar tucked away in a far-off corner. The phenomenon of Koreans operating Japanese restaurants was fairly common in New York City when I was a kid. I now see it all over the country. If you're anywhere just outside a major city, chances are your favorite sushi restaurant is run by Korean immigrants pretending to be Japanese. Identity appropriation when it comes to food is nothing new in America. Swiss immigrants opened German and French restaurants. Muslims from all over the Middle East serve Lebanese food. Bangladeshi people are known to operate Indian restaurants. Still, I find something particularly insidious about this brand of identity disguise. It started in the 1980s, when sushi started to catch on like wildfire and Koreans saw a business opportunity. A generation of Korean immigrants who still remembered being mistreated and colonized by an imperialist Japanese regime arrived in a new country only to imitate the identity of their oppressors to make a living. What does that do to the psyche of a generation of immigrant Koreans?

Sarah and I peruse the menu: volcano roll, caterpillar roll, firecracker roll—all these atrocious interpretations of a maki roll, dipped and slathered in sweet sauce and mayo with more garnishes than a teenager on prom night. This is not the work of a Japanese person, I say to Sarah. A Japanese chef would never desecrate his culture like this. But for most Americans, when we think of sushi, this is what we picture. I, too, have been guilty of indulging in these rolls smothered in Sriracha sauce, topped with panko crumbs, stuffed with fake crabmeat and pollock roe dyed to a neon red. You taste nothing but sweet sauce and cold, vinegared rice. It is an affront to the craft of sushi. And then it hit me: was this the Korean way of getting back at the Japanese? What better revenge than to come to America and steal the cultural identity of a country's most respected culinary craft by stuffing it with cream cheese and dousing it in cheap teriyaki sauce—all the while pretending to be Japanese and thwarting a hallowed aesthetic that Japanese immigrants have been trying to preserve for decades?

Sarah and I are eating a pot of pig's feet and drinking beer. The walls of the restaurant are lined with garish neon signs, and K-pop plays on the radio. Everyone here is speaking Korean. The sushi chef politely refuses to answer my questions. For all intents and purposes, we could be Americans in Seoul, but we are in Montgomery, Alabama. And that is the story for me: this idea of an American identity draped around an immigrant population deep in the South. The waitstaff is composed mostly of Korean American college students, and they answer our questions with a smile and a shrug. We give up asking and return to our food. We are huddled in the safety of our shared language, pretending to be expatriates in a foreign land.

The next day, Sarah is up early to record the Kim sisters prepping box lunches in their kitchen. By the time I arrive, Mrs. Kim, the elder, is cutting up acorn jelly for a salad. A spicy miso stew is simmering in a kettle in the corner. *Banchan* are being apportioned and wrapped. The ladies are wearing colorful aprons and spongy work shoes. They move in tandem. They are not fast, they are not strong, they are not even particularly efficient, but they are persistent. They move on to the next task without hesitation. Not once do they stop moving or chopping or cleaning. You can get so much done when you work without breaks.

Shilla was the third Korean restaurant to open in Montgomery, more than twenty-five years ago, long before the Hyundai plant arrived. The Kim sisters work from 6:00 a.m. to 10:00 p.m. every day except Sunday. That is their day off, but once a month Mrs. Kim will take a day to drive to Atlanta to stock up on ingredients. She is wearing a lace hairnet and lipstick; her husband sells beauty supplies. She won't do this forever, she says. She'll retire one day and take cruises around the world with her husband. I ask her where she learned all her recipes. She tells me that it is just something all Korean women know; it is a shared knowledge. There is nothing precious about her food. Anyone can make this food, she says. She just does it with a little more precision. Still, I can tell she is proud of her work. She tells me that she makes these box lunches five days a week and never repeats a menu within a month's time. She shows me a calendar of her menus; it reads like a tutorial on Korean food.

I ask if her kids can cook all these different dishes. No, she says, but that's okay. They came to America for a different life, a better life, so they can take advantage of all the opportunities here. Mrs. Kim could be my mother. Her story is not very different. I run out of questions to ask her, mostly because I already know the answers.

We leave Shilla and go for lunch at Budnamu. The menu is the same as that of the other restaurants we've tried, but it's the best version of it so far. The *nak-jibokum*, *kalbi*, homemade kimchi, and *doenjang* stew are all deeply satisfying. We talk to the owner, who gives us rehearsed answers about the food. I peek inside the kitchen and see a lone woman meticulously plating food. She's too busy to talk to us but smiles profusely.

I ask them to wrap up three dishes for me, so I can bring them to the women at the Davis Café. *Bulgogi*, thin slices of marinated beef sautéed with onions and peppers, will be the crowd-pleaser. *Doenjang guk*, an umami-rich miso soup with stewed vegetables and chunks of pork, will be a little more challenging for the ladies but still within the realm of familiarity. The last is *nakji bokum*, chewy curls of octopus tentacles sautéed with vegetables and a spicy fermented chile sauce. I figure if the ladies at the Davis try the first two dishes without incident, I can up the ante with this one.

We have to wait until Cynthia is finished in the kitchen. She seems surprised to see me again. She did not save me any pie. It takes her a few minutes to get up the nerve to try the *bulgogi* from Budnamu. She takes a bite the size of a peanut. Then she goes in for a bigger bite. She's never eaten any other kind of food but soul food, she says, so this is a big step for her. She takes a sip of the miso soup as her sisters watch in horrified anticipation. She frowns immediately. Not for me, she says. She then opens the Styrofoam box of octopus and looks at me, incredulous.

"What is it?" she asks. I tell her. "Oh, hell noooo," she says.

We all have a good laugh. Even the customers are having fun with it, but no one will try the octopus. Everyone is daring Cynthia to try it, but she won't budge. I see that Sarah is diligently recording, though I'm not sure how much of this interaction will make it into her story.

I've been studying the way Sarah interviews people. Her questions are direct and precise, but her delivery is disarming. She gives her subjects the space to speak. If there is a silence, she allows it. She doesn't jump in to fill the void. She's patient. She lets the person come to the question at her own pace. If she doesn't answer a question, she moves on to the next one. I decide to take a stab at interviewing Cynthia myself while she's in a good mood.

Q. What scares you about Korean food?

A. I just grew up with simple food. We didn't go out to eat, so I never ate nothing but what we cooked.

Q. Will you go to a Korean restaurant now that you know what to order?

A. Maybe. I'll see. I don't have much time to myself. This place takes everything.

Q. If not you, then who else can run this place?

A. Nobody. It's just me and my sisters. When we go, the restaurant goes as well.

Q. Will you be sad if this goes away, this restaurant?

A. No, honey. Everything comes to an end. I won't be sad one bit. My children will do something better. Doing all this day in, day out is hard. I don't want my kids to have this life.

Q. But who will keep up the tradition?

A. They all cook at home. Every black family cooks at home around here. The tradition ain't going nowhere. It will live on in their homes.

Q. But not for someone like me. What happens when I want this food?

A. Hmm . . .

Q. What makes a woman better in the kitchen than a man?

A. Well, a woman's gonna stick it out until the end. A man is more likely to go away when things get tough. You see, if a marriage don't work out, a man's gonna leave and start a new family and leave the other one behind. A woman's gonna stick it out and see it through till the end. That's why we all sisters running this business.

Q. Do you like what you do?

A. Yes. My mamma would have been proud of me, but I don't want this for my kids.

Q. How much longer can you do this?

A. I will do this till God tells me I can't do it no more. I don't want to do anything else. This is my work. God gave me the strength to do this every single day, and He will tell me when I can't do it no more.

I ask for a hug, and Cynthia comes out from behind the counter. She is a large woman, and her embrace feels good. It feels real. Then she tells me in a calm but stern voice, "It's been real nice talking to you, but I have to go clean up now." She walks away, but just before she disappears into the kitchen, she turns her head sharply toward me and says, "And don't forget to take that octopus back with you, now."

SARAH AND I ARE STANDING on the street in front of Davis when we say good-bye. It is a sunny day, but the light feels drab, melancholic. It's odd for me to tell someone I just met two days ago that I'll miss her, so I don't. She has another interview lined up, and she hurries on her way.

Driving out of Montgomery, I drop by the Waffle House in Prattville, which is famous for its singing waitress. Her name is Valerie. I order a bowl of chili and hash browns, smothered and covered. Valerie's daughter works alongside her. The entire staff here is composed of women. Valerie works the griddle station and belts out rock-and-roll classics all the while, changing the lyrics to make waffle and egg references. She has a deep, soulful voice and a bright energy that seems impossible to sustain for an entire shift.

I ask her when she started singing. She tells me it was during an overnight shift. There were a bunch of drunk men getting ready to fight. She started singing to defuse the situation, and it worked. She's been singing ever since.

Next to me at the counter is an old cowboy in a wheelchair. There's a young couple in a booth with a baby in a stroller. Another man, sitting across from me, is obviously a regular. He banters back and forth with Valerie. Customers drop in and say hello. The women behind the counter seem to know them all. I end up staying for an hour and talking to everyone in the store. They ask me what I'm doing, and they wish me good luck. Valerie's daughter gets off early because she has a class. Everyone waves good-bye to her. Valerie starts belting out another tune; I recognize the lyrics of a Whitney Houston song.

I TRY TO KEEP AN OPEN MIND when I visit a new place, but I already have stories in my head that I want to tell. I want these stories to be perfect. I want the outcome to be just what I set out to prove. But it rarely works out that way. Inside this Waffle House, a chain restaurant, I find the culture I wish I had found inside all those Korean restaurants. All these people come here for a reason, not just for Valerie, but for the food, the social comfort, the intimacy. I wish I hadn't found this intimacy sitting in a chain restaurant next to a Shell station and across from a McDonald's. But maybe this is the culture as it stands right now in America. I could spend the rest of my life eating in Michelin-starred restaurants, or I could start to include places like this one in my deeper understanding of food in America. I wish Sarah were here so we could argue this out. There are many questions I should have asked her but forgot to. I could fill a room with all the regrets I collect.

In 2014, Sarah produced a story for NPR about a photographer who asked pairs of random strangers to pose for a picture together. It's a fascinating story. The photos are rich and haunting. Two random strangers pose in an embrace, then they go about their lives. There is nothing but this captured moment that connects the two people, and yet, in many of the photographs, they seem to have a real bond. Sarah says she sees real intimacy between these strangers, even though she knows it's not really there. It's only imagined, for a fleeting moment. Yet I see it, too, as does everyone who looks at the photos. Maybe it's because we want to see it, because we want to believe that an instant of intimacy can exist. I've listened to this NPR story many times, and each time, it makes me smile. Maybe it's because something that is so hard to find in the real world can easily exist in a fictional photograph. That is enough to keep me going.

Finding the intersection of soul food and Korean food is easy for me, almost second nature. I find the rhythms to be similar, the simplicity, the frugality. A lot of the raw ingredients are shared: pig's feet, cabbage, sweet potato, peanuts. Koreans food tends to ferment more, while soul food tends to cook low and slow. Yet both evoke the same range of feelings in the end. I love nothing more than combining the technique of a low-and-slow food with something fermented. That is the most perfect dish I can think of because it is the best of two worlds I care deeply about.

OCTOPUS STIR-FRY
(NAK-JI BOKUM)

This octopus stir-fry is a mainstay in every Korean restaurant. The octopus is stir-fried quickly until just cooked, with a chewy but pleasant texture. Do not overcook the octopus, or it will become impossibly rubbery. Have all your ingredients cut and ready to go. Use a large skillet or wok over high heat to get your pan screaming hot.

SERVES 4 AS A FIRST COURSE

GOCHUJANG SAUCE

3 tablespoons soy sauce

2½ tablespoons gochujang (Korean chile paste)

2 tablespoons toasted sesame oil

2 tablespoons fresh lemon juice

2 teaspoons fish sauce

1 tablespoon gochugaru (Korean chile powder) or other ground chile

5 garlic cloves, minced

1 tablespoon sugar

One 1½- to 2-pound octopus, cleaned

3 tablespoons vegetable oil

1 tablespoon toasted sesame oil

1 garlic clove, minced

1 carrot, thinly sliced

½ medium onion, thinly sliced

2 jalapeño peppers, seeded and thinly sliced

1 red bell pepper, seeded and cut into thin strips

4 shiitake mushrooms, stemmed and thinly sliced

1 tablespoon toasted sesame seeds, for garnish

2 scallions, thinly sliced, for garnish

TO MAKE THE SAUCE: In a small bowl, combine the soy sauce, gochujang, sesame oil, lemon juice, fish sauce, gochugaru, garlic, and sugar and mix well. Set aside.

Run the octopus under cold running water. Cut the tentacles away from the head and slice into 2-inch pieces. Slice the head into small pieces. Pat the octopus dry with paper towels.

Heat a large skillet or wok over high heat and add half the vegetable oil. When the oil is screaming hot, add the octopus and stir-fry for 1 minute. Remove from the pan and set aside on a plate.

(CONTINUED)

Add the remaining vegetable oil to the pan, along with the sesame oil, and heat until very hot. Add the garlic, carrot, onion, peppers, and mushrooms and stir-fry for 4 to 5 minutes, until the vegetables are softened and lightly browned but not caramelized. Add the octopus and the sauce to the pan and cook for 2 to 3 minutes more, mixing well. If the sauce is too thick, add 1 tablespoon water to loosen it.

Transfer the octopus to a platter and garnish with the sesame seeds and scallions. Serve immediately.

SALT-ROASTED SWEET POTATOES WITH KALBI BUTTER AND GOCHUJANG SAUCE

The sweet potato is a root vegetable beloved equally by Korean and soul food cooks. I love to find the intersection of two cultures by blending techniques and flavors, and to me, this recipe is the best of both worlds: buttery roasted sweet potatoes meet Korean flavors.

This dish uses the stir-fry sauce from the Octopus Stir-Fry (page 153). *Kalbi* is a Korean marinade for beef, but here it's used to make a compound butter. Make the *kalbi* butter ahead of time, even the day before, to allow the flavors to blend.

SERVES 4 AS A FIRST COURSE OR SIDE

4 sweet potatoes, scrubbed	About 6 tablespoons Kalbi Butter (recipe follows), softened
¼ cup corn oil	
Sea salt	Chopped scallions, for garnish
¼ cup Gochujang Sauce (page 153)	

Preheat the oven to 375°F.

Put the potatoes on a plate and rub generously with the corn oil, then roll in the sea salt.

Wrap each potato in aluminum foil and put on an oven rack. Bake for 1 hour, or until the potatoes are soft to the touch. Remove from the oven and let cool for about 5 minutes.

Unwrap the potatoes and transfer to a platter. Split each potato open with a paring knife. With your fingers, gently press on the ends of the potato so the split widens. Add a small spoonful of the gochujang sauce to each sweet potato, then add a large spoonful of the kalbi butter. Sprinkle the scallions over the butter and serve immediately, as the butter will start to melt into the sweet potatoes (which is a good thing).

KALBI BUTTER | MAKES 4 CUPS

¾ cup soy sauce
¼ cup granulated sugar
2 tablespoons packed brown sugar
2 tablespoons toasted sesame oil
6 garlic cloves, chopped

3 tablespoons minced fresh ginger
3 scallions, finely chopped
2 teaspoons gochugaru (Korean chile powder) or other ground chile powder
2 pounds (8 sticks) unsalted butter, softened

In a medium saucepan, combine the soy sauce, both sugars, and the sesame oil and bring to a boil, stirring to dissolve the sugar, then boil for 3 minutes. Let cool until room temperature but not cold.

Put the garlic, ginger, scallions, and gochugaru in a food processor and pulse until thoroughly blended into a paste. With the machine running, add the softened butter and process until fully combined. Drizzle in the warm soy sauce mixture, processing until fully combined.

Transfer the compound butter to a covered container and refrigerate until thoroughly chilled, at least 1 hour. You can make the butter up to a day ahead.

CHAPTER 9

A LESSON IN SMEN

I DREAM OF WHITE CLAM PIZZA. TINY PEBBLES OF GARLIC, dried oregano, freshly chopped littleneck clams, and a child-size fistful of grated pecorino on a warm crust of charred, puffed dough. The briny steam is the first thing that hits your nose; a light drizzle of olive oil makes the entire pie shimmer. Whenever I'm in Connecticut, I eat my weight in clam pizza.

It's snowing today, a dense, silent snowfall that makes the world seem hushed. I'm driving to Westport, a tony suburban town known more for its quiet family life than its cuisine. But there is a Frank Pepe pizzeria in nearby Fairfield, and while everyone says it's not as good as the original, in New Haven, I'm sure it'll do just fine. People always say the sequel is never as good as the original. The snow is wet and thick, and has slowed traffic to a dismal forty miles per hour on the highway. My windshield is frosted around the edges. I'm dreaming of pizza, but I'm thinking of Morocco. I'm here for the *smen*.

Smen, a long-fermented butter, technically illegal to sell commercially in the United States, is not something you can buy at your local gourmet shop. I've searched in vain for a black market in *smen* dealers. I've winked at waitresses at Moroccan restaurants, hinting that I would be willing to pay a hefty sum for a taste of it. I've tried to make it at home, but there is scant literature on the subject. Recently, a blogger friend of mine connected me to someone who had attended a dinner party in Westport thrown by a young Moroccan woman who had recently moved to America. A few e-mails later, I was introduced to Amal. She's from Marrakesh. She's been here for six months and is living with her brother. She is said to possess great cooking talent. A few more e-mails, and I secure an invitation to her home. She promises to show me how to make *smen*. It is an ancient tradition in every Moroccan home, she tells me. I knew that. I worked with a Moroccan chef once, and I've been obsessed with the idea of *smen* ever since.

One of my first jobs in a professional kitchen was at a trendy French Moroccan restaurant in New York City's East Village. Frank Crispo was my boss. He's a no-nonsense blue-collar chef from Philadelphia. His mind is an encyclopedia of Western cooking: French, Italian, Spanish, and even some German classics. He would cook with the angry intensity of a bull and the delicacy of a ballerina. Frank taught me how to compete for my place on the line. He taught me how to win with nothing more than the willingness to work harder than the guy next to me. "Come an hour before anyone else does, and stay an hour late." Frank would say things like that to me all the time.

Before the grand opening, the owners hired a husband-and-wife team from Morocco to teach us their cuisine. They were chefs from Fez, handsome and fashionable. They fought night and day. A kitchen is loud enough anyway, but the noise level in ours was magnified by their vibrating arguments. It would start with a whispered comment from her; then he would cut back with a sharp retort. Things would quickly escalate into a shouting match, her upraised fingers jerking with every pronounced insult while he shrugged his shoulders, letting out a nasal moan of exasperation. The husband went by the name Ben; I don't remember his wife's name. Sometimes, in the middle of their heated arguments, he would look at me and smirk. None of us in the kitchen understood a word they were saying, so we never knew how serious the arguments were. "It is just passion," Ben would say to me later. "I love her, but she is so strong."

I was the young *commis*, or junior chef, so it was my job to entertain them on Sundays, my only day off. I would take them sightseeing, shopping, whatever they wanted. We walked to the Twin Towers one morning only to find out that Ben had a moral disdain for paying to see the top of any building. "I can buy a postcard," he kept saying. We walked back to the restaurant while his wife berated him for thirty blocks.

Ben and I muddled through in broken English, and became friends. I started to look forward to our Sundays together. One Sunday, while his wife was out shopping, he and I went for a walk. He loved walks. He was a tall, gentle man with graying hair that made him look wise. But he was always quiet—too timid, I thought, to talk to me much when his wife was nearby. I took him to Katz's Deli and Russ and Daughters, places where his wife would not want him to eat. We sat in a nearby playground and unwrapped our corned beef sandwich, pastrami salmon on a bagel with scallion cream cheese, and two different kinds of rugelach. Ben liked watching the children run around us screaming. Their high-pitched shrieks didn't bother him. He never had children, and I think that saddened him more than anything else in the world. He told me that the food he was teaching me was for tourists. It wasn't the real food of Morocco. It was what the owners wanted. My jaw dropped. Every day, for the past month, I had been diligently rolling *braewats* and *bisteeyas*, pureeing sundry versions of *chermoula*, and tending to a five-gallon tub of harissa, which went on everything. I thought I was learning something authentic. I felt betrayed. How could he be so nonchalant about it? And why would he bother telling me this? He could easily have finished out his time here without breaking a young cook's spirit.

"You need real spices, you need *ras el hanout*," he said to me quietly, as if we were trading secrets. "And you need *smen*."

As we ate lunch that day, he told me tales of this enigmatic butter that magically improved everything it touched. You can keep for it many years, he said. He had a jar of it at home that was five years old. It is the smell of Morocco, he said. I had never heard of anything like this. In between bites of pastrami salmon, he told me how to make it. He would speak a little, then take a bite of the salmon, close his eyes, and lose his train of thought. After every bite, I'd have to remind him where he'd left off. I wrote everything down on the back of a receipt. I asked him to show me later how to make it, in the kitchen. He shook his head as if to say it's better that no one know about this conversation. He wrapped up the remaining half of his corned beef sandwich and put it in his apron pocket. He didn't talk to me much after that afternoon. At the end of the month, he and his wife returned to Morocco. We vowed to keep in touch but never did. I lost the receipt, and for years I couldn't remember the name of that butter we spoke of that day in the safety of a crowd of screaming children in the East Village.

AMAL'S HOUSE is at the end of a cul-de-sac on a plain-looking street. Westport is a serene, wealthy family town. The houses here are mostly Colonials with two-car garages and pristine driveways. The snow makes every house look like a postcard of a perfect New England suburb. Amal answers the door quickly. She is vibrant and talkative, eager to show me her recipes. Although she already has a degree in economics, she wants to go to an American university. She wants to go to New York City. Westport is a little slow for her, she tells me. She's twenty-six and a modest, religious woman. She doesn't want to disappoint her parents, who worry about her back home in Marrakesh. She has a kind voice and tells me all this in near-perfect English. I ask her how she learned English so quickly. From movies, she says. As a child, she watched Hollywood movies over and over again until she could repeat every word of dialogue.

I ask her to tell me about her life in Marrakesh.

"Every day, you gather with families and friends for meals. You stroll through the markets and smell spices. Everywhere you look, you see colors that remind you of nature. You drink mint tea in cafés and talk all day till the sun goes down. Meals are celebrations, enjoyed in large groups. In America, everyone eats alone. It seems so lonely." She smiles as if to soften the negative remark.

I remind her that Westport is not representative of all of America.

"In Morocco," she tells me, "you are never alone. You are never far from the sound of laughter." Amal is the youngest of nine children. She is the adventurous one. As she's telling me this, I look out the window behind her, at trees covered in snow, at the yard devoid of any human activity. For a moment, we gaze at the lonely scene together, then she lets out a frustrated yelp. "I miss Marrakesh," she tells me. Then she quickly snaps back to her lively demeanor and tells me that, for now, being an American is most important for her.

The first step of any learning process is mimicry. It is how Amal learned English. It is how I learned to cook. With the Internet and cookbooks, it seems that we can learn everything from reading and observing. But there are still mysteries in the kitchen, like sourdough, or croissants you can't master through a set of instructions. *Smen* falls into this category. It is impossible to explain all the nuances in words. The process of making *smen* is simple, but it is all in the hands. There is a rhythm to it, a movement learned through repetition. But not everyone has a Moroccan friend they can learn from.

The following is a description of Amal making *smen*. It is an attempt to put into words something that is, at its core, ineffable.

Amal reaches for a small pot and fills it with about three cups of tap water without measuring. She brings this to a simmer over a gas burner that hisses gently. She opens a glass jar of dried thyme leaves and spoons about three tablespoons into the pot. She then contemplates the ratio and adds another immodest pinch. It is a lot of thyme. As the water simmers, the kitchen fills with the herbaceous smell of wet, fecund earth. Thyme is delicate in small amounts; it is light and green to the nose.

This amount of thyme is aggressive and tannic. I feel as if I'm smelling thyme for the first time.

After fifteen minutes, she strains the liquid into a shallow bowl and discards the spent leaves. She spoons a little into her mouth, to approve of the flavor. She moves this bowl off to the side. She wants it to cool so she can work it into the butter without melting it. But it can't be too cold, either, or it'll chill the butter to a stiffness that would feel "discourteous" to her hands.

In a large ceramic bowl, she rests six sticks of unsalted butter that have been waiting all morning to be touched. She pours two cups of cold water into the bowl and, with both hands, begins to knead together the butter and water. She calls this process "washing." Slowly and method-ically, she squeezes the butter through her fingers. The idea is to clean the butter by removing the milky residue that the butter-making process leaves behind. As she kneads the butter with her hands, the water turns cloudy. Her hands clench and relax in a motion that seems as rehearsed as an ancient dance. When the water turns cloudy enough that we can't see the bottom of the bowl, she drains the water into the sink. She then adds a little more clean water and repeats the process.

Amal is telling me about life in Marrakesh, about her cousins and friends. When a memory makes her laugh, she stops to enjoy the moment. The water turns cloudy again. She repeats this washing process three times, until the water remains clear, then drains the bowl. Next, she adds half the thyme water, which has cooled to room temperature. She uses the balls of her hands to press and smear the butter against the bottom of the bowl. The thyme water is mingling with the surface area of the butter but not emulsifying into it. Watching Amal's hands is like watching a baker knead bread dough, but in slow motion. It is circular, soothing, and sensual. After about ten minutes of this kneading, she drains the thyme water. She adds the salt now. It looks to me to be about three tablespoons; it looks like too much. She pushes it gently but firmly into the amenable butter. We taste it. The *smen* tastes oversalted, but Amal says it's perfect.

She then adds the remaining thyme water to the butter. She presses the butter flat and covers it with plastic wrap. She tells me to let it rest at room temperature for four hours at least or, better yet, overnight.

While we wait, Amal shows me some of her family pictures. They are blurry photos of smiling men and women in bright-colored clothes, always with some kind of food nearby. We prep the ingredients for the dishes we are about to cook together.

When the *smen* is ready, she drains off the thyme water. She chooses a clean glass jar that will hold all the butter. With her right hand, she picks up a small fistful of the butter and the last remaining drops of water trapped inside before pressing it into the jar. Another small handful goes into the jar, pressed into a corner. She continues this process about fifteen times, until the butter reaches the top of the jar. She lays a small circle of cheesecloth over the top of the butter, then screws the lid on tight and wipes the outside clean. The *smen* is done now. She puts the jar in the back of her cupboard and tells me it will be ready in thirty days, but you can leave it for as long as you want. And that is *smen*.

I REMEMBER MY FIRST DAY in the French Moroccan kitchen. Frank asked me if I knew how to make a chocolate mousse cake. I said yes, too afraid to disappoint him. Jaime, an Ecuadorian and Frank's right-hand man for the past five years, was chopping leeks at a station next to mine. He and Frank knew each other's movements like an unspoken language. As soon as Frank left the kitchen, I gathered my *mise en place* for the chocolate mousse cake: chocolate pistoles, eggs, heavy cream, and sugar. That's all I knew. I didn't know where to start. So I asked Jaime what he liked to put in his chocolate mousse.

"You gotta melt the chocolate, man."

"Yeah, of course, I know that, but I just wanted to see if you did it that way, too."

After a few more questions, Jaime knew I had no idea what I was doing. With each step, he'd roll his eyes and show me another technique.

I followed his every move, from turning egg whites into a meringue to whipping heavy cream to a light cloud to folding the batter together in slow figure eights. Jaime barely spoke to me. He didn't have to. A kitchen crew can communicate without words. Later that night, the cake was a hit. Frank came back into the kitchen and congratulated me. "That's a good recipe," he announced loudly, so everyone could hear. I cringed. "Make sure to give the recipe to Jaime," he said. "I don't think he can make a mousse this good." I was speechless. Frank winked at Jaime, who chuckled under his knife hand. I slinked away. That was Frank. He didn't tell you how wrong you were. He let you dig your own grave.

BEFORE AMAL TEACHES ME her family recipes, she pulls out a jar of *smen* that she had brought back from Morocco. It is about eight months old. It smells like the inside of a worn leather satchel. I ask her if *smen* can be made by flavoring the water with something other than thyme. No, she says, this is the only way to make it. It is tradition. My mind wanders to what other flavors could work: basil, red peppercorn, corncobs. This is the difference between us. She has a tradition; I don't. As much as I envy the confidence and faith she has in her traditions, I know I can't be her. Maybe part of being American is releasing the anchor that we have to our heritage so we can drift directionless into the unknown waters of identity. Maybe the more we watch Hollywood movies, the more we lose a connection to something ancient and pious. Maybe it is this very conflict that defines who we are.

Amal tells me that her mother has a jar of *smen* that is more than thirty years old. No one is allowed to touch it. No one even knows where her mother keeps it. She will rub a little on your chest when you're sick or sparingly massage it on a swollen ankle. Amal talks about it with the amazement of a child. I can't imagine holding on to anything for that long. I ask her what it smells like, what it tastes like. There are no words, she tells me.

Amal teaches me a dish she calls *djaj mhamer*, chicken thighs spiced with ground ginger, turmeric, saffron, fresh garlic, and minced preserved lemon. They go into a braising pan together and cook for about an hour. The spices are intoxicating. In her cupboard, she keeps jars of spices she has brought here from Morocco. The cumin is heady and oily; the turmeric is absorbed into my fingers at the slightest touch. Even the black pepper has an extra voltage to it that awakens my nerves. She carefully unwraps a silk kerchief to show me a small vial containing saffron. Amal knows exactly how many threads are in that vial. She counts them as she uses them. When she runs out of a spice, she uses what she can find at the local supermarket. She has to add more of the supermarket stuff than she would like; the flavors are just not the same. As the chicken simmers, she adds a small spoonful of *smen*. That is all you need, she says. It gives the dish its identity. It gives it that haunting flavor that makes her homesick. The *smen* bridges the spices with the preserved lemon so that no single ingredient is detectable. They all come together as one unified flavor. The chicken itself is incidental. It is the sauce that I want to bathe myself in.

The next dish we make is even better: *lham bel barekouk*, thin cuts of beef shoulder braised with black pepper, ground ginger, turmeric, cinnamon, and *smen*. It is topped with prunes and dried apricots that have been rehydrated in a mixture of water, vinegar, and spices. Aromatic fried almonds finish the dish. The textures are refined. The colors of the dish are like a watercolor painting. The French influence here is unmistakable, yet the taste is distinctly Moroccan.

"The French mix the sweet and the salty," Amal says. "It is a flavor we like."

The *lham bel barekouk* will be served with couscous. Amal brews mint tea, which she ceremoniously pours from high above her head into a small tea glass gilded with an ornate leaf pattern.

The ladies of the neighborhood arrive, shaking the snow off their shoulders. Claudia is Amal's sister-in-law; she is from Paraguay. Laura is from New York City, and Susan is originally from Venezuela but has lived in Westport for more than ten years. I've been enjoying my quiet time with Amal, but it's clear that this is turning into a dinner party. Claudia makes peach margaritas and plays Taylor Swift. They each question me about who I am. The ladies are protective of Amal. They look out for her as if she were their own daughter. They adore her food.

As we sip cocktails, I ask them if they've introduced Amal to white clam pizza yet. They tell me no. I shake my head in dismay. These ladies, who've been entrusted with Amal's transition into American culture, have been withholding one of our greatest national treasures. There is time for a snack before dinner, so we order a large pie from Frank Pepe. Claudia volunteers to pick it up.

Frank Pepe is the oldest pizzeria in New Haven. The founder, Frank Pepe, came to America from Maiori, on the Amalfi Coast, when he was sixteen years old. He spoke no English. He opened a bakery in 1925 in New Haven and, as the story goes, started to make pizza with the extra dough he had. His pizza got so popular that, by 1936, he had bought the building next door and, with his wife, Filomena, opened it as a pizzeria. They also served Rhode Island clams on the half shell, which, back then, were plentiful and cheap. In the alleys of New Haven you could find clam carts where you could buy them freshly shucked. There are many versions of the white clam pizza origin story. One of them is from Gary Bimonte, the third generation of the Frank Pepe clan to operate the pizzeria. Gary tells me that his cousin Anthony knew of a bookie by the name of Nick Desport who was a regular at the pizzeria and would always eat clams. One day, Desport asked Frank, "Why don't you put these on a pizza?" Frank did, and the rest, as they say, is history. It seems so obvious now, but it took a long time to combine the two things: clams and pizza dough. This discovery fascinates me—the slow and gradual interconnection between two cultures, in this case, Italian and New England. When you look at the evolution of American cuisine, you always find this tension between tradition and innovation, a tension that produces the foods we crave most. It is in that intersection of the home we leave and the home we adopt that we find a dish that defines who we really are.

As soon as Claudia returns from the pizzeria, we rip open the box and start devouring the pie. Amal eats a slice in three bites. It is true what they say: this Frank Pepe is not quite as good as the original in New Haven, but this is still white clam pizza, and it makes us happy. A small pot of Amal's family *smen* is melting on the stove. I take a spoonful and drizzle it over the pizza. The butter soaks right into the anthracite burnt crust. The cheese and the *smen* work in tandem. The pungent aroma of the *smen* gives the clams a funkiness that wasn't there before. Amal seems slightly mortified that I've just melted a tablespoon of her family butter on a slice of pizza, but she admits that the combination is good.

Tastes like Moroccan pizza, she says.

Like Neapolitan Connecticut Moroccan pizza, I think.

Frank Crispo taught me a lot in the kitchen. He would say things such as "A fish stinks from the head back" and "Always treat your customers like you would treat your mom." He had a lot of sayings like that. He taught me a foolproof recipe for *pot de crème* (a French dessert custard). He also taught me to respect myself. He taught me to be self-reliant. In many ways, we kitchen urchins go into the business looking for a chef and find a father figure—a mentor, I guess you would call him. The first day I walked into Frank's kitchen, I was sporting a long ponytail, mascara, and combat boots. By the time I left, I had cut my hair short and wore my chef's coat with pride. I didn't adorn myself with anything else. I shed any notion of an adolescent identity and started from scratch. I entrusted Frank with that identity. In his own way, he nurtured me into the person I am today. I reminded myself of Frank just the other week, when I asked one of my new cooks to go find me a parsley peeler while the other cooks snickered.

Amal seems unwavering in her identity. "I can marry anyone, but he must be Muslim," she tells me. She loves Josh Hartnett, a Hollywood heartthrob.

Would you marry him, I ask her?

"He would have to become Muslim." She giggles at the thought of it.

Claudia and Amal's brother have a young son. He barely speaks Moroccan. I ask the ladies what we lose with each generation. They seem to agree: usually language goes first, then memories of relatives and grandparents, then traditions, then longing for home, then a sense of identity. What do we have left? A wedding ritual, a few old photos? For me, what is left is our connection to food. Our food traditions are the last things we hold on to. They are not just recipes; they are a connection to the nameless ancestors who gave us our DNA. That's why our traditional foods are so important. The stories, the memories, the movements that have been performed for generations—without them, we lose our direction.

We sit around the dinner table and feast in the Moroccan tradition. We use our hands to share big bowls of Amal's cooking. The ladies here have dined like this before, and they know all the rules. Everyone jumps in to explain to me how to behave at the table.

"You eat less when you eat together," Amal tells me. "It tastes better with friends. It tastes better when you eat with your hands."

There are many rules for the Moroccan meal. First, you must always grab the food with bread, never your fingers. Use only your right hand to touch your food, never your left. Each bowl is loosely divided into sections; you are allowed to eat only the section nearest to you. Never veer off into someone else's space. And never touch the hand of the person next to you. Someone can offer you more food if you finish your portion, but you must never pull a piece of meat from another person's section. Your hands will get dirty, but you must never suck your fingers and then dip your hands back into the bowl. If there is a last bite left in the bowl, always offer it to the elders first. And never leave your plate full, which is wasteful.

We sip mint tea, and the conversation turns into unbridled laughter as the ladies tell stories about one another's missteps.

It is early evening. I'm having so much fun, I stop taking notes. The tender beef and the sweet prunes feel so natural together that I'm amazed

I have never had this combination of flavors before. I make a mental note to try it at home. We may be in Westport, not Marrakesh, but the feeling of communing over a table of good food and conversation is universal. It happens everywhere people gather. Even in this too-quiet town, buried under inches of snow, there is a glowing table of warmth and spice that makes me long to return.

I ask Amal if she would ever open a restaurant. She says that would be her dream, of course. Your food is completely unique, I tell her. I would travel any distance for it. She blushes. Maybe one day. She says she cooks three times a week because it helps her remember the food. She cooks without recipes. The memory of *smen* is still fresh in her hands, and she doesn't want to lose it. When she makes it, it's all through muscle memory and feel. I ask her how many dishes she can make from memory. She looks at me, confused. I've never counted, she says.

At my restaurant, we have a binder where we collect all the recipes we've created. Sometimes I'll flip through it and count them all. How silly that must seem to Amal.

I wonder what the restaurant business would do to her. Would it drain her identity? Would she flourish under the tutelage of someone like Frank? Would her restaurant succeed in an industry so dominated by a culture of established process? She doesn't know what a brigade is, a sous chef, a convection oven. Does she need to? What do we lose when we gain the knowledge of process? Of portion size? Of uniformity? And is it possible to hold on to something that is both ancient and modern that lives in your hands? These are questions that keep me up at night. I came to Amal's house to learn how to make *smen*, and I'm glad I did. But I leave with more questions than answers. I also leave with the jar of *smen* we made together. Yet I can't help pining for a nibble of that thirty-year-old *smen* that stays hidden in a room somewhere in Marrakesh.

I make *smen* all the time now. There are jars of it all over my cupboard, and some in the back of my fridge. I've tried it many different ways—with rosemary, hyssop, bourbon (it was delicious). I understand how profane it must be to combine a Moroccan recipe with alcohol, so I call this a washed butter rather than *smen*. The bourbon-washed butter is so good it can be used on anything from oysters to grilled vegetables. Put it on toast in the morning, or drip it over a slice of warm Pullman bread. The bourbon-washed butter gets softer as time goes by, but only time will tell what happens as it ages. In the meantime, I still have the jar of *smen* Amal and I made together. This one is precious to me. Perhaps I'll keep it for the next thirty years.

BAKED CLAMS WITH SAFFRON AND BOURBON-WASHED BUTTER

Briny baked clams are a perfect pairing for Bourbon-Washed Butter. Aside from the aged butter, the clams don't need much more than a pinch of saffron, which serves as a nod to the butter's Moroccan origins.

This Bourbon-Washed Butter is a variation on the traditional *smen* that I learned from Amal. It's a way to age butter so that it develops a slightly funky, fermented flavor. This version also takes on a smokiness from the bourbon. The aging process is straightforward, but it takes time: put the washed butter in an airtight container and leave it, undisturbed, in a cupboard or other dark place for at least 15 days. But that's just a starting point—it can go for as long as a year or more if you make it right and there is no excess water or air pockets to spoil the butter. I would recommend about 2 months to get a flavor that is definitely funky but isn't overpowering.

SERVES 4 AS A FIRST COURSE

Rock salt

12 cherrystone clams, scrubbed clean

About ¼ cup Bourbon-Washed Butter (recipe follows)

3 tablespoons grated Parmesan cheese

12 saffron threads

Lemon wedges, for serving

Preheat the oven to 450°F. Spread a layer of rock salt on a baking sheet.

Nestle the clams in the rock salt. Bake the clams for about 5 minutes, just until the top shells release from the bottom shells. Take the clams out of the oven and carefully remove the top shells and discard them.

Put the clams back into the rock salt. Add a little bourbon butter to each clam. Top each one with a scant teaspoon of the grated Parmesan and garnish with a saffron thread. Put back in the oven and warm just until the butter and cheese are melted, about 90 seconds. Serve immediately, with lemon wedges on the side.

BOURBON-WASHED BUTTER | MAKES 2 POUNDS

One 1-liter bottle bourbon, preferably a 5-year-aged one 1 tablespoon sugar	2 pounds (8 sticks) unsalted butter 4 teaspoons salt

Pour the bourbon and sugar in a large deep pot, bring to a simmer over medium heat, and simmer until the bourbon has reduced to about 2 cups. The alcohol will ignite, so have a tight-fitting lid next to the stove, and do not ever peek into the pot. When the bourbon does ignite, simply cover the pot to put out the flames, but it is important to take the lid off as soon as the flames have subsided. If you don't, pressure will build inside the pot and the alcohol will reignite the next time you lift up the lid. If the bourbon ignites immediately, turn down the heat and let it simmer more slowly. The whole process will take 15 to 20 minutes. Transfer the bourbon to a large bowl and refrigerate until it is cool to the touch.

Add the butter to the bourbon and start to knead it, really massaging the butter and bourbon together. You want to knead it for about 10 minutes nonstop, but be careful not to let the butter warm up too much, or it will start to melt. If the butter seems as if it is starting to melt in your hands, add a few ice cubes to the bowl and keep kneading. Once the butter is ready, cover the bowl with plastic wrap and let it sit at room temperature for 24 hours.

The next day, drain off and discard the bourbon. Add the salt to the butter and knead it in thoroughly. Transfer the butter to a 2-quart glass jar and put several layers of cheesecloth over the top, then screw the lid on tight. Let age in a dark place at room temperature for at least 15 days before using, but I recommend about 20 days. If done correctly, it can last indefinitely in the jar. It will smell funky, and that's a good thing. There is a chance the butter will spoil. You will know if it does, as it will smell like ammonia. Once you open the jar, the butter can continue to age in your fridge for months.

SEARED BEEF RIB-EYE WITH PRUNES, ALMONDS, AND BOURBON-WASHED BUTTER

I had never thought to pair prunes and beef before I met Amal, and now I can't get the combination out of my head. Alone, prunes can sometimes seem too sweet; but as part of a sauce braised with vinegar and aromatics, they develop an earthiness that gives the meat an otherworldly taste. You might forget you're eating beef.

SERVES 2 AS A MAIN COURSE

Two 10-ounce rib-eye steaks

Salt and freshly ground black pepper

2 tablespoons canola oil

½ cup chopped onion

2 garlic cloves, minced

1 teaspoon ground coriander

½ teaspoon ground ginger

¼ teaspoon ground cinnamon

2 cups chicken stock

2 teaspoons apple cider vinegar

1 cup pitted prunes

4 teaspoons Bourbon-Washed Butter (page 171)

¼ cup blanched whole almonds

2 teaspoons chopped fresh mint, for garnish

Trim off any excess fat from the rib-eye steaks. Season well with salt and pepper. Let sit at room temperature for 30 minutes while you make the sauce.

Heat 1 tablespoon of the canola oil in a large saucepan over high heat. Add the onion and garlic and sauté for about 4 minutes, stirring often, until the onion gently caramelizes. Add the coriander, ginger, and cinnamon, stir, and cook for 2 minutes, or until very aromatic. Add the chicken stock and vinegar and bring to a simmer. Add the prunes, cover, and simmer for 20 minutes.

Take the lid off the pan and simmer for another 10 minutes, or until the sauce has reduced to a light gravy-like texture. Turn off the heat, add the bourbon-washed butter, and stir to melt it into the sauce. Season with salt and pepper. Keep warm.

In a large sauté pan, heat the remaining 1 tablespoon oil until hot. Add the steaks and cook for 3 minutes, or until they have browned nicely on the first side. Flip the steaks and cook for 3 minutes more. Scatter the almonds around the steaks and toast them for 2 minutes, until nicely browned. Remove the almonds when you remove the steaks from the pan. Drain on paper towels.

Check the steaks. They should be medium-rare at this point. Turn the heat to low, put 2 teaspoons of the bourbon butter on top of each steak, and let it melt. Transfer the steaks to serving plates and let rest for 2 minutes.

Spoon the prune sauce over the steaks and scatter the toasted almonds on top. Garnish with the chopped mint and serve immediately.

CHAPTER 10

DEATH AND AQUAVIT

'VE BEEN TO SEATTLE ONLY TWICE: ONCE FOR A BOOK tour and now again to premiere a documentary film called *Fermented*. The first time I landed there, I knew little about the city beyond grunge, Starbucks, and Microsoft. I was once a fan of Shawn Kemp of the Seattle SuperSonics, who, in the 1990s, was supposed to dethrone Michael Jordan but never did. I'd heard about Pike Place Market and the restaurant Canlis. I'd heard it would rain a lot. I was on tour to promote my cookbook *Smoke & Pickles*. I had just opened a new restaurant, and my daughter was barely three months old. I was in town for only a night. I figured I would eat a lot of salmon and drink buckets of micro-roast coffee. I never imagined I would make a connection to the city that would haunt me for years. That first trip was clouded by my dad's death. Seattle became the place in my mind that I associated with dying. It took me four years to get back there and find an affirmation of life.

It's the morning after my film premiere, and last night's whiskey is still pulsing through my arteries. I'm up early for the pancake breakfast at the Swedish Club. I was told the line gets long after 9:00 a.m. I'm discovering Seattle's rich history of Scandinavian roots, mostly centered in the neighborhood of Ballard, where there is a large Nordic Museum and Larsen's Danish Bakery, which sells *kringle*, a pretzel-shaped flaky pastry filled with marzipan and coated with white icing. There is also Scandinavian Specialties, a small, cheerful shop where you can buy a toothpaste-type dispenser full of smoked cod roe and cream. At the Leif Erikson Lodge, you can celebrate everything from Viking traditions to Midsommarfest with a plate of traditional Swedish meatballs. Otherwise, there is little evidence today that Ballard was once a city formed and driven by Scandinavian immigrants starting in the 1860s. They were lured here mostly by the fishing industry of Salmon Bay and Puget Sound. Norwegians developed the halibut fisheries, while Icelanders fished more for cod. Finns and Swedes focused on trolling. Logging and farming were also important trades familiar to the Nordic peoples. If there was any landscape in America that fit right into the Nordic ethos, it was here in Seattle.

My taxi pulls up to the Swedish Club. The creamy Swedish-blue façade has a calming effect on my headache. The building looks like something you'd find in an Olympic village, modern but functional. I can hear music and conversation coming from the basement. I walk down and find two hundred people already gathered around plastic folding tables. The basement looks like a community center, with drop ceiling tiles, unforgiving fluorescent lights, and a linoleum floor. I stand in line for pancakes. My head is throbbing from my hangover, and I'm craving hot coffee, but I don't want to lose my place in the growing line.

On a stage up front, two ladies seated on folding chairs are playing accordions, a kind of Nordic polka music. It is merry. The only people dancing are an older couple; they are shuffling across the floor in choreographed twirls and struts. The lady has on a long blue dress that rises and falls with every turn. Her silver hair matches the white knit blouse she's wearing, and she smiles in time with the music. I'm enthralled by her movements.

When I get to the front of the buffet line, I'm handed a plate of pancakes that are actually crepes, rolled and stacked. A fistful of lingonberry preserve is spooned over them, and a ladleful of whipped cream finishes the plate. I get a Styrofoam cup of black coffee and stand in the middle of the cavernous room. I look around for the dancing couple; they're now sitting with friends at a table near the stage. I walk up to them and ask if I may sit with them.

Their names are Bob and Sarah. I tell them how much I liked their waltz. Sarah corrects me and says they were also doing the *hambo*, the *schottisch*, and the *springar*. The entire table is part of a dance group that meets regularly. They tell me that social dancing was common in Seattle in the 1970s. The Swedish Club was a place to convene and meet new friends. Many people met and married through these social clubs. There used to be clubs for Danes and Norwegians back then, too. The Swedish Club is the only one left. But it isn't just for Swedes; anyone can join. They just have to want to be a part of the Scandinavian tradition.

I ask Sarah what it means to be Scandinavian.

"We're not a soup, we're a stew," she says emphatically. "Each Scandinavian country is distinct, but together, we form an identity that is generally harmonious. We swim around in the same bowl, but we're not homogenous."

Her husband, Bob, gaunt and freckled, has little hair left. He is picking at his pancakes, not talking to anyone. He doesn't care much for meeting new people, Sarah explains to me. This is a Scandinavian trait, I am told. It is an aloofness rooted in isolation, not rudeness.

"If this was the seventies and you came up to us and asked to sit with us, no one would have looked at you," Sarah tells me.

I ask her why no one else is dancing.

They are just getting warmed up, she tells me. She asks me if I want to dance. I respond by saying I don't know the first thing about polka dancing.

"It's easy. If you know how to ride a skateboard, I can teach you a basic buzzstep."

She pulls me out of my chair and leads me into a dance. I must be eighty pounds heavier than she is, but she is twirling me around like a doll. First, she shows me the buzzstep, then she guides me into a simple waltz. My rhythm is off. She tells me to shut out the world and just listen to the music. She instructs me to step in time with the beat, but my hangover is preventing me from hearing the music clearly. I'm sure I look as stiff as a wooden board, but I'm having fun. My eyes are closed, and Sarah's hands have a tight grip on my palms. I can feel my cheeks stretch into a smile. I peer over at the table. Bob is not watching us.

I don't remember the flavor of the pancakes. They were cold, and the lingonberry jam was overly sweet. That's all that stood out. But the people are not here for the food. On a Sunday morning, a day with humid-free sunny weather, there are three hundred people packed into a basement listening to Nordic polka music. Many of them are not Swedish. I can't say for certain why they commune here, but they are sharing an experience. Sarah cannot finds the words to explain what a Scandinavian identity is, but she tells me it is something that is felt, not described. I am glad I came here. Even though the pancakes were forgettable, I got to dance with Sarah.

Bob reminds me of my father. He is old and taciturn. He doesn't smile for anyone. I suspect he has a million great stories to tell, but he is not about to waste any of them on me. He takes Sarah back out to the dance floor, and as he spins her about, her dress swings out like a blooming Nordic flower in a cold, gray room.

FOUR YEARS AGO, Seattle was the last city on a leg of book tour that started with a few cities in California. By the time I reached Seattle, I was looking forward to going home. When I arrived, it was raining, but it was not like any rain I was accustomed to. It was a downward mist that never stopped. The city smelled like moss and sounded like Gore-Tex. No one used umbrellas. They accepted the rain not as weather but as *terroir*.

I was not prepared to deal with my dad dying while I was there. Seattle is about as far as one can be from the modest New Jersey suburb of Leonia, where my parents lived. I was enjoying a late lunch with a local food writer and Gina, who, along with her father, Armandino, operates Salumi Artisan Cured Meats, the city's best spot for Italian salami. My phone rang, and I saw my sister's name pop up. I already knew why she was calling. In the few seconds it took me to excuse myself from the table and walk outside, I went from fear to anxiety to relief to resentment to acceptance. I was exhausted as I stepped out into the gentle rain.

"Hello?"

My dad wouldn't make it through the night. It was different this time. I had to come, now. I said yes. I let my sister cry on the phone as if it were my shoulder, and then I hung up. I went back inside. There's no way to politely tell two people you've just met that your father is dying, so I just blurted it out. They understood, they said, if I had to go. I didn't, though. I wanted to finish my platter. I was hungry. I found comfort in the tangy meat flecked with salted fats, chewy and wrinkled around the edges. I ate the brined olives and the pickles. I consumed every slice of the *coppa*, *culatello*, *finocchiona*, and *mole* salami. I savored every last bite—unrushed.

When I left, Gina gave me a link of the *mole* salami, and I gave her a copy of my book. The flight to Newark would be long and lonely, crowded and private. I calculated that my dad would pass away while I was cresting over Minnesota or Wisconsin or any other place we'd never been together.

He never wanted me to be a chef. He came from an old Korea where chefs were cooks and cooks were servants. For immigrant parents, the notion of being a cook was a huge step in the wrong direction. When I was a kid, my dad would drive me to West Point, hoping I'd one day wear the gray-and-black cadet uniform. I'm named after Ted Kennedy. My father's dream for me was to become an American diplomat.

It was not a fun day when I told him I wanted to cook for a living. I was still in college. I had dropped out for a year, to travel. I was finishing my last semester, but more for my parents than for me. We didn't fight about my career decision, and he never disowned me. We just rarely spoke much after that day.

I COULDN'T SLEEP on the flight to Newark. I ate everything offered to me by the flight attendant: the sterile turkey sandwich with yellow mustard, the salted peanuts, the murky coffee, even the rancid pretzels that tasted like burnt sand. My breath aged a week overnight. I had to chew a pack of wintergreen gum before I entered the hospital. The rest of the family had been there through the night. Miraculously, my dad was still clinging to life.

There's a good Korean restaurant not far from the hospital, with a fake waterfall and toad sculptures around the entrance. Mom told me to take my niece and nephew there for lunch. My dad was weak, his body swollen from painkillers. He couldn't speak, but his eyes were asking for mercy. The nurse came in to adjust his IV, and the heart monitor went blank for a moment. To the horror of the nurse, my mom asked with inappropriate eagerness, "He finished?"

My sister yelled at our mother in Korean. I smirked. Mom had nursed my dad through his illnesses for years, so death was not unexpected. In that distracted moment, it was probably a relief.

When the heart monitor kicked back online, Mom insisted I take the kids out for Korean barbecue and bring her back some. Dad seemed very close to dying now, and she didn't want the kids to see it. I wanted to stay, though. I wanted to hear him apologize to me for ignoring me all those years, for never allowing himself to become the father I needed.

I approached the bed. The only parts of him that looked the same were his hands. They were always big and strong. Even in his weakened state, they still looked masculine. I lifted one of his limp hands and put mine underneath it, not palm to palm; I just let his palm rest on my knuckles. He was too weak to clench my fingers. I got to kiss my dad on the forehead and tell him it was okay for him to leave us, that we'd be all right.

Then I took the kids out for lunch.

My dad didn't needlessly hang on to life. He passed away before we got our first round of grilled meat. Mom didn't call us to let us know. She wanted us to enjoy our lunch.

OVER THE NEXT FEW DAYS, I helped Mom sort through my dad's things. My sister was the only one who cried. I think she did it because no one else did. We went through his closet of possessions. My sister wanted to keep a pair of his golf shoes. We found some old black-and-white photos that went to the "keep" pile, but most of what we found was junk. Old magazines, English-to-Korean dictionaries, and an abacus he had never used. I found no letter telling me how secretly proud he was of me, no box where he kept all my old report cards. He was not sentimental. Much of his life had been marred by drinking, and he had few friends left in his older years.

We did, however, find a large box of dollar coins and a stack of two-dollar bills he'd collected over the years, probably a few hundred dollars' worth. Before my mom could take them to the bank, I swiped one of the bills. It lives in my wallet now. I'm not sure why, because I, too, am not all that sentimental.

THE SWEDISH PANCAKES remind me of the foods my father ate. I ask the people sitting around the table at the Swedish Club why they like the pancakes so much, and they tell me they remind them of their childhoods. They ate the same thing when they were young. I don't think anyone here actually believes these pancakes are delicious, but they trigger memories. Even for me, someone who has no relation to Seattle or Swedish culture, eating these pancakes feels like a link to a generation my father lived through.

My dad was never much of a gourmand. His food was always very utilitarian. You ate just enough to make you feel full, but you didn't overindulge and you certainly didn't use the dinner table for pleasure. He never talked about food as anything more than something he needed to consume to survive. Most nights, eating seemed like more of a chore than anything else.

Still, there was one dish he'd ask for on occasion. It was an army stew called *budae jjigae*. It was invented during the Korean War, when ingredients were scarce and many families improvised meals based on the food rations handed out by the American army. My dad spent a few years in the Korean army, though he never talked about it, and I was always instructed never to ask.

When Mom made him this stew, he would eat it quietly, slurping up every last drop. No one else wanted it. Mom's versions included everything from Spam to hot dogs to processed American cheese. For many Koreans, budae jjigae represents an impoverished time in Korea, something not to be celebrated. We don't eat these kinds of frugal dishes anymore. Some old-school Korean restaurants serve a modern version of it, but for the most part, the dish was forgotten as Koreans became upwardly mobile.

I grew up believing that it was only my dad who had such lousy taste in food, but a lot of my parents' generation ate poorly regardless of nationality or wealth. Much has been written about the ills of the commercial food industry and the rise of fast food that dominated the 1960s and '70s in America. My dad was a part of that generation, and for him, eating at McDonald's was what you did if you wanted to assimilate into American culture. It was a borderline act of patriotism, as were canned soup, TV dinners, and Coca-Cola. His was also a generation where immigrants could lift themselves out of poverty if they worked hard. My parents worked seven days a week. They worked late into the evenings. The joys of the dinner table were not a priority. I ask the older people at the Swedish Club what they ate when they were younger. Meatballs, salmon, and Jell-O are the popular answers.

THE PANCAKES have settled my hangover, and I go for a walk. It is a rare sunny day in Seattle, and people are out in droves. I'm curious about a shop called the Old Ballard Liquor Co., which sells locally made aquavit. It is a small distillery and café housed in a warehouse building on the docks of the Lake Washington Ship Canal. This is an industrial part of the city. A business nearby sells drinking tours on a bicycle trolley. People get on sober and come back exhausted and drunk.

When I arrive at the distillery, I find a sign on the door saying that party bicycle customers are not welcome. I immediately like this place. Inside, there is a small table that seats eight and a bar the size of a broom closet. You can see the entire distilling operation here. It's made up mostly of storage bins, a small distiller, and a rudimentary pump system to fill the bottles. There's a small kitchen in which an unsmiling woman in her thirties is preparing cured meats. Her name is Lexi. She is the owner, distiller, chef, and tour guide. She's hurrying back and forth from the bottling duties to slicing charcuterie to answering questions from the other four people in the place. I see Magnus Nilsson's *The Nordic Cookbook* on her shelf.

"We have what I call the Ikea Rule," Lexi explains to me rather quickly as I peruse her menu. "If it's served at Ikea, we won't serve it here. Not because I dislike Ikea, but there's no reason to limit yourself to the same five stereotypical dishes over and over. We want to encourage people to think outside of the stereotypes."

She introduces me to Jane, which is her name for the twenty-seven-gallon immersion-heated still. "I couldn't do this without her," Lexi says. She bought the still from a family in Barlow, Kentucky. "I figured that a family of moonshiners who'd never stopped making stills, Prohibition be damned, would know more about it than just about anybody."

I tell her I'm from Kentucky. "I know," she says. She has watched every season of *The Mind of a Chef*, I learn. The food community is still a small world. I was able to walk and dance anonymously through a huge crowd at the Swedish Club, but here, Lexi and I are part of a much smaller club.

I ask her to show me how to make aquavit. She points out a custom spice basket she built. It has a mesh bottom that fits directly over the still kettle. She fills the basket with caraway seeds or fresh dill or rhubarb. As the flavorless alcohol boils off, the steam passes through the spices on its way to the condensing arm and picks up the oils and flavors of whatever is in the basket. What comes out is a clear, flavored, distilled aquavit, or what Lexi calls a *taffel*.

"We can dilute the *taffel* to eighty proof and bottle it as is, or we can infuse more spices and fruits into it for a richer set of flavors. At that point, it stops being a *taffel* and just becomes aquavit, and is how we make most of our products. Think of the word *taffel* like white dog, and *aquavit* like whiskey."

I taste all five of her aquavit selections from small wineglasses. The flavors are clean and aromatic. The dill aquavit is like a walk through a green pasture in spring. I can feel the aquavit bringing life back to my chest cavity.

I ask Lexi what I should eat, and she recommends her *sill* board: pickled herring prepared five different ways and presented on a wooden board, simple and measured. It looks less like Scandinavian food and more like a sashimi plate. Lexi explains the iterations to me: classic pickled herring with onion, coriander cream herring, tarragon herring with flake salt, smoked herring in a lemon-chive cream, and strawberry pickled herring.

"If you visit a restaurant in Scandinavia that advertises pickled herring and they don't have at least ten flavors, people won't eat there," she tells me.

There is a lull in the store, and Lexi sits with me. She is young, but carries the intellectual burden of someone much older. She tells me she lived in Sweden for six years and just recently returned to the States. She is serious when she talks. I ask her why her food is so vastly different from the pancakes I had earlier today.

"We have a large number of Scandinavian-born expats who were raised on post–World War II processed foods and are now in their seventies and eighties. Much of this community prefers frozen meatballs and packaged gravies and familiar, consistent flavors. There's also a healthy dose of nostalgia there; we humans tend to spend more and more time thinking about the past as we get older, and these sort of familiar, nostalgic foods are real touchstones for many folks."

Lexi is not Swedish by birth, but she's upholding a tradition she imported from present-day Scandinavia. Her knowledge of Scandinavian

foodways is vast and cerebral. It is unyielding, too. To some, her atti-
tude may come off as arrogant. Somewhere between the old immigrant
culture of Ballard and the new Nordic culture that is influencing food
culture globally, there is an obvious chasm. Lexi is not descended from
that generation of immigrants who settled in Ballard. She does not feel
the need to uphold their traditions. In fact, she's upending them. She
runs the only Scandinavian restaurant in Seattle, yet the people I was
with at the Swedish Club rarely, if ever, come visit her.

Even though Lexi and the Swedish Club represent the same cuisine,
they do not serve the same food. Generational changes are far more
impactful than the bonds of a national cuisine. The foods of the Swedish
Club are about nostalgia; Lexi's food is about a passion for a lost art of
technique. In some ways, both are reaching back. They just point to a
different time. Lexi speaks of centuries-old traditions, and the folks at
the Scandinavian Specialties store speak of their childhood. I don't think
one is more correct than the other. Lexi's food tastes better, but that's
just my opinion. Culture expands at such a rapid rate in these modern
times, I can understand why a generation of people would want to retreat
to something familiar and comforting, such as a plate of flabby pancakes
and sweet jam. I look down at my table: there are a dozen empty glasses
in front of me. I devour a cured meat board and a slice of sweet, aromatic
cardamom cake.

I love what Lexi is doing at the Old Ballard Liquor Co. It is unexpected and rebellious. It takes a courageous person to follow a road
that contradicts the food of her childhood. Lexi doesn't want to do the
familiar immigrant food she ate as a child, but neither does she want
to make the food of Noma, the dizzyingly progressive Nordic cuisine of
René Redzepi that has taken the world by storm. She wants to bring the
familiar flavors of Scandinavia but with a technique and precision seldom
seen in Seattle or America. She has taken Scandinavian food out of the
predictable framework of the immigrant's struggle. It is not a cuisine of
frugality or necessity. It is an uncompromising dedication to technique.

The irony of all this is that Lexi's business is struggling. She has a small shop in a neighborhood without much foot traffic, and her only neighbors are drunk kids who get off a party bicycle looking for a place to pee. It is a hard life, but one she chose for herself. She tells me she grew up poor on a farm outside the city. I'm sure her parents weren't thrilled at her decision to make aquavit for a living. Her choices in life may seem frivolous to a generation that had to work long hours and sacrifice life's earthly pleasures for a can of pickled fish, but that doesn't make her struggle any less real. Indeed, in a world where it is easy to sell real estate and buy a home in the suburbs, it is a sublime act of conviction to willingly choose this challenging a life.

The aquavit has made me light-headed, and I get emotional when I'm tipsy. I ask Lexi for some recipes, and we hug. Right before I leave, she tells me, "Morality plays a big part in cultural cuisine. Scandinavian culture disapproved of food for a long time. It was sustenance, not something to be enjoyed. Not something to luxuriate in."

I have to blink several times when she says this. She could be talking about the Korean culture of my dad's generation. If my dad were Swedish, all he would want would be a bowl of dry meatballs with sweet lingonberry sauce.

I WALK ACROSS THE BRIDGE over the canal. I think about my father again. I will probably always think about him when I'm in Seattle, but I won't do it with sadness. I don't know if there was anything in his life that moved him to tears. He had a hard life, and he was tough on his children. Still, I forgave him everything in that New Jersey hospital room. I wish he could have had something that made him as happy as I am now. A few glasses of aquavit and some pickled herring are enough for me. I will always remember him as a strong, complex person who never found the peace he needed until the very end.

I can't help thinking about Shawn Kemp, the basketball player. Shawn had all the raw talent to be the best in the NBA. He had a good run, but he just couldn't avoid the drugs, and they eventually ended his career. He could have been so much better. I used to get angry at him every time the story of another cocaine arrest came out. I realize now that it's not my place to judge. He did with his life the best he could, with the tools he had. As a kid, I had a poster of him over my bed. He is dunking a ball with the Seattle skyline in the background. Maybe his career ended in disappointment, but I still believe that for a few brief, shining moments, he was the best there ever was.

BUDAE JJIGAE WITH FRIED BOLOGNA

Budae jjigae was my dad's favorite thing to eat. He used to have it with Spam and hot dogs, but I make it with fried bologna. I use American cheese, because there is no real substitute for it. This is a good soup, and I think its ingenuity is still relevant. It represents a utilitarian kind of cuisine that I don't want to forget. Not everything has to be glossy and precious. Sometimes food *is* just a no-frills gustatory experience. This is also one of the best hangover meals.

SERVES 4 AS A MAIN COURSE

SAUCE

2 tablespoons mirin

1 tablespoon soy sauce

2 tablespoons gochugaru (Korean chile powder) or other ground chile powder

1 tablespoon minced garlic

1½ teaspoons sugar

1½ teaspoons gochujang (Korean chile paste)

¼ teaspoon freshly ground black pepper

BUDAE JJIGAE

1 tablespoon vegetable oil

6 ounces sliced bologna

1 cup large-diced onion

1 cup bite-size pieces kimchi, with its juices

2 scallions, sliced into 2-inch lengths

4 ounces enoki mushrooms

3 ounces shiitake mushroom caps, thinly sliced

7 ounces firm tofu, sliced ½-inch thick

4 to 5 ounces (2 packages) instant ramen noodles

5 cups chicken stock

4 large eggs

4 slices American cheese

TO MAKE THE SAUCE: In a small bowl, mix together the mirin, soy sauce, gochugaru, garlic, sugar, gochujang, and black pepper. Set aside.

TO MAKE THE BUDAE JJIGAE: Heat a medium skillet over medium-high heat. Add the oil, and when it's hot, add a couple of slices of the bologna in a single layer and fry, turning once, for 2 minutes on each side. Transfer to a plate and cook the remaining bologna. Slice the bologna into finger-sized batons and set aside.

Assemble the jjigae in a medium rondeau or other low-sided pot. Scatter the onion evenly over the bottom of the pot. Add the kimchi and scallions and pour over the reserved sauce. Add the mushrooms, followed by the tofu. Arrange the fried bologna on top. Scatter the ramen noodles over it and pour in the chicken stock.

Place the pot over high heat and bring the jjigae to a boil. Reduce the heat and simmer for 8 to 10 minutes, until the noodles are almost cooked. Crack the eggs into the simmering broth and cook for 2 to 3 minutes, until the noodles are tender and the eggs are cooked to your liking.

Ladle the soup into four serving bowls, top each with a slice of cheese, and serve.

PICKLED SALMON

Lexi's recipe for pickled herring was the inspiration for this dish. It's hard to find fresh herring outside of the Pacific Northwest, so I swapped in salmon. Try to get a fatty wild salmon like king or coho. The pickled salmon is great for a variety of snacks and appetizers. You can simply serve it with good dark bread and sour cream. It is also lovely as a topping for salads, or served as an open-faced sandwich with lots of fresh lettuce. For an elegant first course for a party, see the recipe for Pickled Salmon with Strawberries, Dill, and Horseradish Cream on Pancakes on page 190.

The salmon takes a week to cure, so plan accordingly. It is well worth the effort. I like to make it in a large quantity, but you can cut this recipe in half if you prefer. Once the salmon is pickled, you can wrap it tightly and keep it for a few weeks in the fridge.

SERVES 8 TO 10 AS A FIRST COURSE

SALT BRINE	PICKLING BRINE
4 cups water	2 cups sugar
1 cup sea salt	2 cups distilled white vinegar
	1 cup water
One 2-pound skin-on salmon fillet, cleaned of scales and pin bones	2 tablespoons allspice berries
	4 bay leaves, crumbled
	1 whole clove
	1 small onion, thinly sliced
	1 small bunch dill

TO MAKE THE SALT BRINE: In a medium saucepan, combine the water and salt and bring to a boil, stirring to dissolve the salt. Transfer to a bowl and refrigerate until thoroughly chilled, at least an hour.

Put the salmon in a nonreactive container, such as a shallow baking dish, and pour the salt brine over it. Cover and brine in the refrigerator for 3 days.

Remove the salmon from the salt brine, transfer to another container, and cover with fresh cold water. Soak the salmon in the refrigerator for 1 hour, then change the water and soak the salmon for another hour.

MEANWHILE, TO MAKE THE PICKLING BRINE: In a medium saucepan, combine the sugar, vinegar, water, allspice berries, bay leaves, and clove and bring to a boil, stirring to dissolve the sugar. Turn off the heat and steep for 30 minutes, then pour into a bowl and refrigerate until thoroughly chilled, at least 1 hour.

Remove the salmon from the freshwater soak and put it in another nonreactive container. Cover with the pickling brine and refrigerate for another 3 days.

(CONTINUED)

Remove the salmon from the pickling brine and pat dry. Remove the skin and the gray fat layer underneath the skin.

Place half the sliced onion and dill on a large sheet of plastic wrap, arranging them in a rectangle about the size of the salmon fillet. Put the salmon on top and cover with the remaining onion and dill. Wrap tightly in the plastic wrap and refrigerate for at least 1 day before serving.

Discard the onion and dill. Slice the salmon thinly on a diagonal and serve. If keeping the salmon longer, remove the onion and dill and rewrap.

PICKLED SALMON WITH STRAWBERRIES, DILL, AND HORSERADISH CREAM ON SAVORY PANCAKES

Pickled salmon has a complex set of flavors, so I love to use it as part of an elevated first course. The dill and horseradish—flavors of Scandinavia—marry perfectly with the oily notes of the salmon.

SERVES 8 TO 10 AS A FIRST COURSE

HORSERADISH CREAM

1 cup sour cream

¼ cup cold water

2 tablespoons grated fresh horseradish

Pinch of sugar

Pinch of sea salt

Pinch of freshly ground black pepper

PANCAKES

¼ cup warm water (about 112°F)

2 teaspoons active dry yeast

1 cup whole milk

¾ cup sour cream

1 tablespoon unsalted butter, melted, plus more for the pan

2 large eggs

1 cup all-purpose flour

1 cup whole wheat flour

1 teaspoon salt

1 teaspoon grated lemon zest

12 ounces Pickled Salmon (page 188), thinly sliced

6 strawberries, hulled and thinly sliced

Pinch of sea salt

Small dill sprigs

TO MAKE THE HORSERADISH CREAM: In a small bowl, whisk together the sour cream, water, horseradish, sugar, sea salt, and pepper. Cover and refrigerate until ready to use.

TO MAKE THE PANCAKES: In a small bowl, combine the warm water and yeast and let stand for 10 minutes, or until foamy.

In a small saucepan, combine the milk, sour cream, and butter and heat over low heat, stirring gently, just until the butter is melted and the mixture is smooth; do not allow to boil.

Lightly beat the eggs in a medium bowl. Slowly drizzle in the milk mixture, whisking gently, then whisk in the yeast mixture.

In a large bowl, whisk together both flours, the salt, and the lemon zest. Add the wet ingredients, mixing until a loose batter forms.

Heat a medium skillet over medium heat and add 1 tablespoon butter. Heat until the butter starts to foam, then ladle in ¼ cup of the batter, tilting the pan to spread the batter. Let cook for 3 minutes, then flip the pancake and cook for another minute, until golden brown. Transfer to a paper towel–lined plate or baking sheet. Repeat with the remaining batter, adding butter as needed. You should get 10 to 12 pancakes.

TO ASSEMBLE THE DISH: Lay a warm pancake on a serving plate. Layer some slices of the pickled salmon over the pancake. Arrange some sliced strawberries over the salmon. Sprinkle a pinch of sea salt over the strawberries, drizzle a little horseradish cream over the strawberries, and finish with a scattering of dill sprigs. Repeat with the remaining pancakes and enjoy right away.

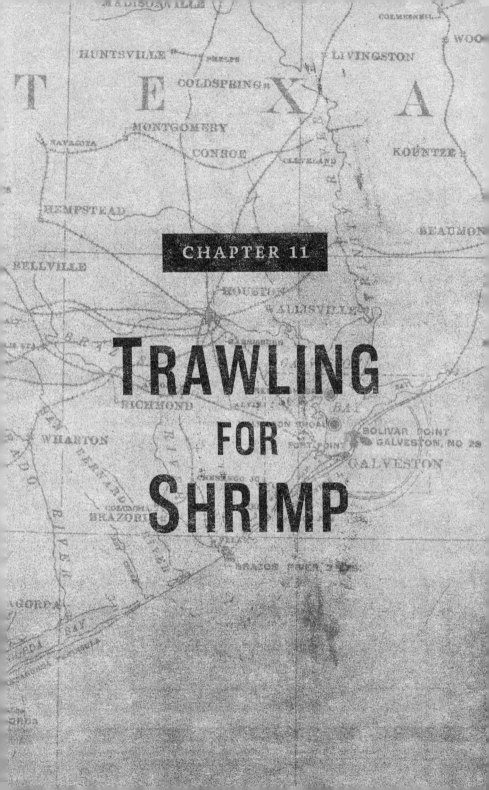

CHAPTER 11

TRAWLING
FOR
SHRIMP

CROSSING FROM SEABROOK INTO KEMAH, FOR A moment I get the feeling I'm floating on air—the highway elevates so swiftly over the piers. To my left is a clear view of the rich blue waters that stretch into Galveston Bay. The color mirrors the Texas sky. I am on my way to Galveston to secure a shipment of Gulf shrimp for my restaurant. It is something I have to have on my menu. Shrimp crosses all culinary borders. From the pages of Nathalie Dupree's *Shrimp and Grits Cookbook* to the melamine plates of Vietnamese crepes stuffed with shrimp and pork to chilled martini glasses of shrimp cocktail served at every steak house in America, shrimp are adored everywhere. I've tried to avoid shrimp on my menus, but the demand is just too high. Americans consume about 1.3 billion pounds of shrimp annually. So here I am in shrimp country, to see with my own eyes an industry that has been much maligned. If I'm going to cook with shrimp, I need to find a source I can trust.

If you eat shrimp regularly, chances are they come from Southeast Asia, where they were most likely farmed in overcrowded mud ponds manned by poor subsistence workers barely able to eke out a living. These shrimp swim in a toxic cocktail of fertilizers and antibiotics, to ward off the host of diseases that infect these monoculture-breeding facilities. Still, chances are the shrimp don't taste all that bad. Most farmed shrimp from Asia have no detectable flavor, good or bad. Once you dust them with paprika and cumin and blacken them in a cast-iron pan, or drown them in a spicy sweet-and-sour sauce, it matters little how flavorless they are. It is easy to overlook the chemical bath they were treated in before they arrived in frozen five-pound bricks. Shrimp are a cheap commodity, the equivalent of aquatic vermin.

I pull into a Vietnamese restaurant in Kemah. All along the Gulf Coast, from Seabrook to Galveston to Palacios, Vietnamese fishermen have settled into communities that started when thousands of refugees were relocated here after the Vietnam War. I sit down and order *báhn xèo*, a popular dish on the menu in every Vietnamese restaurant in America. It is a light, crispy crepe of turmeric and rice flour folded over shrimp, pork, and bean sprouts and served with a sweet dipping sauce. The place is bright and airy. The customers are white and working class and polite. On my table is the familiar plastic chopstick holder that opens up when you pull a knob on the lid. Bottles of Sriracha and soy sauce sit on a plastic tray. My waitress goes back and forth between taking orders and studying an oversize textbook.

When the crepe arrives, I can tell the shrimp is not from the Gulf. I ask the waitress, but she tells me she doesn't know. I'm hungry, so I finish what's on my plate, wondering as I eat if it is more authentic for a Vietnamese restaurant to use frozen shrimp farmed in Vietnam than Gulf shrimp. Then I wonder if any of the restaurants here use the local shrimp, or if the lure of cheap imports is just too tempting. The waitress tells me she is a college student studying for an exam. This is her uncle's restaurant; her aunt is the cook. I tell her I'm here to interview Vietnamese shrimpers and could she ask her uncle if he knows any. She doesn't hesitate to answer.

"They will not talk to you," she says bluntly. "Mostly, they want to be left alone."

"Is it because of all the racial stuff that happened here in the past?"

The relationship between the Vietnamese fishermen and the local Texas fishermen has long been punctuated by controversy; skirmishes have boiled over into fights and even murders. After the Vietnam War, when thousands of refugees were placed along the Texas Gulf, many did what they knew how to do best: fish. This was a time before stringent regulations, and the Vietnamese, desperate to make a living, broke many of the unwritten rules of the bay. They skirted laws, they ignored limits, they transformed an old Texas profession into a cutthroat business. This behavior coincided with the rage many Texans felt over unfair demonization of American Vietnam War veterans. Though the immigrants were on the same side of the fight in Vietnam as Americans, here in Texas, tensions between Vietnamese and white fishermen ran hot like a breezeless summer night. The strife was further complicated by a growing industry of cheap farmed shrimp from Southeast Asia flooding the American market, driving shrimp prices to all-time lows. Many of the Texas old-timers were pushed out of business. Many blamed the Vietnamese for eroding a way of life that, on the Gulf Coast, was more than just a profession; it was a tradition. Others argued that the shrimp industry was already in decline with or without the Vietnamese. Even so, the tensions ignited into violence. Vietnamese shrimp boats were burned, shots were fired, rallies were held, and at one point, the KKK got involved. A generation of mistrust and resentment ensued.

This was more than thirty years ago, and the hatred has subsided, I'm told. Still, the local industry has been steadily constrained by catch limits, overfishing, oil spills, and increasing environmental regulations, and all the while, the amount of imported shrimp continues to rise. The Vietnamese shrimpers fare no better today than anyone else suffering in an industry that is being choked from all sides. I'm told that nowadays everyone gets along because no one is doing any better than the next guy.

"That was a long time ago," the waitress says. "I'm too young to remember all that."

Her aunt comes out of the kitchen, and I awkwardly thank her for a delicious meal. She doesn't speak much English, and my waitress, eager to get back to her studies, does not volunteer to interpret. I pack up my notebook, but then, just as I am about to leave, the young waitress turns to me suddenly and says, "During the war, everyone came to Vietnam and burned it down, so they had no choice but to leave. They came here to work, not to fight."

SAN LEON is a quiet coastal town a bit farther down from Kemah. It occupies a peninsula that juts out like the tip of an oyster knife piercing Galveston Bay. It is a town of mobile home parks and modest houses built on stilts, a backwater resort where one can get away from the noise of everyday life. On the Bayshore side are restaurants and a few nautical-themed bars, such as Gilhooley's, a perfect place to waste an afternoon drinking tequila and slurping down Gulf oysters. The other side of the peninsula is where the commercial fishing boats dock. I drive along the edge of the water looking for people to talk to. Near an oyster processing plant, I see a few Mexican workers wrapping up for the day. The crying of the seagulls drowns out any other noise as they circle and dart menacingly. As I approach, the men rise to their feet. I ask them where I can find Vietnamese shrimpers. They tell me if I want to catch up with them, I have to go to Twenty-Second Street an hour before dawn. I pencil that into my notebook. The men don't sit down again until I'm back in my car.

I drive down the coast another thirty minutes, to Galveston. I'm meeting up with Kenny from Katie's Seafood Market on Pier 19, a small storefront operation that is actually one of the largest fish purveyors in the Gulf. Katie's is a proud family-owned business made famous by Buddy Guindon, a larger-than-life figure and an outspoken proponent of the Gulf. "Kenny" is the brother who works behind the scenes. He is thoughtful and generous with his time. He looks like he hasn't combed his hair in weeks. His hands are black from working a forklift all day.

Kenny tells me that the real money in the Gulf is in snapper and big-game fish farther offshore; the shrimp business is a lost cause. We walk around his shop looking at all the varieties of shrimp he has displayed on mountains of crushed ice. White shrimp from the bay, brown shrimp from deep waters, small bait shrimp, and Royal Reds from Louisiana. I taste the ones from the bay. They are small, white, and delicate. I prefer them to the larger varieties. Most of the bay shrimp goes straight to bait shops, where they are used to fish for larger game. This is a shame. These little guys are special, nothing like the spongy, flavorless curls of flesh that went into my *bánh xèo*. Kenny tells me the shrimpers can't make enough money selling these shrimp to wholesalers. In an industry flooded with cheap imports, there is no demand for these tasty bay shrimp. There may come a day, he laments, when they close the bay to commercial fishing altogether.

It is easy to get discouraged. In my experience, people in the fishing industry are a depressing lot. Their world is always on the brink of Armageddon and has been that way for as long as Kenny can remember. Kenny is quick to share with me a world of problems, but he has a shine in his eyes. He gets it from the water. He tells me he will pass along my order to his brother, Buddy. Right now, he has to get back to work. The forklift has been acting up all day. He winces at the sound of a truck backing up to his property. He's got to load up a large order of tilefish for a customer in Houston. As he walks away, I see he has a slight limp, but something in his eyes tells me he'll outlive the rest of us who lose our minds every time our wireless Internet goes awry.

THE NEXT DAY, I drive back to San Leon at 5:00 a.m. I arrive at the docks while the Vietnamese shrimpers are preparing their boats. It is still night. The winds are invisible in the dark, but I can feel them building strength above my head. There are about twenty shrimp boats docked in a makeshift marina of crooked pilings and rotting wooden planks. A squat cinder-block building provides the only light. The shrimp boats are rocking back and forth in the wind. All these boats are small single-engine trawlers no more than forty feet long with a boom and a net. They are in varying degrees of disarray. Only a few boats have turned on their work lights, which are perched high above the cabin. I can see a few men working on nets or drinking coffee. They're listening to the weather report on their radios. No one is willing to talk to me. I pace the docks trying to look as unsuspicious and trustworthy as I know how. I get to the end of one side of the dock and watch a boat go out, sputtering smoke as it slowly grinds through the choppy waters. I can hear flags whipping in the wind somewhere behind me. There are distant lights on the other side of the bay, and they seem like a planet away. I want to get out on the water, though I know my chances are slim. I turn around to make another pass around the docks. Just then, a man jumps off his boat to have a cigarette. I offer him one of mine. It's hard to light the cigarette in this wind, so I huddle in close. His face is worn and wrinkled. I can't tell how old he might be because the sea seems to have aged him beyond his years. His cheeks are brown and shapeless, his eyes emotionless. I can see tufts of graying hair under the brim of his Texans baseball cap. He is wearing a windbreaker, polyester slacks, and sandals on his feet—not exactly the uniform of an experienced sailor. His name is Mr. Ton. He tells me he works the entire boat himself, which is dangerous. Seagulls alight on the boats as if wakened by the motors around us.

I pretend to complain about the weather. He is not going out, he says. Too windy. His pickup truck is parked nearby, and he disappears into it for a while, talking loudly into his cell phone. Then he returns, and before he can get back on his boat, I grab his arm and ask him if he'll take me out on his boat. I offer him money. He shakes his head to tell me it is a preposterous idea. His work light is flickering, so he gets on his boat to fix it. Two more boats go out, and my chances of getting on one are dwindling. There is a small window to go out and catch shrimp while they are motionless, in the dark hours before dawn. The wind brings to shore a gust of low-pressure air that fills my lungs with salt. Mr. Ton ignores me, but I wait by his boat drinking tepid coffee and looking like a lost pet.

Suddenly, he looks up at me and waves me onto his boat. He will make one pass, that's it. He tells me to stay out of his way. He starts the engine, and we head out behind another boat that is spitting diesel smoke into the air. Mr. Ton tells me to wait in a small area of the boat next to the winch and the engine room. The sky is still dark. I can hear the sloshing of water, but otherwise, I'm blind to what is around me. I can see only what is happening on the boat.

Mr. Ton is agile for a man his age, whatever that may be. He runs back and forth between the captain's chair and the back of the boat as he lowers the outriggers. The mechanisms on these boats are very simple, not like those for the large commercial boats that go offshore deep into the Gulf. We drive slowly to a spot not far from the docks. Mr. Ton guides heavy metal doors, each one weighing about four hundred pounds, out over the black water. The nylon shrimp net goes out over the sides, and he lowers the doors into the bay. The net will unfurl into a conical shape and drag across the bottom of the bay. The doors keep the trawl net spread open. A tickler chain runs ahead of the net to stir up the floor and kick the shrimp out of the mud.

Mr. Ton moves the boat slowly over the water. He looks into the choppy waves as though he can see what is happening underneath. He is calm now, smoking a cigarette. He tells me he bought this boat for forty thousand dollars over twenty years ago. It has been a good living, he tells me, but not so much anymore. His kids are grown up, and he fishes only when the catch is good, which is not often. On a day like this, everyone loses money. He points to the corks floating on the water, but I can't understand what he's saying. He looks out over the water and shakes his head repeatedly.

A small sliver of dawn is pushing up from the horizon. Mr. Ton pushes me aside to start the winch. It has been only thirty minutes, but he has decided to pull up his net. The gulls go crazy as the net emerges from the water. Mr. Ton guides the net over the holding box. He releases the slipknots tied to the bottom of the net. A small catch of shrimp falls into the box. It isn't much. Maybe twenty pounds. Mr. Ton is disappointed but shrugs as if to say he knew as much. The winds are picking up. He is eager to get back. He points to the other boats and gestures to tell me they are wasting their time. He reties the rope around the net and sets it aside.

Knots serve many functions. The obvious one is to connect two things. Most of the knots we use in our day-to-day lives have some origin in nautical history. Before mechanization, a sailor's life depended on knots. The trick of a good knot is making a pattern you can control. Anyone can tie a knot that binds. Anyone can use friction to create tension. The real skill is tying a knot that doesn't move but will easily release when you need it to. In an age of steel and motors, knot making is a dying art. On a boat like this, you probably need to know only a few knots to perform all the tasks needed. Mr. Ton uses a clove hitch to tie the boat up to the piling. It is a remarkably simple knot that clamps under its own loop. I'm sure he doesn't know the name of this knot that he has tied countless times in his life, at least not in English.

I help Mr. Ton transfer his catch into a plastic bucket, which he loads onto the back of his pickup truck. This will go straight to a bait shop. I offer him money for his time. He smiles at me for the first time and refuses. I give him the rest of my cigarettes. He says good-bye unceremoniously and drives off, his tires kicking dust onto my jeans. It is just getting light. A lot of the other boats start to come back, with little to show for their efforts. The wind has whipped up into a circular motion. The palm tree leaves are clapping violently. Seagulls cackle in protest.

Hurricane Ike still haunts this region like a nightmare. In 2008, a tropical cyclone swelled into a Category 4 storm that made landfall in Galveston on September 13. The storm winds ripped away trees. They leveled everything. Dozens of people lost their lives, and the storm left billions of dollars in damage. People here refer to time as before Ike or after Ike. After Ike, everything had to be rebuilt, so everything here looks almost new. But there are still remnants of empty plots of land where houses once stood. And then there are these battle-scarred shrimp boats. Some survived the storm intact; others were repaired or rebuilt. To the Vietnamese immigrants here, this was their livelihood, and they would patch it and get back to work. They were the first ones back on the water after the storm. Their boats look tattered, but they work. They creak and they cough. In the light of the new morning, they look like ghost ships kept afloat against their will.

The fishermen hurry to their cars and drive off. For a moment, I think about following them in my car. But what would I do if I caught up to one of them? I can offer nothing they want. And what I want from them—their privacy, their trust—is as elusive as darting fish in an oil-black sea.

I can't find any Vietnamese restaurants in San Leon, so I stop at a Mexican restaurant for breakfast. I see *migas* on the menu and order it. Crispy corn tortillas mixed with eggs, *pico de gallo* served with refried beans and soft warm tortillas—it is a filling breakfast. At another table, a couple is eating breakfast with their small child playing at their feet. On the wall over the kitchen pass is a picture of Pancho Villa decorated like a shrine. The cook hands me a bottle of Cholula hot sauce, and the familiarity of it makes me happy. The restaurant is filling up with what seem like workers whose day has been cut short by the restless winds. The cook is also taking orders, and he's getting in the weeds. His father, seated at a table next to the TV, is watching CNN. He turns to look helplessly at his son, who's trying to write down the orders as fast as he can. I bus my own dirty plates and wipe down my table so a group of men in work boots can sit down.

I TAKE A LONG NAP in my car and wake to the shrill cries of seagulls. It is lunchtime, so I head to a restaurant called Topwater Grill, at the end of Ninth Street, looking out over the bay. It looks like your typical fun-loving wharf eatery, complete with fishing tackle decorations and the Zach Brown Band blaring from the speakers. The building sits on a piece of dock historically known as April Fool Point. It was one of the points of entry for slave ships from Africa. Just past the entrance is a display of T-shirts, hats, and beer koozies for sale. Places like this are typically not where you go for great seafood, but Topwater Grill has a stellar reputation, and I want to check the place out. Behind the restaurant is a small loading dock, mostly for small sport-fishing boats. The owner of the restaurant is Captain Wally, and everyone in San Leon knows him. You can find him here, but no one knows exactly when. You just have to catch him on his rounds. He doesn't like to stay in one place very long, the manager tells me.

I leave my name and number with the hostess so she can call me when Captain Wally arrives. I sit down for lunch. I start with Gulf oysters roasted with garlic and oil. Then I devour a basket of steamed Royal Red shrimp with drawn butter and a little Texas Pete hot sauce. The menu runs the gamut from Camerones Rancheros to Boudin Balls. The redfish with Ponchartrain sauce is delicious. As I am finishing up, a waitress comes by to tell me there has been a Captain Wally sighting. I wait for a long time to see if he'll come by my table. He finally does. He is wearing a clean outfit of shorts and a sport windbreaker. He is a kind-looking man with wrinkled sea skin and a thick Polish accent. He asks if I'm Edward. I tell him yes, and he stares at me with some suspicion. What is it exactly I'm looking for, he asks. I tell him about my book, and he reluctantly sits with me. He starts by telling me he doesn't have a lot of time. He has to meet with some contractors about a new development.

We talk about the food, and I thank him for his commitment to serving fish from the Gulf. He shows me a wall with all the accolades he has received over the years. He tells me he had many more but that those got washed away with Ike. We talk about fishing and life in San Leon. I ask him if he gets along with the Vietnamese shrimpers. Yes, he tells me. He works with them all, and they are his friends.

"But it's hard for the old-timers," he tells me. "Their kids do fine, they become American, but the older ones, they have a hard time letting go. I tell them, 'This here is America. Why do you want to make this place Vietnam?' I've had my own story, you know, but when I got here, I said to myself, I am going to embrace this country."

I ask him what his story is. He lets out a sigh. It's too long to recount.

"Anyway," he says, "I'll just give you the short version. It was 1940 when the Russians came into Tarnopol. I was five years old at the time. They gave us twenty minutes to pack, mostly clothes, some provisions. They put us on a sled and took us to the railroad station. We were transported for two to three weeks. We had never left Poland before, and here we were, traveling weeks by rail with little food and no medicine and nowhere to sleep. When we got out of the train, we found out we were in Siberia. My parents were forced to work in a labor camp in the forest. We didn't think we would survive. Some months later, they were transporting us again by train, to another labor camp even deeper into Siberia. The train doors were left open, and my father decided we would jump. He went first and the children went next, and last was my mother. We walked to a nearby village in the snow. A woman, God bless her, allowed us to stay with her.

"This was 1942, and the Germans were beating up on the Russians. The Germans were recruiting all Polish men to fight with them, and if they did, they promised that their families could return to Poland. So my father joined. They took him away, and we didn't see him for a long time. We heard he was fighting in Persia. Well, we were still in Siberia thinking we would go back to Poland, but then my mother heard of a group of families that were heading to Iran. We jumped aboard a train in the direction of the Caspian Sea. To this day, I still don't know how my mother found the strength and will to keep my brother and me safe on that journey. We didn't have papers; we didn't have money. My brother and I hid under the seat compartments almost the whole trip. When we got off the train, we took oxcarts and trolleys. We were walking along a deserted road when we saw a military truck drive by. They were Polish soldiers, and when they realized we were from Poland, they let us on the truck and took us to Tashkent. From there we somehow got to a port on the Caspian Sea, where we waited to board a boat for Iran. Well, we finally got to Iran, where we lived in a tent city for many months."

I'm writing very fast, trying to get every detail of his story right. I'm not concerned with the facts or the question of how he could know so many details of his life from the age of five. It is clear to me he has told this story before, but that makes it no less fascinating.

"I saw my father once, for two days, during all that time, and then we didn't see him again for another seven years after that. We moved to Tehran, where we lived in a refugee camp. They set up Polish schools, and we lived six months there. Then we got on lorries and traveled through some very dangerous parts to get to the Persian Gulf. They put us on a boat to Karachi, which was then India; now it's Pakistan. We stayed there for four months, then got on another boat, to Mombasa, Africa. Then we boarded a train, first to Nairobi, then to Uganda, where we lived in a Polish settlement camp on Lake Victoria. We stayed here for over five years. They built schools for us, and we were treated well here. When the war ended, we went back to Poland. We heard our father had somehow made his way to England. So we went there to join him. We stayed there for three years, until about 1952, when we decided to make a new life in America. We had a sponsor who lived in Indiana, and we made the long trip, on the *Queen Elizabeth*, landing on Ellis Island. We took a Greyhound bus to Hammond, Indiana, and my father got a job as a welder. When I got older, I found work as a draftsman for the telephone company. In 1957, I was drafted into the U.S. Army, and I was sent to Washington, D.C., as a tech engineer. I was discharged in 1959, and I went back to work for the telephone company. Back then, the solid-state transistor radio was becoming popular, and my manager allowed me to experiment on the devices. I developed a few patents and got promoted. In 1972, I got a call to come to Houston to work for an oil rig company, doing their electronics systems. I would come down here to San Leon to fish, and I liked it very much. I had a small shrimp boat back then, and I made some money doing it on the side. In 1975, this marina came up for sale, and I bought it. At the time, I was also going to Ecuador for work, so I didn't focus too much on this property. In 1983, I started to be here more full-time. I bought a fleet of shrimp boats, and we did that business for a while. When I built this restaurant, it was just a small place that served the seafood we would catch from the bay. Then, in 2008, Hurricane Ike took it all away. We rebuilt the restaurant, and now my son runs the show here, and it is doing very well."

I'm trying to keep eye contact with him while madly scribbling. I ask him about the gold anchor around his neck. His wife got it for him a long time ago.

"I'll tell you a funny story about my wife," he says. "When I was in the U.S. Army, some friends set us up on a blind date because we were both Polish. We started talking on that first date, and wouldn't you know it, we had lived in all the same places at the same time. Our families knew each other, and I had actually met her once when she was just eight days old. Her family had been on the same journey as mine. She was in Siberia when I was there, she went across the Caspian Sea to Iran, and she lived in the same camp in Africa when I was there. She came to the United States a year after I did. When we were dating, I showed her a picture I had kept from Africa. There was a man who had killed a great crocodile, and all the kids in the camp surrounded the animal to take pictures. I showed her the picture, and wouldn't you know it, she was in the picture."

He grows quiet for a brief moment. "There was a reason for all this, for meeting my wife. I am blessed. Too many times I should not have made it out alive. Now I have my own family, and I feel like it was all for a purpose. I am eighty-three, and no question I have lived a blessed life."

My hand is cramping from writing so fast, my fingers trembling. I ask him where he keeps that picture of the man with the crocodile. He tells me he lost it during Ike. Like everyone here, he lost almost everything.

"Well, this was much more than I intended on saying," he tells me. "I think you only wanted to know about my restaurant."

I put down my pen and close my notebook. There is nothing more to write. I shake hands with him and wish him a healthy life. He seems tired from talking. His phone rings as he gets up to leave the table. I watch him as he walks around his restaurant, shaking hands with customers and wiping down a stained menu. Through the glass walls of the restaurant, I watch him go back to the marina, where he helps a fisherman bring his boat out of the water. A brown pelican sits perched on a rock, patiently waiting for the scraps to be thrown its way.

I don't know what these various cultures have in common other than the bay that provides them work and, I assume, some deeper satisfaction of living. And hot sauce—they all seem to like hot sauce. As Kenny said, when you're on the water, the rules of the land don't apply. It's as if you get to leave the planet for a while. Other problems arise on a boat, but they are mechanical or else involve battles with weather or annoying gulls. For most of the fishermen I talked to, the biggest problem is that the laws of the land have slowly but heavily crept onto the boats in the water, making that sweet journey of escape barely possible anymore.

In 2017, Hurricane Harvey battered the Gulf Coast, leaving most of the coastal towns in devastating floodwaters. It was the worst storm since Ike. But the folks on the coast will rebuild. From the shrimp trawlers to the Mexican cooks to Captain Wally, they will return to their bond with the water; they will once again harvest their livelihoods from the bay.

Shrimpers are squeezed all around by the cost of operating a boat in the United States, the cost of meeting regulations, and competition with low-price, low-quality shrimp from Asia. The price of shrimp has become so cheap that we have devalued the flavor of shrimp. We think of it as an everyday food that we consume without a second thought. But if you like shrimp, you should get your hands on some Galveston Bay white shrimp. The boats never go out for more than a day, so the shrimp don't get frozen. They come in fresh and are sold right away. They are delicate and taste of the bay. You will find that you don't need to blacken them or bury them in a blanket of sauce. And you'll know what the pelican knows: that shrimp are best eaten fresh and simply prepared.

VIETNAMESE CREPES WITH SHRIMP, PORK, AND HERBS
(BANH XEO WITH NUOC CHAM)

Banh xeo is a traditional Vietnamese stuffed crepe dish, served with lettuce and herbs on the side. You wrap the crepe in lettuce and dip it into the sauce known as *nuoc cham*. But for this version, I serve the crepes open-faced, with the lettuce and herbs on top. Serve this as a casual first course along with a crisp light beer.

SERVES 4 AS A FIRST COURSE

BATTER

2 cups rice flour

2 tablespoons plus scant
    1 teaspoon cornstarch

1 teaspoon salt

¼ teaspoon ground turmeric

½ scallion, thinly sliced

⅓ cup coconut milk

2 cups water

FILLING

1½ teaspoons fish sauce

½ teaspoon sugar

½ teaspoon salt

⅛ teaspoon freshly ground
    black pepper

12 ounces pork shoulder,
    sliced into thin strips

12 ounces small shrimp,
    preferably white Gulf
    shrimp

½ small yellow onion,
    thinly sliced

¼ cup vegetable oil

2 cups bean sprouts, rinsed

GARNISH

1 grapefruit, cut into
    suprêmes, juice reserved
    (see Nuoc Cham recipe,
    page 209)

1 bunch mint, roughly
    chopped

1 bunch cilantro

1 bunch Thai basil, chopped

1 cup chopped romaine lettuce

Nuoc Cham (recipe follows)

TO MAKE THE BATTER: In a medium bowl, combine the rice flour, cornstarch, salt, turmeric, and scallion. Add the coconut milk and water and whisk well. Set aside at room temperature for 1 hour. The batter will thicken slightly as it sits.

MEANWHILE, MARINATE THE PORK FOR THE FILLING: In a small bowl, combine the fish sauce, sugar, salt, and pepper. Add the pork, tossing to coat, cover, and refrigerate.

When ready to cook, drain the pork and divide the pork, shrimp, and onion into 4 portions each.

Heat a 10-inch nonstick skillet over medium-high heat. Add 2 teaspoons of the oil to the pan, then add one portion each of the pork, shrimp, and onion and sauté for about 1 minute, stirring often, until the pork is slightly browned. Remove the pork and shrimp from the pan and reserve warm until ready to plate.

Give the batter a good stir with a ladle, pour about ⅓ cup of the batter into the center of the skillet, and swirl the skillet to cover the bottom; the batter should sizzle and bubble as you pour it in. After 30 seconds, pile ½ cup of the bean sprouts onto the crepe, lower the heat to medium, and place a lid on the pan. Cook for 2 to 3 minutes, until the sprouts have wilted slightly.

Remove the lid. Pour 1 teaspoon of the oil around the edges of the crepe and cook for 3 minutes more, or until the crepe is crispy and golden on the bottom. Slide the crepe onto a serving plate. Repeat with the remaining batter and filling, putting each crepe on a serving plate.

Divide the pork and shrimp evenly between crepes. Arrange the grapefruit segments, herbs, and lettuce over the crepe—build the greens nice and high. Drizzle the nuoc cham sauce over the herbs and crepe. Serve immediately, with more nuoc cham on the side if you want.

NUOC CHAM | This is a great dipping sauce for spring rolls and lettuce wraps. The grapefruit juice is optional, but it really makes the sauce vibrant. MAKES ABOUT 1½ CUPS

⅔ cup lukewarm water
3 tablespoons sugar
⅓ cup fresh lime juice
5 to 6 tablespoons fish sauce
1 or 2 Thai bird chiles,
    thinly sliced
	2 garlic cloves, minced
	Reserved juices from the
	    grapefruit suprêmes
	    (from the Crepe recipe,
	    page 207)

In a small bowl, whisk together the water and sugar to dissolve the sugar. Add the lime juice, fish sauce, chiles, and garlic and whisk to combine. Add the reserved grapefruit juice.

BOURBON NUOC CHAM-ROASTED OYSTERS

Try to get lovely big, fat Gulf oysters for this recipe if you can. They aren't as briny as some other varieties, but they are juicy and they cook really nicely.

The oysters are topped with the same basic dipping sauce I serve with the crepes on page 207, but I replace the water with bourbon. It adds smokiness and depth to the sauce. When you cook with bourbon, you can't just substitute it in equal parts for water. You have to cook the alcohol out of the bourbon.

SERVES 6 AS A FIRST COURSE

Rock salt
12 oysters, preferably from the
    Gulf, scrubbed clean
	¼ cup Bourbon Nuoc Cham
	    (recipe follows)

Preheat the oven to 500°F, or as hot as it will go.

Spread a layer of rock salt on a baking sheet and nestle the oysters in the salt, with the flat sides facing up. Put the oysters in the oven and watch them carefully as they cook, as they will only take 3 to 5 minutes. As soon as the oysters start to open up and you see a small bit of the oyster liquor bubbling around the sides, they are ready. Take the oysters out of the oven. Wearing heatproof gloves, lift each oyster and pop the top shells off; they should come off easily. (I don't even use an oyster knife for this, just a sturdy paring knife.)

Arrange the oysters on a serving plate and drizzle the bourbon nuoc cham right over the oysters. Serve immediately.

BOURBON NUOC CHAM | MAKES ABOUT 1 CUP

2 cups bourbon, preferably a 5-year-aged one 3 tablespoons sugar ⅓ cup fresh lime juice	5 to 6 tablespoons fish sauce 1 or 2 Thai bird chiles, thinly sliced 2 garlic cloves, minced

Put the bourbon in a medium pot, bring to a simmer over low heat, and simmer slowly until it has reduced to about ½ cup. The bourbon will ignite, so have a tight-fitting lid next to the stove, and do not ever peek into the pot. When the bourbon ignites, simply put the lid over the pot to put out the fire; remove the lid as soon as the fire is doused. The alcohol may ignite once or twice more; just cover the pot to extinguish the flames.

When the bourbon has reduced, pour it into a heatproof measuring cup, then add water until you have ⅔ cup reduced bourbon water.

Pour the bourbon water into a bowl and add the sugar, lime juice, fish sauce, chiles, and garlic. The nuoc cham will keep in your fridge, covered, for up to 2 weeks.

CHAPTER 12

THE IMMORTALITY OF PATERSON

WHAT IS IT ABOUT A WATERFALL THAT MAKES people want to jump? Is it the calm waters suddenly cascading into a collision of violence? Is it the release in that freefall, the churning energy that began long before we were here and that will continue long after we're gone? I have these thoughts as I'm standing in front of the Great Falls of the Passaic River in Paterson, New Jersey. It is early in the morning and, aside from a few joggers, I'm alone. After staring at the waterfall for a few minutes, I start to see an optical illusion. I see stillness, yet I know there is constant movement. I see an eternity in the patterns of the water.

A man walking his dogs tells me that someone jumped to his death just last week. It happened in broad daylight, he tells me. A man just jumped off the Wayne Avenue Bridge. It happens a lot, he tells me. There is a footbridge over the falls from where you can see the river up close. The water cascades more than sixty feet in random patterns over the Watchung Mountains to unforgiving rocks below. It is a majestic and frightening thing to behold. I choose not to go across the bridge. No need to tempt my impulsive nature. I'm surprised at how desolate it is here. On a good day, Paterson is a thirty-minute drive from Manhattan, but there appears not to be a single tourist. If this were in Brooklyn, there'd be a throng of visitors all day long. I see a lot of contradictions in this waterfall, tucked inside a city that has seen better days. Stillness and motion, life and death, solitude and connection.

Because of this waterfall, Paterson was once a center of industrial innovation. The falls gave birth to a once-thriving city of immigrants and laborers. Alexander Hamilton was the first one to laud the potential of the Passaic River, to imagine the harnessing of its raw power to fuel his vision of an America that would lead the world in manufacturing. Paterson became an industrialist's dream, a land of unregulated factories driven by cheap labor and abundant raw materials. Thomas Edison, Samuel Colt, Rogers Locomotive, engineers, inventors, and entrepreneurs congregated in Paterson to shape the future of a relentless America that would meet the demand for everything from guns to textiles. By 1870, the mills of Paterson produced more than 50 percent of the silk made in this country, giving Paterson the nickname Silk City. The first wave of immigrants to work the factories came from Europe and founded new neighborhoods such as Dublin, an Irish American enclave along the east bank of the Passaic River. They were quickly followed by Italian, Polish, Hungarian, and Greek immigrants desperate for jobs. The rise and fall of Paterson traced the greater story of American manufacturing. Strikes, stricter labor laws, and unions made conditions better for these workers but also spurred the industry titans to move their factories elsewhere. The fate of Paterson's industrial era was doomed by an algorithm of maximum production powered by immigrants working at the lowest possible wages.

These days, the immigrants to Paterson come from the Dominican Republic, Cuba, Haiti, India, Palestine, and Peru. There are still factory jobs but only a fraction of what were once here. The city is a relic of giant abandoned factories where the people outnumber available jobs. I am walking along the historic meat market in downtown Paterson. Through the window of a corner market, I see hundreds of live chickens crammed into holding pens. I go inside and ask the man behind the counter what they sell. He's from Cuba. He's wearing a white tank top undershirt and a gold chain around his neck. He points to a handwritten menu that lists chickens, ducks, guinea hens, turkeys, and "heavy fowl," which are just older chickens. I am instructed not to take pictures. In order for me to stay, I have to buy something, so I order a white chicken, and the man behind the counter reaches into a cage and pulls one out by its neck. He weighs the chicken and sends it to the processing line. From where I stand, I can see only a stainless-steel sink and a few men with cleavers. But the feathers on the concrete floor tell me everything. I pay for my bird, and he tells me it will be ten minutes. The waiting room is painted a teal blue, and there is nothing in it but a few plastic chairs. When my freshly killed bird is ready, he hands it to me neatly wrapped in butcher paper inside a brown paper bag. I don't know what I'm going to do with it. I'm staying in a hotel. I have no need for a raw bird. I leave the shop and think for a moment about throwing it away, but I can't. This bird just gave its life for me.

The reputation of Paterson these days is one of crime and unemployment. It is a city where history seems to have sputtered to an end. Writers do not write about Paterson anymore; tourists do not sightsee here. Folks who are fortunate enough to have jobs work for little pay, and the idle remain idle. Paterson reminds me of the immigrant streets I grew up in, where children folded up their innocent childhoods and buried them deep beneath the concrete. But a strength rises out of the cracks in the sidewalks of these immigrant neighborhoods. The Paterson I see today is vibrant, with the din of a hundred languages and the aromas of myriad spices. The rapper Fetty Wap is from Paterson, and you can hear his music blaring from cars as they coast through downtown. He is a hometown hero, one who made it. His mournful tones, like an anthem, ring throughout the patchwork city.

The restaurants of Paterson are as diverse as the people. Older immigrants, such as the Greeks, once popularized a hot dog they inexplicably called the Texas wiener, which is basically a chili cheese dog. There are a few places, such as Libby's, that still serve a tasty version of it. The more recent immigrants have their own restaurants now. I could write a story about any of them, but I'm here for the Peruvian experience.

The city is home to the largest concentration of Peruvian restaurants in the country. Peruvian immigrants started showing up in Paterson for factory jobs in the 1960s, but their numbers were modest. Then, in the 1980s, a militant communist faction called the Shining Path terrorized Peru with a violent campaign that lasted almost twenty years. Many Peruvians died; the ones who didn't saw their economy dismantled. Peruvian immigration to Paterson skyrocketed. When factory jobs started to dwindle, Peruvian Americans opened shops and restaurants to cater to their growing numbers, creating a cultural replica of their home country. This small section of Paterson is called Little Lima. No one knows exactly how many Peruvians live in Paterson today. The figures fluctuate between fifteen and thirty thousand, depending on whom you ask. There are said to be about sixty Peruvian restaurants in Paterson.

You could spend a month here and eat every meal at a different restaurant. I have two days, maybe three. If I'm ambitious, I can fit in about five meals a day. It will be impossible for me to taste all the food I want to, so I come up with a strategy. The first thing I do is look online for the restaurant with the best ratings. I find La Tia Delia, a place that has been in Paterson forever and is most recommended by travel sites. I cross that one off my list. I'll pick the second or third most popular, such as Griselda's, because it will give me a baseline for the cuisine and I'll run into fewer tourists there. I try a wide selection of dishes there: ceviche; *anticuchos*, which are marinated and grilled beef skewers; and *lomo saltado*, a Peruvian stir-fry of beef in Chinese oyster sauce often served with French fries. The food is tasty but a little underseasoned. I don't eat everything, just a few bites of each dish, unless I really enjoy it. The rest I wrap up and carry around with me in case I want to retry it after I've had another version of the same dish. Also, I hate leaving a plate of uneaten food. The second part of my strategy is to talk to as many locals as I can. Locals usually give me a bunch of recommendations. Lastly, I leave time and room in my belly for wandering around. It is amazing how many times I'll find a wonderful eatery when I'm not searching for one. One more thing: I look for restaurants that specialize in one dish. This is always a reliable indicator of good food.

D'Carbon is famous for its Peruvian rotisserie chicken, known as Pollo a la Brasa. You can smell the wood-burning oven from a block away. It is only 10:30 a.m., but the place is already busy. I sit down to an early lunch with my dead chicken as my companion. Everyone gets the same thing here, so ordering is not a tormented process. I ask for a whole chicken, not a half, because I don't want a chicken that has been precut and drained of its juices. The chicken is marinated in garlic, cumin, paprika, oregano, black pepper, and lime juice. It spins slowly on a spit until the skin gets crispy. The flesh inside turns into a cooked suspension of protein and meat juice that steams with the first bite. There is something profane about eating a cooked chicken while a raw one sits nearby, so I move the bag to the seat across from me. The rotisserie chicken comes with a sauce called *aji verde*, which is salty, spicy, garlicky, and green. I could drink a gallon of this sauce. Every five minutes, the restaurant's smoke alarm goes off, blaring out a mind-numbing pattern of rings, but no one seems to notice. They all go about the meal undisturbed. I accompany my chicken with Yucca a la Huancaina, which is fried hunks of yucca root the size of a truck driver's fingers doused with a yellow cheese sauce. It's hard to keep myself from eating the whole bird, it is so good, but I have to save my appetite. At the end of my meal, I ask my waitress if I can give her my raw chicken. I explain the circumstances, but she refuses, angrily. She thinks I'm trying to leave a chicken carcass as a tip. I walk out with two chickens under my arm, one cooked, one still raw.

The first time I had Peruvian food was at Mo-Chica, Ricardo Zarate's pioneering restaurant in Los Angeles. It's been closed for years now, but

I remember the food vividly. Ricardo made his *salchicas*, which are pork sausages made with pork blood. His Oxtail Risotto was rich and gelatinous and his Salmon Tiradito with Yuzukoshi was as pretty to look at as it was ethereal to eat. His was refined food with a peasant's heart. It made me curious about the roots of Peruvian food and about Ricardo's story. It turns out he grew up in northern Lima with an identity as diverse as Peru itself: Inca and Chinese on his mother's side and Spanish Basque on his father's side. If you could build a human in a lab with the most covetous culinary DNA, Ricardo would be it. He fled Lima during the revolution, when he was nineteen. His sister's apartment had been bombed; he had lost friends to gun violence. He moved to London and worked in the kitchen of the famed Japanese Australian chef Tetsuya Wakuda. When he relocated to Los Angeles in the mid-1990s, he found a city bursting with immigrant culture and poised for a restaurant renaissance. Mo-Chica put Zarate on the map, and he, in turn, put Peruvian food on the stage of a city that was just emerging as a culinary destination.

Ricardo was a mature chef by the time he opened Mo-Chica, and his food was Peruvian painted with an artist's brush. He could cook French and Italian. He had already become familiar with Asian flavors in Lima, but he refined them in London. His food was a cultural awakening for most Americans, but for him, it was just the food of his youth. "I took all the favorite foods of my childhood in Lima and then I put my twist on them," he told me. I wanted to eat the foods of Ricardo's youth before he manipulated them. I wanted to strip away the artist and see the immature sketches of Peruvian food. I could tell Ricardo had a rich well of raw materials from which he derived all this creativity, and I wanted to peek inside that well. I was greedy for it. I could have gone to Peru, but I chose Paterson instead.

I always feel conflicted by the notion of authenticity. I am here in Paterson for some version of Peruvian food that is authentic, but what does that mean? In many ways, the food of immigrants is not authentic but frozen in time, reflecting the culinary moment when the wave of immigrants left their homes. This is the food of nostalgia. It gives an immigrant population a connection to its home country. Meanwhile, in Peru, the cuisine and the identity of the nation have continued to evolve. Chefs such as Gastón Acurio were not cooking their expressive cuisine when Ricardo fled Lima. Ricardo's generation of Peruvians took with them the cuisine of that time and relocated it to places such as Paterson. I'm sure there are restaurants in Lima today that still cook in the old style, but the evolution of Lima has altered the culinary landscape forever. Today it is a wealthy, thriving city, and home to a number of Michelin-starred restaurants. In an odd twist of history, the Lima of Ricardo's youth now lives here in Paterson. So what does that make this food? Authentic? Is it Peruvian with a hyphenated "American" next to it?

I ask Ricardo for an explanation. He nods and starts to speak slowly but quickly builds up speed as he gestures with his big hands.

"When people ask me what is Peruvian food, I have the hardest time to explain. I say to them, 'Peruvian food is a pot that has been simmering for five hundred years.' The first ingredients were the Incas and the Spaniards. Then we added Africa and Morocco to the pot. Next is Italian, with a little German and French. Then a lot of Chinese. The last ingredient is Japanese. And the pot is still simmering."

I love that description. It is a perfect metaphor. One day, I hope we can describe American cuisine in the same wide-open way.

JUST UP THE STREET from D'Carbon is a little bright spot called El Rompe y Raja. I meet Eduardo, who is both the chef and the cashier. I tell him I'm an "Eduardo," too. His ceviche is fresh and unadorned. It comes with a thin slice of roasted sweet potato that is served chilled. He tells me to go back and forth from the tilapia to the sweet potato. I have never had ceviche like this, so perfectly balanced, the acidity of the lime juice tempered by the sweet flesh of the potato. Eduardo's father had a restaurant in Lima. They left when he was a teenager, and Eduardo spent a decade working in Italian restaurants in New York City. He started this place just last year. I ask him why he would open another Peruvian restaurant in a city that already has so many.

"'Cause I'm fucking crazy. It's suicide, I know."

"You could have opened in Paramus or Clifton."

"I thought about that, but then, I also like it here. This is my home. I don't want to be anywhere else."

I ask him what his restaurant's name—"El Rompe y Raja"—means:

"It's music. You know sometimes you go to a club and the music is rocking and you have a great fucking time? That's a *rompe y raja*. It's a slang."

The menu reads the same as that in many of the other Peruvian restaurants in Paterson, but the food is different, more ambitious. It has swagger, like Eduardo. I reach into my backpack for a small flask of whiskey I've been saving for later. We share a drink; then he pours me a glass of purple corn juice, which is sweeter than the sweetest Kool-Aid. He goes back into the kitchen and makes me a plate of *cau cau*, chunks of cow intestine with soft-boiled potatoes in green sauce. The intestines melt in my mouth. I drink more purple corn juice and whiskey. This is the best bite of food I've had so far.

"You Chinese?" he asks me. No, I say. "When I first saw you, I thought you were Chinese from Peru."

IN THE NINETEENTH CENTURY, Chinese laborers from Canton arrived in Peru to work the sugar plantations and coastal guano mines, dank caves of sea bird shit that made for valuable fertilizer. They were contract laborers, or "coolies." Essentially they were legal slaves. Almost all of them were male. They numbered in the hundreds of thousands. When their contracts were paid up, many of them settled with Peruvian women and adopted their wives' last names. They started to establish restaurants called *chifas*, the word for Chinese food that arose out of Peruvian ingredients. Calle Capón, Lima's Chinatown, also known as Barrio Chino de Lima, became one of the Western Hemisphere's earliest Chinatowns.

During the wave of immigration to Paterson, a small number of these Chinese Peruvians arrived here and opened Cantonese restaurants serving *chifa* food. But their *chifa* cuisine has always been overshadowed by the Chinese American experience, which began with early settlers coming to California from Guangzhou during the Gold Rush. In 1882, the Chinese Exclusion Act was passed, essentially closing America's doors to Chinese immigration. By 1902, Chinese immigration to the United States was made permanently illegal, and remained so until the 1940s. What makes all this interesting from a culinary standpoint is that what most Americans knew about Chinese food came from this small region of Guangzhou, which Americans called Canton. Even today, the idea of Chinese American food is still woefully limited to a miscalculated Cantonese cuisine. The *chifa* cuisine, when it came to America, was limited to the pantry that was accessible here, which did not include many Peruvian ingredients. So *chifa* cooks were forced to use the ingredients of the American Chinese pantry. As a result, there is little to distinguish the *chifa* restaurant from the countless Chinese American restaurants that likewise serve a Cantonese-inflected menu. The two restaurants seem at first almost identical, but there are subtle differences. If all this sounds complicated, well, it is.

For *chifa*, Eduardo tells me to go to a place called Eat in Happy Restaurant, which I jot down in my notebook as the best name for a restaurant I've ever heard. It is good *chifa*, he tells me.

I put my dead chicken and my other leftovers on the chair next to me. It is starting to give off a tepid odor. The place is painted dark and the tables are spaced out for maximum seating. The walls are spare to the point of being unwelcoming. The menu, aside from a small section called "Platos Especiales," reads like any other Chinese American menu. I order Kam Lou Wantan, which is just sweet-and-sour pork with wontons. Chi Jau Kay is chicken stir-fry with oyster sauce. General Tso Pollo is, well, you know. The one dish that seems different is the restaurant's *lomo saltado*, a Peruvian national favorite on every menu in Paterson. It consists of thick strips of beef sautéed with onion, fresh tomatoes, and scallions, and tossed with French fries in a light sweet-and-sour oyster sauce. The meat is dark and delicious, and the fries get soggy in a good way. I'm full, but I can't stop eating. The flavor is salty and sweet-and-sour and brutally honest. It is better than the version I tried at Griselda's.

The persistence of this version of Chinese food presents a conundrum. It seems identical to many Chinese American restaurants. Can *chifa* even exist in America if, by its very definition, it is the hybrid of China and Peru? I order a dish called Chaufa, which is the same fried rice I've eaten a thousand times. I look out the window of Eat in Happy Restaurant and see, just a block away, a Chinese American restaurant that I am sure is serving the same fried rice—except it is also not the same. According to Leibniz's law on the identity of indiscernibles, if they were actually the same, I would not recognize them as being distinct. But I do. The two dishes might use the same ingredients, but by arriving in Paterson through two distinct paths, they are ontologically separate. Both started in Guangzhou and arrived in Paterson, but before they arrived in America, they evolved in two separate cultures. As Immanuel Kant would say, even if two things are the same, if they are at two different places at the same time, they are numerically different. Because of this, I can taste a difference.

At China Chilcano, in Washington, D.C., José Andrés makes a version of *lomo saltado* that is much better than what I'm eating at Eat in Happy Restaurant—well, maybe not better, but more complex, more creative, and more focused. It is not "authentic," but neither is what I'm eating here, and neither is what is served in Lima. This is what I find so infuriating about the impulse to classify food as authentic. It implies that there is a right and a wrong. It implies that tradition is static and that there can be no evolution. It implies that a culture can stand still. There is nothing about this place in Paterson, New Jersey, with its paint chipping off the walls, that resembles José's stunning restaurant in Penn Quarter in D.C., and yet they are connected. I'm happy to be here in this working-class restaurant eating this proletarian version of *lomo saltado*. If José is taking this dish to its highest potential, then this is where it starts. I clean my plate. I can feel the tremble-causing MSG creeping into my bloodstream. I have a love-hate relationship with MSG. I love what it does to my mouth, not so much my nervous system.

I'm so full that my eyelids start to flutter. I cannot eat any more today. I get in a cab because it hurts to walk. I'm carrying bags of food that are starting to give off a smell that is unrecognizable and nauseating. I don't have a destination. I ask the driver to take me through a few neighborhoods; I'm about to fall asleep. Just then, I notice an awning for a bakery that reads "Los Immortales" in a font that is part German Gothic, part Mexican gang. I ask the cabbie to stop. I almost ask him if he wants my chicken, but I have grown attached to it now.

Los Immortales is a bakery that also sells meat and grocery items. The shelves are filled with Inca Kola, which is Peruvian soda made with lemon verbena. The place used to be a pool hall, and there is still a small bar area where a young man serves beer, coffee, and lottery tickets. Behind the counter are trays of fresh-baked *pan chuta*, *alfajores*, and a row of pastries that look vaguely Gallic. A small group of men are drinking beer and talking loudly. On every inch of every wall are photos of soccer teams from Peru's past. This place is a museum of vintage photos, trophies, and jerseys wrapped in protective plastic sheets. I look closely at a black-and-white photo entitled "Alianza Lima." The faces of the men in their striped uniform are stoic, the photographic print foggy, with a silver cast. They are "the immortals." I ask one of the men there about the memorabilia. He tells me that many retired professional soccer players live in Paterson. Whenever they go home, they bring back a picture or a jersey and donate it to the bakery. It all goes on the walls.

Soccer (or football) was introduced to Peru by English sailors in the late nineteenth century. The story goes that it was during these early games that the Chalacan strike was invented. Now popularly known as the bicycle kick, the Chalacan strike is an acrobatic move where a player kicks the ball over his head while upside down in the air. It is the most flamboyant and difficult move in soccer today. Peruvians have an immense pride in their national team, which was first formed in 1927. Despite the team having never won a World Cup, Peruvians are deeply loyal. Ricardo Zarate laments to me that he has not yet seen the Peruvian team qualify for a World Cup in his lifetime. "If they ever do," he says with all the fervor of a starving man, "I will drop whatever I am doing to go."

One of the men at Los Inmortales tells me that on warm evenings, you can go to nearby Pennington Park and watch them play. Victor Hurtado, Freddie Ravelo, Julio Aliaga—he rattles off more names I don't recognize.

"They are old now, but they can still curve a ball like crazy. It is beautiful to watch."

Pennington Park sits along the Passaic about a mile downriver from the Great Falls. It is not much of a park, but there is a great, wide soccer field. By the time I get there, the light is fading, but children are running around and playing soccer in random pickup games. The parking lot is filled with cars and people. The atmosphere is festive. I sit in the stands with the bags of leftover food I've collected throughout the day and watch the matches. Two men are kicking a ball back and forth almost the length of the soccer field. The trajectory of the ball looks illogical. It seems to suspend itself in the air and change course. I wonder if these men are the retired players I was told about, but I choose not to ask. It is beautiful to watch them play, and I don't want to disturb them. On my left, Paterson rises over a steep hill; the houses look flat and luminous as the sun sets behind them. To my right is the Passaic River, calm and murky. Soon it will be too dark to see. I've been warned to get out of Paterson before dark. It's not safe, I've been told.

I notice there is a hole in the bottom of the bag holding my raw chicken. The chicken is gone. It must have fallen out, and I didn't notice it with all the other bags I was carrying. I retrace my steps, back to Los Inmortales, but it isn't there. It is dark now, and the streets are lit up with neon signs and traffic lights. I don't know why I'm looking for that chicken. It's not as if I was going to keep it, but I've been carrying it with me all day. I wanted to be the one to decide its fate, but sometimes the world decides these things for you. The streets are crowded with people, and the restaurants are packed with patrons. The city feels alive, more awake than in the daytime. I discard the rest of my bags and feel liberated. Without the capacity to eat any more, I'm free to just roam without purpose.

I'll be back in Paterson tomorrow, and I'll eat at five more restaurants. I'm sure that some of the meals will feel like the same ones I had today. Nevertheless, I'm looking forward to it. Walking back through the city at night, I think about the great American poet William Carlos Williams and his epic poem *Paterson*, which he published in five separate volumes from 1946 to 1958. I plan on reading some of it tonight. Williams was an experimental poet who changed not just the course of American poetry but also how we view everyday objects such as red wheelbarrows. His name sounds funny because his first and last names are the same, almost. In 2016, Jim Jarmusch released a movie called *Paterson*, which was shot entirely here. In the movie, the main character's name is Paterson, and he lives in Paterson, New Jersey. The actor's name is Adam Driver, and in the movie he plays a bus driver. In the distance, I think I hear the clamor of the waterfall, but it is only the sound of a truck moving slowly through traffic. The man who jumped off the bridge on February 21, 2017, remains unidentified.

I remember when I first heard about *chifa* cuisine. I imagined what could happen if Chinese food collided with Peruvian ingredients. I imagined a great number of new flavors and layers of color and texture, but I never got that. The collaboration between China and Peru is a part of their history, and not mine to manipulate. But what if the imagination were free to explore the connections without the constraints of history? Without the concern for the purity of tradition? It is in Paterson where I find the confidence to explore that question. I could have imagined a fictional *chifa* dish without ever traveling to Paterson, but it would not have had the same respect for the people. It is always about the people, the Peruvians and Chinese who came together to form the roots of a cuisine that chefs stand on top of; the transplanted people here in Paterson who are creating another branch of Peruvian food culture, parallel and distinct from what they left behind in Lima. When I think about *chifa* today, I think about Lima. I think about Ricardo and José and all the people in Paterson who cooked for me and opened up a world I never knew existed.

POLLO A LA BRASA

True *pollo a la brasa* is slow-cooked over charcoal, and if you have a charcoal grill, you should cook your chicken on it, rather than in the oven, as in this recipe. But it is the marinade that makes this dish so special. The chicken must be marinated overnight, which makes the chicken tender and juicy with a crust that is caramelized and salty, just the way chicken skin should be. I use Korean gochujang in the marinade because it closely resembles the Peruvian chile that is hard to find in the States.

SERVES 2 OR 3 AS A MAIN COURSE

MARINADE

¼ cup soy sauce

2 tablespoons gochujang
(Korean chile paste)

2 tablespoons olive oil

Juice of 3 limes

5 garlic cloves

2 teaspoons minced fresh
ginger

2 teaspoons ground cumin

1½ teaspoons smoked hot
paprika

1 teaspoon dried oregano

1 teaspoon dried rosemary

1 teaspoon salt

½ teaspoon freshly ground
black pepper

1 whole chicken
(about 2½ pounds),
preferably organic

Green Ají Sauce
(recipe follows)

TO MAKE THE MARINADE: In a food processor, combine the soy sauce, gochujang, olive oil, lime juice, garlic, ginger, cumin, smoked paprika, oregano, rosemary, salt, and pepper and process until smooth.

(CONTINUED)

Put the chicken in a large casserole dish. Loosen the skin of the chicken over the breasts and thighs. Rub the marinade both under the skin and over it. Let the chicken sit in the marinade, covered, in the fridge overnight.

The next day, remove the chicken from the fridge about 30 minutes before putting it the oven. Preheat the oven to 450°F.

Put the chicken in a roasting pan and roast for 15 minutes. Reduce the oven temperature to 350°F and cook the chicken for 45 minutes, or until the skin is dark and caramelized. To test for doneness, insert a knife into the chicken where the thigh bone meets the backbone; if the juice runs clear, the chicken is ready. Let rest for 10 minutes before carving.

Serve the chicken with the green ají sauce on the side.

GREEN AJÍ SAUCE | MAKES ½ CUP

1 bunch cilantro, root ends trimmed	3 garlic cloves
3 jalapeño peppers, seeded and minced	½ teaspoon salt
	¼ cup olive oil
	¼ cup mayonnaise

In a blender, combine the cilantro, jalapeño peppers, garlic, salt, olive oil, and mayonnaise and puree until just smooth (be careful not to overmix, or the sauce may break). Transfer to a glass or plastic container and refrigerate until ready to use.

GREEN FRIED RICE WITH CHICKEN, CILANTRO, AND AJÍ SAUCE

Think of this as Chinese fried rice with the flavors of South America.
I am not going to claim that this rice has anything to do with Peru, but
it has everything to do with Paterson, New Jersey. This recipe incor-
porates many of the flavors I discovered there: plantains, ají sauce,
and *pollo a la brasa*. The avocados give the rice a funky green tinge,
and I swapped out the traditional carrots for broccoli to reinforce that
greenness. Make this with leftovers from Pollo a la Brasa (page 225)
or other roast chicken.

SERVES 2 AS A MAIN COURSE

1 cup short-grain rice

1⅓ cups water

¼ teaspoon salt

2 tablespoons vegetable oil

1 plantain, peeled and coarsely
  chopped

½ cup finely diced onion

½ cup finely diced red bell
  pepper

½ cup finely chopped broccoli
  florets

½ cup peas

1½ tablespoons toasted sesame
  oil

1 teaspoon grated garlic
  (use a Microplane)

1 teaspoon grated fresh ginger

3 tablespoons soy sauce

2 cups pulled chicken from
  Pollo a la Brasa (page 225;
  or see Note)

1 tablespoon fish sauce

2 ripe avocados, halved,
  pitted, peeled, and roughly
  chopped

2 tablespoons chopped fresh
  cilantro

2 tablespoons chopped
  scallions

In a medium saucepan, combine the rice, water, and salt and bring to
a boil. Reduce the heat as low as it will go, cover, and cook for 20 to
25 minutes, until all the liquid has been absorbed. The rice should be
tender and fluffy; if it is not, add 2 tablespoons water to the pan and
let it cook a little longer. Turn off the heat and let stand for 10 minutes.

Spread the rice out on a baking sheet and refrigerate for 1 hour, or until
thoroughly chilled.

Heat a wok or a large skillet over high heat. Add 1 tablespoon of the
vegetable oil and heat until hot, then add the plantain and fry, stirring

and tossing it, until browned and crispy. Remove from the pan and set aside on a paper towel–lined plate.

Add the remaining 1 tablespoon vegetable oil to the pan and heat until hot. Add the onion and stir-fry for 1 minute. Add the bell pepper and broccoli and stir-fry for 2 minutes. Add the peas and cook for 1 minute. Transfer the vegetables to a plate and set aside.

Add the sesame oil to the wok and heat until hot. Add the chilled rice and stir-fry for 3 minutes. Add the garlic and ginger and stir-fry for 1 minute. Add half the soy sauce and stir to color the rice. Add the chicken, the remaining soy sauce, and the fish sauce and stir-fry for 2 minutes. Add the reserved vegetables and toss everything together, then add the avocado chunks and stir-fry for another minute.

Stir in the cilantro and scallions and serve right away.

NOTE: If you don't have leftover chicken on hand, a store-bought roast chicken will do just fine.

CHAPTER 13

NIGERIAN HUSTLE

LIVE INSIDE THE HEM OF THE AMERICAN SOUTH, ALONG
the edge of many cultures and influences. Midwestern values
press down from above, the Appalachian influence pushes
from the east, the antebellum South rises from below. In the
Bluegrass State, I can find salt-risen bread in Harlan, mutton barbecue in the western region of Owensboro, and sorghum farms in
Winchester. I can tell you where to find country hams smoked and
cured in a practice that goes back generations. The fabric of this
culinary tradition folds over me and comforts me. At the same time,
I can also go to a wonderful Japanese restaurant in Lexington and
humble but delicious Mexican cafeterias all over Louisville, or get
Persian food in Covington. There isn't a checkered tablecloth big
enough to hold all the dishes that come from this place.

Kentucky has always had one foot in the South and the other foot
pointing outward. The Ohio River is the main tributary of the vast
Mississippi River, and it birthed a vibrant commerce city, an inland
port, in Louisville. From its early days of furs, hides, and salt to its dark
era as a major slave-trading marketplace, Louisville has been a port of

entry for diverse cultures. It has never been afraid of outsiders, from the French to the Jews to, more recently, Persians and Somalis. And after three hundred years, Louisville is still figuring out its identity.

I am explaining this to chef Tunde Wey as we drive back from the airport. Tunde has been traveling the country hosting dinners to talk about race and identity in America. Most of the dinners have been in big cities. I wanted to bring him to Louisville, a city much smaller in scale, more intimate in feel, and more polite in its politics. Tunde does not hold back his opinions, and he doesn't couch his words in soft vocabulary. He is blunt and honest and scathing. It makes me nervous to know that he will be leading a discussion about race in front of my clientele, my friends, and my neighbors. And that is exactly why I extended the invitation for him to come here.

This is the first time I've done anything like this. I've always held the opinion that a restaurant should be a place free of politics. I've always believed that the role of a chef is removed from ideology. My table has always been, and always will be, a place welcoming to all. But as of late, the sad events in our country have been gnawing at my soul. The shooting of young black men, the incarceration of teens, the dehumanization of the LGBTQ community, the xenophobia, the hate. I have begun to feel that as chefs, we no longer have the luxury of being neutral. I look to Tunde for guidance.

Before he arrived here, he let me know that he wanted to explore Louisville on his own and get to know the city.

"I got you a car for the week, so you can get around freely," I tell him.

"I don't drive, man," he informs me. "I can't risk getting pulled over by the law."

I FIRST READ ABOUT TUNDE WEY from an article he coauthored with John T. Edge of the Southern Foodways Alliance. Tunde uses food to voice his protest. In the article, he came out punching, against white appropriation of what he deemed inherently African American food traditions. While I don't fully agree with his arguments, I'm drawn in by his bravado. We began a series of phone calls. I'd call him on his cell phone, and he'd say all the right things to me. I'd open up to him about the issues troubling me, and he'd console me in just the right way. He would also make sweeping inflammatory statements that made me blush. He'd reprimand me, and it felt justified. It was like an Internet dating scam: I was taken in by his words. Tunde was somber and scholarly, but he also had an arsenal of brutal words that hinted at dismantling the system, a system I'm deeply entrenched in. I was seduced, and yet, at any given moment, I couldn't decide whether he was hustling me or enlightening me.

In one phone conversation, he told me that his inspiration for cooking was Fela, the Nigerian musician who invented Afrobeat, a dizzying sound of percussion, improvisation, and scalding lyrics. Fela's music is like James Brown, Bob Marley, Muhammad Ali, Che Guevara, and the Preservation Hall Jazz Band all converged into one frenetic nucleus of energy. Fela's music was protest music, unleashed onto the streets of Nigeria at a time of post-colonial struggle, when the militant government was clashing daily with the struggling population. I bought Fela's albums because of Tunde. I listen to them the way Tunde instructed me to.

"Expensive Shit" is a thirteen-minute song recounting the story of when Fela swallowed his marijuana stash during a raid of his home, with the cops searching through his shit, literally and figuratively. It starts out with tempting percussion and keyboard chords that portend something dire to come. The horns come in at the two-minute mark, tight as a G-string. You don't hear a single voice for six minutes, and when you do, it is a hoarse moan of anguish and release. The lyrics go back and forth from English to Yoruba to Pidgin English. A chorus of young women follows Fela's lead. The music is so exhausting, so taut and blinding, you need musical breaks, if only to give your emotions a chance to breathe. But it never really lets go of its grip on you. I can feel the fingernails of Fela's vocals in my throat.

"Fela used music as a weapon to protest the government of Nigeria," Tunde tells me, "but it was also riveting music that you can dance to. I want to do the same with my food. It is not embellished in any way. It is the food of Nigeria, but it serves a purpose that is more than just eating."

Fela was an irascible, mercurial man of unending machismo who once notoriously married twenty-seven women in one ceremony. Tunde may be a disciple, but he is very different. He absorbs energy. He walks with a swagger that is both juvenile and confident. He wears political T-shirts; his dreadlocks are hipster. When he speaks, his voice has the cadence and gravity of a poet's. He pulls you into him and charms you with words, simple but meaningful words. He can infuriate you one moment and disarm you the next. Anyone can make radical statements. Tunde makes you believe in them. He has a laugh that lights up a room, even over the phone.

EVERY MORNING, I pick up Tunde and we talk on the drive to breakfast or to the market. On this morning, I tell him over breakfast that I wished more African Americans felt welcome eating at my restaurant. It is not a statement driven by profit or politics. It is just something I've noticed over the years running a fine-dining restaurant. I've hosted guest dinners with soul food chefs and still could not get a majority of African Americans to attend. I ask Tunde if it's something I'm doing or not doing.

"It is about community," he tells me. "You present a world where innovation is the by-product of your status quo. The reason you don't have black people at your restaurant is because what they want is something familiar. It could be the food or it could be the community. Your restaurant is pompous, and it offers neither of these things."

I choke on my croissant.

TUNDE AND I go to an African market I never knew existed in Louisville. We buy grains and palm oil and spices I've never used before. We get twenty pounds of frozen goat meat with the skin attached. Tunde is excited by the skin. It is rare for me to go into a market and be so unfamiliar with the ingredients. The only thing I know for sure how to cook is the twenty-pound box of plantains we haul away. Afterward, I take Tunde to my favorite fried chicken joint, Indi's, a local mini-chain that was started by a Trinidadian family almost twenty years ago. We order fried chicken, potato wedges, broccoli-and-cheese casserole, collard greens, and boiled string beans. I ask Tunde if he sees any connection between this soul food and the food of his West African roots.

"We don't eat much fried food. That is the biggest difference. But I see similarities, too. The North Carolina red rice is basically *jollof* rice. I see it in collard greens, in the way Southerners cook okra, and in many of the stewed vegetable dishes."

After lunch, Tunde gets an upset stomach and has to go down for a nap. It is the fried food, he tells me. He isn't used to eating so much of it.

WE HOST HIS DINNER at a cafeteria in Louisville's West End, a predominantly African American neighborhood. The place is packed and diverse and humming with anticipation. Tunde makes *jollof* rice; goat curry stew; *fufu*, a steamed bread made from cassava flour; yam pottage; and plantains. After the dinner, we don't talk about the food. Instead, Tunde guides a discussion around what it means to be black in America, in Louisville. At one point, he asks the white people in the room, "What are you personally willing to give up so that I may have success?" This quiets the room. He lets the silence linger like the smell of curry on our fingertips.

It is nerve-racking to watch Tunde at work. I know he will at some point say something to rile up the crowd. He is nervously waiting for someone to respond. I understand what he's trying to do, but at the same time, this is not the Tunde who just this morning made tea for me and joked about how insecure he was about his cooking. There is a side to him that is generous and vulnerable and funny.

I'm sitting in the back row and whispering with Josh, Tunde's friend from Nigeria. They went to college together in Detroit. Josh lives here in Louisville and works for Ford, as an engineer. Josh plays rugby. He keeps his hair buzzed short. He is half-listening to Tunde while looking at girls on his Tinder feed. We talk about the food, and Josh says to me, half-jokingly, "You know, I am a better cook than Tunde."

I'm taken aback. I ask him how that's possible.

"In Nigeria, many men know how to cook. It is our tradition. Tunde is good, don't get me wrong, but my food is better."

"Then why don't you do what he is doing?"

"Because I want to make money and have a good life. Tunde is a philosopher. It is not always the best cook that opens the restaurant. In your culture that may be the case, but for us, each one of us chooses what life we want to have."

Josh tells me to go to Houston if I want really authentic Nigerian food. There I will find the intersection of commerce and craft. He shows me a picture of a beautiful young woman on his Tinder feed who wants to meet up with him.

THE NEXT DAY, Tunde is off to eastern Kentucky, to cook another dinner, this time with Lora Smith, cofounder of the Appalachian Food Summit. Director at PhilCap Fund, a support organization for Appalachian-run businesses, a hemp seed grower, an activist, a farmer, and a mother, Lora lives and works on Big Switch Farm in Egypt, Kentucky. She drives two and a half hours to pick up Tunde from my restaurant. He gets into her car like a king stepping into a chariot.

I have known Lora for a few years. She is a private person. She blushes when she speaks in front of a crowd, even though her words can hold a room breathless. There is a bounce to her voice, and she laughs easily, a guttural laugh like a stream that suddenly bends. Her protest is not in the public forum, like Tunde's, but behind the scenes. She works tirelessly for her land, her crops, her people. She sees resistance in the pragmatic choices we make in everyday living.

"Eating cornbread can be an act of protest," she says. "If you know where it all comes from and you are trying to make a difference in how you spend your money."

She talks of preserving the resources of Appalachia. Her mission is to convince people to invest in the region. She sees romance as a means of funding. "I want people to fall in love with Appalachia because that's the only way to get people to invest in it. And that is how I can protect and preserve this land."

Big Switch Farm is on lush, fertile soil, with soft hills and grasses that bend as the winds change direction. It is a place where you know your neighbors but may not see them for days. Dinners in these parts are either quick calories in between work or long celebrations and gatherings. There is no middle ground.

Tunde's dinner with Lora is a small gathering of artists, community leaders, and activists. They come for the food and, more than that, the dialogue. Later, Tunde writes about his experience with Lora in an article for *Oxford American*. It reads like a love letter. He rhapsodizes about eastern Kentucky as an idyllic place of farmland and dreams and good people. For all his steaming criticism of America, Tunde is a man who reacts to kindness. And Kentucky was kind to him, at least the small sample of it he interacted with. The next time I see Lora, we talk for a long time about Tunde, about his childish imperfections, his propensity for naps, his wit, and his brilliance. I jokingly tell her that I would love to live in the version of eastern Kentucky Tunde so tenderly portrays in that article.

HOUSTON IS NEITHER TEXAS nor the South. It is often referred to as the melting pot of the South. When I tell people in Houston that their city reminds me of Louisville, I get strange looks. Maybe it's a stretch, but I see Houston as a place of many identities, diverse commerce, and international communities. Houstonians' connection to the American South, as in Louisville, is as fragile as the windswept seeds from a dandelion puffball.

Houston is home to the largest population of Nigerians in America, estimated at around 150,000. Many of the African restaurants dot Bissonnet Street, behind the flashy car dealerships and underneath the canopy of Houston's intricate highway system. It is a place where most of my friends in Houston have never been. This is, in the local vernacular, a rough neighborhood. I am surprised at how openly the sex workers walk the street corners at dusk, propositioning men in cars.

My first stop is a place called Afrikiko, a plain storefront in a strip mall that looks deserted. The restaurant seats about fifteen people. The only other people here are two men shooting the breeze, drinking Heineken. I ask them for food recommendations, and they invite me to join them. Anthony and Patrick are both from Lagos. Nigerians are friendly people, they say to me. It seems like a sweeping generalization, and one that I don't typically pay attention to, but they insist it's true. I tell them about my controversial friend Tunde. Patrick tells me to call Tunde on the phone. "I will have him laughing in no time," he tells me. I put my phone on speaker and make the call. Tunde answers, and Patrick goes on a rant I can't understand. He speaks a mix of Yoruba and Pidgin English. Within seconds, the two are bantering, and I can hear Tunde laughing on the other end of the line. Patrick is making fun of Tunde's name. I don't get why, but it has something to do with calling into question the nature of Tunde's identity—is he really Nigerian? They call each other out on where in Nigeria they're from, which tribe, what lineage. It is all in good fun, but as soon as Patrick hangs up the phone, he turns to me and says, "Your friend, he needs to learn what it means to be Nigerian."

I find this an odd statement coming from a man who has just spoken with someone in his native tongue. Patrick is in his late fifties, but even in his laughter, he seems like a man who has not shed the demons of his youth. He tells me that if I want to know about Nigeria, I must buy him and his friend a round of beers. He says it jokingly but does not refuse the beers when I order them.

Anthony is helpful with the menu. We go through the entire thing, and he explains every dish to me. He recommends I order the Goat Pepper Soup, a spicy concoction with tender braised goat in a scotch-bonnet-and-tomato broth. I also get the Peanut Soup, which is nothing like what it sounds like. It is not thick and creamy. The smell is distinctly roasted peanuts, but the texture is light and watery, with a surface broken by bubbles of chili oil. This dish is popular in the northern region of Nigeria. The flavor is earthy and familiar at first; then the punch of spice is jarring. It takes a few spoonfuls to get used to the flavor combination, but once my tongue acclimates, the taste is addictive.

Egusi is a soup made from ground melon seed; the flavor is tough and medicinal. The soup is spicy, mealy, with braised greens that remind me of collards. It feels healthy. Each dish here is served with a ball of *fufu* the size of my fist, kept warm by a single layer of cellophane wrapped around it. *Fufu* is the staple steamed bread that is eaten with pretty much everything. Made from cassava and plantain flour, it is soft, chewy, and pillowy, not unlike the dough of the Chinese steamed buns I used to eat in Chinatown as a child. It calms the mouth after every bite of spiciness—for example, of the beef stew with tomatoes and *jollof* rice I can't stop eating.

Ophelia is the chef. She is young and plump and wears a colorful head wrap. She comes out to greet us but won't tell me how she makes her food. Patrick urges her to be careful, because I might be a spy. He laughs so loudly it disturbs everyone in the restaurant, including her husband, who is glued to the TV watching a soccer match. I tell her I'm not a journalist, but she doesn't believe me. She doesn't want me to write about the secret ingredients she uses in her stew. We pose for a picture, but she says her recipes are her own and not for sharing. Patrick tells me to bribe her with beer. I order another round, and Patrick's laughter fills the tiny restaurant.

THE NEXT DAY, I wake up early to meet with Tunde's sister-in-law Ronny, who has promised to teach me a few Nigerian dishes while I'm in

Houston. Ronny lives in Katy, which is a bit of a drive. These invitations are always precious to me. Just as Lora opened up her home to Tunde, here in Houston, I find myself driving to a stranger's home for no other reason than to cook food. It is humbling to witness the kindness of people. Ronny is a busy woman, but she greets me at the door as if we have known each other for years. She has a young daughter. She works from home and also runs a moving business on the side. During our cooking lesson, she is interrupted by her cell phone every few minutes.

Ronny tells me that Nigerian cooking takes a long time, so we should get started right away. She takes out chunks of beef with cow skin and some chopped-up chicken. She starts to brown them with a little oil in a large pot. She cuts an onion, holding it in her left hand and slicing it with her right by sawing the blade of her knife toward her. This is how we do it in Nigeria, she tells me; we don't need a cutting board. She adds Knorr beef cubes, which she gets from Lagos. They remind her of home. She sprinkles curry powder, dried thyme, and onion powder into the pot. She puts the lid on the pot and lets the meat roast on high heat. No liquid. The juices from the meat are enough to keep everything moist.

She uses a blender to puree red bell peppers, tomatoes, and a scotch bonnet pepper with a little water. Next, she adds the raw onion and blends the mixture until it becomes a chunky liquid. She pours this into another pot and simmers it for thirty minutes. In the first pot, the meat juices have reduced, and the meat is browning. She removes the meat, adds oil, then fries the cow skin until it is crispy. She combines the meat, the skin, and the simmering tomatoes in one pot. She adjusts the seasoning and lets this cook for another thirty to forty-five minutes, until it is tender.

I ask her if she'd play some music, and she turns on Fela. The sharp edges of the protest songs seem tamed in this quiet, pleasant house in the suburbs of Houston. I ask her about Nigeria.

"Nigeria is a big place; we have many identities; Yoruba, Hausa, Igbo, Valaba, and more. But Nigeria as a whole is a fun place. You would know all of your neighbors. If you would have a maid, she would become part of your family. Our clothes are colorful and loud. And so are we."

Then I ask her about Tunde.

She smiles and nods. "His parents wanted him to be a pharmacist. He was always the smartest kid in class. He was always so curious, ever since he was a young kid. We grew up as Christians, but Tunde in high school decided he would be Buddhist. He would lock himself in the bathroom and hum for hours." She laughs out loud. "Tunde is the most honest person I know. He can never lie. His name is Akintunde, 'the warrior that has returned.' It is a good name for him, though in college his girlfriend called him Willie."

She takes out some greens, which she calls *ewedu* (jute leaves), and braises them with a liquid that has been boiled with stock fish and another Knorr cube. The stock fish is a salty dried fish and extremely pungent. It softens when boiled in water. The greens turn mucilaginous like okra; they're stringy, but in a pleasing way. Ronny checks to see that the meat is tender. She spoons the *ewedu* onto a plate, then adds the braised meat in the center of the greens. She serves this with a ball of *fufu* she miraculously whips up in a pot in a matter of seconds. We sit at the kitchen counter and eat together. I ask her what she thinks of Tunde's work, and then about race.

"Tunde is a mystery to us, but I know he is doing what's in his heart. He has a way of complicating things, but I respect him. For me, it is simple. I want my kids to know that being black is not a disadvantage. I don't want to pretend that the prejudices are not real. But I want to focus on the good. My kids will be African American, yes, but that is such a vague word. I want them to know that they are Nigerian American."

Her daughter is sitting on the couch watching cartoons on an iPad, ignoring us but listening, too. And quietly, in the background, she is absorbing the music of Fela as it fills the house with energy. Ronny and I sit and talk for a long time, and Ronny does not look at her phone when it rings. She tells me many stories of her life both in Nigeria and here in Houston. They are too many to recall. I am both enlivened and burdened by our conversation. It is refreshing to talk so openly about race, but uncomfortable, too. I don't think I've ever sat down with a white person in America and opened up a conversation about what it means to be white in America. But perhaps that is necessary, too. Maybe all the times we sit around talking about Lora's fried chicken or Tunde's *jollof* rice, we are also talking about race. Maybe that is what John T. Edge's lasting legacy will be—to get us to confront the history of race in America through the lens of food.

I will miss talking to Ronny, because I don't get to talk this openly with many people. Like passengers on an airplane, we each know that we will go our separate ways, and there is safety in that. I give her and her daughter a hug. As I turn to leave, Ronny asks me if I've been to Sabo Suya Spot yet.

No, I tell her. It was on my list, but I don't have time. I'm headed to the airport.

"You must go there. Ask for Adamu; his food is famous. His *jollof* rice is the best."

THERE IS ALREADY A LINE FORMING when I arrive at Sabo Suya Spot. The smell of spice and roasted peanuts fills the air. Adamu is in the kitchen, and a woman is taking orders at the register. I order three kinds of *suya*, or skewers: beef, lamb, and kidney. They come in Styrofoam clamshell boxes with raw onion and tomatoes. I order *jollof* rice with *ram*, which is the Nigerian vernacular for goat. I talk to Adamu for a short while, and he promises to explain everything to me later by phone.

His skewers are spicy; they get into your chest cavity with a gradual warming that stays with you for hours. The *jollof* rice is hard to put down. It seems as if each individual kernel of rice were cooked separately with tomato and spice. The kidneys are cut into thick chunks and have the aroma of bitter blood. The goat is bursting with the fruitiness that comes from a scotch bonnet pepper. My nasal passages flare up with each bite;

tiny beads of sweat form at my temples. After a few more bites, I realize I haven't been breathing. So I stop to inhale, and the cayenne goes right into my nose. I sneeze loudly. A group of men at a table next to mine laugh out loud. It happens to all of us, they say.

The skewer of beef is from an eye of round cut, thinly sliced. It is marinated in what Adamu calls peanut cake and a mix of curry, cayenne, ginger, clove, salt, and Maggi, which is a spice cube used in many Nigerian dishes that, from what I can tell, is mostly MSG. Adamu marinates his skewers for two hours before they go on the grill. His peanut cake, he says, is the real thing, not like the fake peanut butter many competitors use. He takes raw peanuts and grinds them to a paste; then he squeezes the oil from it, saving it for another use. The peanut paste is fried until crispy, and then pulverized to a granular powder. This is the base for all Adamu's marinades, and what gives the skewer a perfume redolent of peanuts and a taste that is mild and soothing.

Adamu has been making this paste all his life. His father owned a company that made oils, everything from peanut to sesame. His grandfather and uncles had been kings in the Bade Emirate of Northern Nigeria. That would make him a prince. The youngest of four children, he never left his mother's side. When she went into the kitchen to prepare dinner, he followed her, playing with seeds as she picked basketfuls of bitter greens for supper. He learned to cook from her.

"Then I grew to love it. Now I cook better than her."

Trained as an agricultural engineer, Adamu moved to Austin in 1997 to work in applied materials. A few years later, he got into a car business in Nigeria, thinking it would be an easy enterprise to run while he worked in America. Within a few years, though, he lost everything. He was depressed, and unsure of what to do next. He hated his job. He worked all the time and had no friends. America was harder than he had thought.

"Once you lose that stage of childhood where you free and happy, it is harder to make friends. I was in a stage in my life where I had no friends and no money."

His family encouraged him to do what he had always wanted to. He opened Sabo Suya Spot in 2010. Though business was slow at first, and selling skewers for $1.25 apiece was no way to get rich, he continued, working seven days a week and greeting customers on a first-name basis. Word got out about his food. Now there is a line every night. Adamu ships his food to a Nigerian soccer player who lives in London. His food goes to Toronto, to Dubai, he proudly exclaims. His dream is to open a place in New York, to bring Nigerian food to a wider audience.

I order more skewers to take back home with me. The drive to the airport is a foggy haze of watery eyes and swollen tongue. I check my skewers into my luggage. I run to the gate, only to find out my flight is delayed two hours. I settle into a vinyl seat and check my e-mail. My heartbeat slows. I see an e-mail from a Nigerian princess. Normally, I don't open these scam messages, but I can't help myself.

Dear Beloved,

I know this message will come to you as a surprise but permit me of my desire to know you as more than just a friend. I am Amadia Abacha, the daughter of Sani Abacha, the late Nigerian Head of State. I am presently in distress and in needing of your kindness. I am currently under house arrest while my family is undergoing trial in Lagos. The government has frozen all our family assets and auctioned all our properties.

To save our family from total ruin, I have managed to ship through an undercover courier, the sum of US $6,000,000. It is deposited into a secure account which I will disclose the name and contacts to you if I get a positive response.

I have sought you out because you are a man of deep understanding and compassion. I believe that with your positive response, we can move forward to a new life together with all the wealth needed for a happy life. Bear in mind that Love has no colour barrier, no educational back ground barrier, no religious, language, nationality or distance barrier, the only important Thing there is love. For it is in that enduring Love that we can build a new life and finally live in the beauty of new home that accepts the both of us. I am waiting for your e-mail my love.

SLEEP OVERCOMES ME like a warm blanket. When I arrive home, I open my bag to find the skewers missing and a note from the TSA saying they inspected my bag. My anger turns quickly to sadness. I had wanted my wife to taste those skewers. I had planned to give them to my cooks. My packed clothes smell of oil and peanuts and curry. In the familiar surroundings of my Louisville home, it is the only reminder that the food I ate back in Houston was real, not a dream.

It was through my friendship with Tunde that the world of Nigerian food was introduced to me. But it is remarkable how easily accessible it is. I realize that I'm only a few degrees separated from this rich culture that thrives in the southwest part of Houston. It is an easy cab ride there from downtown Houston. The people are friendly, and eager to explain the dishes to you. It is so close and yet it is also a very distant cuisine.

Still, I realize I will never fully learn the true complexity of Nigerian food. Just as I may never understand the motivations of someone such as Tunde. One of the more confusing though delicious things I ate in Houston was a meat pie, a carryover from British colonial times. It was delicious and could easily have come from a London bakery. I wonder how many layers of history the food of Nigeria contains. I've had to learn a lot about Nigeria to understand the food in a way that is different from just noting spices and cooking techniques. I read Nigerian poetry, listen to Nigerian spoken word, recite their names, and study their religions, their history, their music. I learn that Nigeria has hundreds of languages and dialects, many of them without a written alphabet. I learn about Fela.

Studying the food of Nigeria makes me connect to the foods in my backyard. It is true that you don't necessarily need to read the local poetry to enjoy a regional cuisine, but it does give you a greater understanding and respect for it—just as it does for the foods that surround me in Eastern Kentucky. When I think about Lora and her farm in Egypt, Kentucky, I think about Wendell Berry. I hear the music of Michael Cleveland and Bill Monroe. I think about the storytelling and the laughter that surround their dinner table. It is impossible to tell the story of Lora's food outside the context of her culture, and that is why I'm on this journey. It is because every insight I gain from learning about another culture brings me closer to the one I find myself in. This project, this entire process of discovery and adventure, is about trying to find my own America and where I belong in it. For someone like me, who traverses numerous cultures, the answer isn't always obvious. Sometimes that means I wander through the bluegrass hills of Eastern Kentucky. Other times, I have to travel somewhere as foreign to me as a Nigerian café in Houston. Both get me to the same place.

BEEF SKEWERS WITH CASHEWS, CURRY, AND BLACK PEPPER

Trying to re-create a dish you've had at a restaurant is always tricky, especially when it's a dish as fine-tuned as Adamu's skewers. I won't claim to have mastered the techniques that he has taken a lifetime to perfect, but I was so fascinated by his peanut powder that I worked on that one recipe for weeks to get it right. I ultimately liked the flavor of cashew powder best, making it with the technique I learned from Adamu. The cashew powder is key, so focus on making it as fine as you can. Once you get a taste for the spices in this recipe, you can be more adventurous and substitute lamb for the beef, for a gamier flavor.

If you have a charcoal grill, use it for these skewers, but roasting them in the oven works well, too. Use bamboo skewers that have been soaked in water for the best results.

½ cup unsalted raw cashews

1 pound boneless beef short ribs

1 tablespoon salt

1 tablespoon white pepper

1 tablespoon garlic powder

1 tablespoon onion powder

1½ teaspoons smoked hot paprika

Scant 1 teaspoon cayenne pepper

2 tablespoons vegetable oil, plus more for drizzling

GARNISH

Sliced onion

Lemon wedges

Preheat the oven to 400°F. Soak bamboo skewers in warm water for at least 20 minutes.

Pulse the cashews in a food processor until you get a fine, granular powder. Put the ground nuts on a small baking sheet (or in a pie pan) and toast in the oven for 3 to 5 minutes, until dry but not too toasted. Remove and pulse again in the food processor or chop to get the texture even finer. Return to the oven and toast for another 2 minutes. Repeat the process until you have a fine powder that is aromatic and dry to the touch; it should feel like coarse cornmeal. Set aside.

Cut the beef into thin strips and put in a large casserole or baking dish.

In a small bowl, mix the salt, white pepper, garlic powder, onion power, smoked paprika, and cayenne pepper. Wearing latex gloves, massage this spice mix into the beef. Let marinate at room temperature for 20 minutes.

Preheat the oven to 400°F or prepare a hot fire in a charcoal grill.

Mix the cashew powder with the vegetable oil in a small bowl to make a paste. Rub the paste on the meat and let it sit for 10 minutes.

Weave the meat onto the skewers by making an S-shape out of each strip of beef and then piercing the meat with a skewer; leave as much of the rub on the meat as possible.

If using the oven, place the skewers on a baking sheet and drizzle with a little vegetable oil. Bake for 10 minutes, turning once. They are done when the beef is cooked and the cashew rub is toasted and aromatic. If using a grill, oil the grate and grill the skewers, turning once, for 3 minutes on each side. Be careful not to overcook the meat as it will burn quickly.

Serve the skewers warm, with onion slices on top and lemon wedges alongside.

───────

SPICY TOMATO-BRAISED CHICKEN WITH TURMERIC AND CASHEW

Almost every Nigerian restaurant in Houston has a variation of this spicy tomato stew on its menu. Each version I ate was slightly different, yet the flavors were all familiar. Still, the dish was unlike anything I had ever tasted. It is spicy, so beware—if you want a less hot version, cut down on the habanero peppers. This dish gets even better if it sits overnight, so if you can, make it a day ahead and reheat it when you are ready to eat.

Serve the chicken over plain steamed rice. Or, if you're feeling adventurous, get a box of instant *fufu*, the Nigerian steamed bread made from cassava flour; it's easy to find online. Follow the instructions on the box. *Fufu* whips up in minutes and though the flavor is neutral, it has a texture that is perfect for sopping up the rich sauce.

SERVES 4 AS A MAIN COURSE

4 bone-in, skin-on chicken thighs

2 teaspoons salt

1 teaspoon freshly ground black pepper

¼ cup canola oil

1 cup sliced white onion

1 cup sliced celery

3 tablespoons tomato paste

2 garlic cloves, chopped

2 tablespoons ground ginger

¼ cup unsalted raw cashews, ground into powder (see preceding recipe)

2 teaspoons ground turmeric

1½ cups chicken stock

½ cup coconut milk

3 plum tomatoes, coarsely chopped

3 small habanero peppers (leave whole)

5 sprigs fresh thyme

Season the chicken thighs with the salt and black pepper.

Heat 2 tablespoons of the canola oil in a large Dutch oven over medium-high heat. Place the chicken thighs skin-side down in the pan and sear until browned, about 3 minutes on each side. Transfer the chicken to a plate.

Add the remaining 2 tablespoons oil to the pan, then add the onion and celery and cook for 2 minutes. Add the tomato paste, garlic, ginger, cashew powder, and turmeric and cook for 2 minutes, stirring constantly, until the spices give off an aromatic perfume.

Pour the chicken stock and coconut milk into the pan and stir well. Return the chicken thighs to the Dutch oven. Add the tomatoes, habanero peppers, and thyme, cover, and simmer over low heat for 30 minutes, or until the chicken is tender.

Pull out the chicken and keep it warm on a baking sheet covered with aluminum foil. Bring the cooking liquid to a boil over high heat and cook until thickened and reduced by almost half.

Arrange the chicken on four plates. Spoon the sauce over the chicken. Serve with rice or fufu.

CHAPTER 14

GERMAN MUSTARD

O N NEW YEAR'S DAY, MY WIFE ALWAYS COOKS UP A mess of cabbage and black-eyed peas for good luck. I make Korean rice cakes called *duk-bok-ki*. Same reason, different tradition. We always eat my mother-in-law's sauerkraut with some schnitzel because that's what I crave. We squabble about how much food to make. It's our tradition. In the evening, I head over to a local bar by myself. Every year, the bar hosts a Townes Van Zandt tribute. He died on New Year's Day. In remembrance of him, a bunch of musicians get together and perform his songs. One of my favorites is called "German Mustard." It's less of a song and more of a guitar meandering, with nonsense lyrics strewn about. I sit alone at a table in the back nursing a cold beer. It always chokes me up to think about someone dying on New Year's Day. It is the irony of dying at the beginning of a new year, when we are supposed to be hopeful. My grandmother also died on New Year's Day. I always take a few minutes to talk to her on this day, to tell her what I've been up to. The last line of the Townes song comes abruptly: "German Mustard 'tween your jeans . . ."

Why does German food get such a bad rap? I am bewildered that it has never received the same attention that Italian, French, Spanish, or even Scandinavian food enjoys in America. German is one of the great cuisines of Europe. During the 1800s, more than six million Germans immigrated to America, and brought with them many influences that remain ingrained in our cultural systems: kindergarten, Amish furniture, and Santa Claus. We owe our beer culture to German beer barons such as Pabst, Schlitz, and Miller, all of whom were from Milwaukee. German immigrants also brought pretzels, sausages, frankfurters, and hamburgers to America, not to mention a strong tradition of pickles, mustards, and thinly pounded and fried meat. These are all things I love.

When my wife and I travel, we are always on the lookout for German restaurants. We have found some good ones: Metzger's in Ann Arbor, Michigan; Hessen Haus in Des Moines, Illinois; Schnitzelbank in Jasper, Indiana; Laschet's Inn in Chicago; and Wurstküche in Los Angeles. Sadly, most of the German restaurants we try are caricatures of a cuisine now reduced to a menu of rubbery fried meat and store-bought sauerkraut served by surly waiters dressed in lederhosen. We have suffered many a meal knowing that the sauerbraten was not properly marinated, that the strudel dough was not hand-stretched. I've lived an entire life imagining what the pinnacle of German food could be, and I can tell you one thing: it is not to be found in a dusty beer hall decorated with fake antique beer steins and German flags. So much time has elapsed since the early German immigrants settled in American cities and towns that there remain only fading traces of their food's flavor in today's German restaurants. Cuisines such as Cambodian and Persian have a more recent connection to the homeland, and the food is less diluted by generations of assimilation.

Why hasn't a chef taken up the cause of reinvigorating German cuisine for the food-obsessed world we currently live in? This seems like the perfect time for a German food resurgence. Having asked chefs, critics, food writers, and enthusiasts, I have narrowed down the reasons to five common misperceptions about German food. Here they are, in no particular order:

REASON 1: Germans food is heavy, clunky, unsophisticated, and unappetizing.

I turn to my wife, Dianne, over coffee and ask her to come with me to Wisconsin. For what, she asks? German food. She gives me a weary look, the look of someone who has accompanied me on previous food trips. Though it may seem like a riotous good time, the reality of these trips is more about obsessive scheduling, painful overeating, and a lot of driving around looking for places that my GPS doesn't recognize. Then, during dinner, I may ignore her for long stretches while I catalog flavors and ingredients in my notebook. After dinner, I will disappear into the kitchen to talk to the chefs, and usually enjoy a shot of whiskey. Indigestion is common, and mornings are often filled with regret and empty promises not to eat so much.

I tell her this trip will be a lot of fun. Also, I want her opinions of the food. Her family is mostly from the Black Forest and Alsace. She can trace her lineage back to the Dürholtz clan. Yet, after seven generations, she no longer identifies as German. She does not speak German, nor does anyone in her family. They do not travel to Deutschland on vacations; they do not hold fast to any old-world rituals or traditions. But something in the food remains steadfast in their consciousness.

Every fall, Dianne's mother makes sauerkraut with cabbage that she grows in her backyard. And something in my wife's eyes lights up every winter when she bites into a fresh batch of her mom's sauerkraut. It's the best sauerkraut I've ever eaten. With everything else forgotten, Dianne still has the food to link her to her homeland. We celebrate Christmas with stollen (sweet bread), and roast lamb with asparagus and potato dumplings for Easter. "Like Oma used to make it," my wife jokingly says.

THE DRIVE TO WISCONSIN is warm and pleasant. Our four-year-old daughter is singing in her car seat. I have mapped out a dozen places for us to visit. Dianne likes to drive. She takes in the open highway like a bird coasting through a sun-dappled field of corn. I fell in love with Dianne on the day we met, more than fifteen years ago. She has the austere bones of a Teutonic statue, but underneath, she is the embodiment of a love so pure, it makes me cringe.

I am entertaining our daughter with a puppet show. She has my nose, small and bouncy. Having a kid is a challenge for us. We both work a lot; we both travel a lot. And neither of us wants off the hamster wheel. I promised Dianne a vacation in Paris—two years ago. Wisconsin isn't even close, but it's time together. And for a few days, our daughter gets both of us.

Our first stop is in Fitchburg, at a German store called Bavaria Sausage. An unadorned sign outside reads "Makers of Old World German Sausage." Inside, the shelves are packed floor to ceiling with German products: packaged goods from Germany, shelves of mustards, cheeses, frozen strudels, smoked fish, and a dizzying array of sausages and force-meats. Everything is clean, organized, and accurately labeled. My wife squeals with joy. Seeing a neatly labeled store makes her unreasonably happy. Meats are laid out in sections. Summer sausages and smoked meats are in a refrigerated display case right by the entrance. The prepackaged wursts are displayed in another area, behind a glass deli case. Next are the hams and specks. Working my way down the spotless glass case, I see a section of salamis that includes Hungarian salami, pepperoni, and something called gypsy salami. After that is a section of headcheeses and creamy forcemeats, including a veal loaf and *Fleischkäse*, then a thorough selection of fresh brats, wursts, and wieners. Jerkies and smoked livers finish out the display. Everything in this case is made in-house.

I start at one end of the deli case and sample a bite of everything I can. It is late morning, and the shop is starting to get busy. The girl behind the counter hurries me along so that she can get to the next cus-tomer. The clientele is a mix of locals and people who drive in from all over to stock up on their German provisions. I overhear a conversation in German among a group of older women. My wife is in the condiment section, stocking up on more German mustard than we can consume in a year. My daughter is munching on German gummy bears, or, as they call them, *Gummibärchen*.

All the sausages are good, but the *Landjäger* makes my taste buds sing. The small sticks of beef, pork, and lard are mixed with red wine and spices, then smoked and left to overferment so the sourness comes through prominently. *Landjäger* were traditionally eaten by hunters who would take these snacks with them on long trips because they don't require refrigeration. What I love the most about German food is the aggressive sour notes that come from intricate methods of fermentation, not from acid. The flavor is sour, tempered with umami. It is hard to describe it other than to say that it's the flavor of deliciousness. It makes my mouth water. I give Dianne a bite of my *Landjäger*. It is as though generations of dormant DNA just woke up. She hits me in the arm. That is her way of showing me she really likes it. Even our daughter says that these gummy bears are better than the usual ones we get.

This is the art of sausage making at its best. I dare anyone who thinks German food is clunky to taste an array of German cured meats and not detect the subtle differences in fat, sour notes, salt, and spices. The slight adjustments in proportions create wildly different textures and flavors. If the German food at some restaurants is clumsy, it is because of the cook, not the cuisine. The raw materials I find at Bavaria Sausage are nothing short of perfection, as fine-tuned as a professional race car. I leave the store content, with a warm pretzel, a smoked sausage, and a spoonful of mustard.

REASON 2: German food needs an ambassador to bridge the narrative to an American public.

We have an early reservation at Karl Ratzsch in Milwaukee, the second-oldest German restaurant in the city. It opened in 1904, but lately, the food has slipped, and by all accounts, the restaurant is surviving on an aging but loyal clientele who dine there mostly out of nostalgia. Like many old-world German restaurants, Karl Ratzsch was destined for closure. Recently, though, one of Milwaukee's most accomplished young chefs, Thomas Hauck, bought the place and revamped the menu to give the historic restaurant fresh new vigor. Chef Hauck grew up in Milwaukee, and had fond memories of the restaurant. It pained him to see it crumbling away into disgrace. He got rid of the lederhosen and created a menu that bridged the old and the new.

The restaurant is breathtaking, but in the way a museum or a historic home can be breathtaking. The dark oak wood is brooding and waxed to a bowling alley shine. The hard edges of the wood are softened by faded murals of lonely country landscapes painted over the mantels. An intricately carved grandfather clock dominates the center of the dining room like a scene from an E. T. A. Hoffmann fairy tale. My wife loves it. Her tastes range from earthy to church-like. Her ideal home interior would look like a well-made coffin.

The restaurant is empty except for a few tables in front and a birthday party for a man in his eighties. The waiters are dressed elegantly in gingham button-down shirts. The hostess is a mature woman who moves through the restaurant like a matron. She is not the owner, but has worked here a long time. She won't tell me exactly how long, but she assures me she has seen it all. She tells me she doesn't see many young people here anymore. They want things that are trendy, she proclaims with disgust. They have turned their backs on the traditional food of Germany.

The menu here is not traditional, at least not the part of it I order from. Chef Hauck is doing something remarkable: bridging the gap between the traditional and the new. We start with a warm pretzel, which may sound cliché, but it is the best pretzel I have ever had. A feathery-thin crust yields to the slightest touch to reveal a fine-bubbled yeast dough that smells like toasted hay and butterscotch. The pretzel is the size of my child's head. It is brushed with clarified butter and opaque crumbs of white salt. My fingertips glisten with so much salt and butter that I seriously ponder taking a bite of my own hand. The accompanying condiment is not sharp mustard but pickled brown mustard seeds suspended in a sour cream concoction. It seems heretical. It is surprising and delicious.

Next is the sauerkraut. It is like nothing I have ever had. A half-fermented sauerkraut, it is crunchy and fresh, light, and speckled with caraway seeds. It harmonizes seamlessly with the pork schnitzel. The sauerkraut contains gentle juniper and flowery notes that inexplicably make the pork taste light. It is a brilliant redefining of what sauerkraut can be. I order a second helping.

This is the German food I have been looking for: smart, respectful, and innovative without being silly. The bite-size portions of Herbed Lard and Pork Crackling on Pumpernickel are elegant and ethereal while at the same time proudly beating a German drum of flavor. I feel giddy. It is as though I am discovering a new cuisine that the world hasn't seen yet. Chef Hauck has a sauerkraut fritter stuffed with bacon and *Landjäger* on the menu. The kohlrabi and horseradish salad is sharp, precise, and witty. It liberates horseradish from its prison of raw oysters and Bloody Marys. A glass of crisp, daffodil-perfumed Riesling makes the dinner perfect. I look around at the empty restaurant. Where are all the Milwaukee diners who are missing out on this treasure?

The specialty of the house is Knistern Schweinefleisch Schaft, a monstrous pork shank slow-cooked and served with the skin crackling. It is a behemoth plate of food, and we barely make a dent in it. It is the one dish they cannot take off the menu because it is what all the regulars order. It could feed five of them. It is my least favorite dish of the night.

THREE WEEKS after our wonderful meal, and less than a year after Chef Thomas Hauck renovated the menu, I find out that Karl Ratzsch has closed for good after more than 110 years of business. I reach out to Chef Hauck to talk to him about it. "I guess people weren't into change," he tells me. He isn't in the mood to talk much. I get it. Any restaurant closing is sad, but this one is especially tragic. Many things go through my mind about what could have saved Karl Ratzsch. Maybe the food needed to be in a more contemporary setting. Maybe such an innovative German cuisine needed a new décor. Maybe it needed a PR machine behind it. Maybe it needed a big personality. Maybe it needed lederhosen.

I have heard more than once that German food needs an ambassador. At one of my favorite German restaurants, there is a sign at the entrance that reads, "Unattended children will be sold." It is a joke, but not really. Germans are known for many excellent qualities, but being warm and fuzzy is not high on the list. And that kind of humor does not translate well to a wide American audience. I have heard people say that German food needs a Julia Child to reinvent its cold reputation and bring it to the masses. Hauck is a smart, brilliant chef. He is a gentle man, soft-spoken and humble. In a world driven by big media personalities, can a chef like Hauck break through and trumpet a new era of German cuisine?

Does the merit of a cuisine carry only as far as the personality shouting behind it? I wonder where our love for French food would be without a charismatic ambassador like Julia Child. But I also know that we should credit a generation of French restaurants that transformed the traditional cuisine into something that Americans could understand and adore, from the pristine plates of Le Bernardin to the comfort of neighborhood bistros like Le Zoo, L'Acajou, and Café Noir. I think Chef Hauck proved that you don't need to stray too far from the core definitions of German food to create a fresh version of that cuisine, too.

"Germans are not braggadocios," my wife explains to me. She says it in a way that implies that I am. Everything she says implies something. "We are hardworking and honest. Bragging about it is considered beneath us." I shrug and watch a YouTube video of myself on my smartphone.

THE OUTSIDE of Kegel's Inn, on the outskirts of Milwaukee, is painted with a mural of an angry cherub holding a staff in one hand and a beer stein in the other. It is Friday afternoon during Lent, and the noise is reaching a level I have not heard before in a restaurant. Everyone comes here for the fish fry on Fridays. Everyone here seems to know one another. Somewhere an accordion is playing, but I can't see the musician. This restaurant has been here since 1924 and looks like your typical German beer hall. Dark wood, heavy murals by Peter Gries depicting pastoral hunting scenes, and leaded glass combine to make me feel like I am at church—though church was never this raucous. The food is good but nothing to shout about. The lake perch is simply breaded and fried. It comes with coleslaw, tartar sauce, and fresh lemon wedges. A potato pancake and applesauce are served on the side. Still, the feeling in here is good. There is something familial and comforting that has been built up over generations.

The German word *Gemütlichkeit* means friendliness, good cheer, warmth, and a sense of hospitality. It is what you feel at beer halls; it is a sense of community. There is no word in English that quite captures its meaning. It is said to be something uniquely German, but it is also something we can all relate to. If you've ever been in a bar drinking with a roomful of strangers and yet feeling oddly connected to everyone in the room, that is *Gemütlichkeit*.

The service is prompt and accommodating. The food is fine. The walls are austere. No one here has gone out of his way to be nice to us, but I don't want to leave. I want to bask in something I rarely feel in a restaurant: the sense that every one of us is contributing to this feeling of *Gemütlichkeit*. We are participants, not passive observers who expect the restaurant to bring the joy to us. Here, it is us who bring the energy to the restaurant. No longer can I blame the restaurant for a bad experience. It is up to me to have a good time. This is oddly refreshing, liberating.

German food will someday make a comeback in the United States. I believe that one glorious day, it will not be so hard to find a well-made schnitzel and sauerbraten with spaetzle. The person who finally accomplishes the feat won't have to be a celebrity, won't even have to be German, but he or she must embrace the concept of *Gemütlichkeit*. I would drive many, many miles for a place like that.

REASON 3: German food never recovered from the negative attitudes caused by two world wars.

I am walking around the Milwaukee County Historical Society building. Upstairs is an archive of books. Steve is the caretaker of these books. He doesn't get many visitors. I ask him about German food, and he sits down to talk with me. Steve is a meek and scholarly middle-aged man wearing a nondescript blue shirt with two identical pens in the chest pocket. As I look over his shoulder, I see the city of Milwaukee, built by generations of German immigrants who made this rugged, cold land into a thriving city. Steve brings out old books, and we read through them, looking for passages on what the life of German immigrants was like a century ago. Most of these books crack open like petrified fossils being handled for the first time in ages.

I remember the hostess at Karl Ratzsch telling me how its menu evolved during World War I to reflect anti-German sentiments. It was changed to read more like an Austrian restaurant. Hungarian goulash made an appearance. Sauerkraut was called "Liberty Cabbage." In later years, even chicken Parmesan landed on the menu. I mention this to Steve, and he confirms that he has heard these same stories.

"The immigrants didn't necessarily hide their German identity but they didn't flaunt it, either," Steve explains to me. "To be German was difficult in those days."

In 1914, when America's official stance on World War I was neutral, many Germans living in Milwaukee held rallies for the German victims of the war. In March 1916, a weeklong charity bazaar in Milwaukee drew more than 150,000 people to help with war relief for the people of the Fatherland. But in 1917, when America entered the war, anti-German sentiment flared up and quickly turned into a witch hunt for anyone considered a treasonous German. Bach and Beethoven were no longer played in the music halls. The Deutscher Club became the Wisconsin Club. There was a campaign to erase all German references in Milwaukee, which at that time had been known as the German Athens of America, or the center of German culture in the States. Many families fled west, to the countryside, to escape the hysteria. What resulted was a stifling of the thriving German culture in Milwaukee.

With the rise of Hitler and the Second World War, the attitudes of many Americans toward all things German were cemented even more in negativity. Yet by then, many of the German immigrants had assimilated and come to identify as fully American. Disassociating oneself from anything too "German" became a prevailing inclination for generations to come.

ONE OF THE COOLEST PLACES to drink in Milwaukee is Bryant's Cocktail Lounge, a throwback bar that serves up innovative cocktails in a space that makes you feel like you're on a 1970s movie set. If this place were in Manhattan, I'd be surrounded by rude rich people, but here, I'm surrounded by average people just out having a drink. I start a debate with some locals about the best places to eat in Milwaukee. They tell me about a Vietnamese place, a tapas bar, any place by the Bartolotta group. No one mentions any German restaurants, so I ask why not.

"No one wants to eat that stuff anymore," a tipsy woman in her late twenties yells in my left ear. "The only people who eat there are old people and tourists like you."

I ask her to tell me the one definitive food from Wisconsin that everyone can agree on. She doesn't hesitate in her response: brats.

"But isn't that German?"

She shrugs and goes back to her foamy cocktail.

It is getting late. My wife is asleep with our daughter in our quaint hotel room. I don't want her to be angry with me in the morning, so I leave the bar with my whiskey cocktail half full. Outside the bar, there is a BMW parked on the curb. As Americans, we don't have a problem driving German cars or buying German knives or watching German films. But German food has been shunned. I wonder if there was a moment in history that was lost, when the cuisine had a chance to evolve but was quelled at the very moment it could have flourished. Choosing our food is so much more emotional than buying a car or a set of knives. But history is emotion, too. It is memory, and memories are not something that can be reasoned with. They are alive, and they incite fear and anger and hatred, but they can also be tools for reconciliation and joy. As I watch America go through a new cycle of fear and hate, it pains me to see that the lessons of the past have done little to prevent the prejudices of the present. American life has always been defined by the tensions between the old and the new immigrants. Maybe acceptance is a naïve thing to believe in, but isn't it possible that overcoming food prejudices can lead to wider tolerance?

REASON 4: We've already appropriated the best of German food and we call it American food.

We drive to Madison the next day to meet up with Tory Miller, who is the head chef of L'Etoile. Tory is Korean by birth. He was adopted as a child by German American parents, and grew up in Racine, Wisconsin. He has recently opened a Korean-inspired restaurant, and I am curious to see what's on the menu. The place is packed. Bowls of bibimbap, rice bowls topped with marinated vegetables, and ramen are flying out of the kitchen. I sit at the counter and eat spicy rice cakes, noodles, and dumplings. After two days of nonstop German food, this spicy fare feels nice in my belly. Tory sits next to me, and we catch up.

Tory wears his hair in a mini Mohawk, designer glasses, and a sleeve tattoo on his left arm. "Since I look Asian, people think I can cook all this food like it's in my blood," he says, "but I didn't grow up eating this food." He speaks fast and passionately. He is watching all the cooks on the line while we chat. "The Asians come here and judge me all the time," he continues. "They tell me it's not authentic. But that's not what I am doing. I am doing my version of Korean food."

I ask him what he grew up eating. Was it traditional German food?

"I grew up eating brats and kraut and all that stuff, but we never called it German food. We just called it food."

When we eat a hot dog, or drink a beer, or crack into a loaf of multigrain bread, do we think about Germany? German immigrants were one of the first groups to come to the United States, and their contribution to food has been so deeply absorbed that, for the most part, we consider it just American food. Is that the ultimate goal of assimilation? Disappearance? Does the fact that German food has so deeply infiltrated our food identity mean that it succeeded in its goal to assimilate, or in that process, did it fail to carve out its own cultural and historical identity? I wonder if, in a hundred years, Americans will eat bibimbap without knowing where it came from. Isn't that already happening to foods such as tacos and pizza? Or can we go back and recalibrate these beloved foods every time a new wave of immigrants comes to America?

I ask Tory what German or Korean food is once we import it into a place such as Madison. It's about the people, he tells me, and the people now are looking for more diverse flavors.

The food I'm eating has all the flavors of the Korean pantry but tastes nothing like what my grandmother made for me—and that is okay. To believe that there is just one version of Korean food is ridiculous. Tory brings a distinct identity to this vision of Korean food. There is Wisconsin cheddar in his *duk-bok-ki*. There is smoked brisket in his fried rice. This food makes me smile. It would piss my grandmother off, but you can't quell food evolution. In many ways, German food was absorbed into standard American fare or stifled before it had a chance to evolve organically in America. For me, though, that is not the end of the story. German food is not at a dead end in America. It's just dormant.

REASON 5: There are no new German immigrants bringing a renewed cuisine to America.

Immigrants bring their foods and traditions. They create and re-create an unending food narrative here in America. But Germany is not Cambodia or Syria; it is not a country in peril. There are no new waves of German immigrants coming to America. The Germans who do immigrate here are educated. They are more likely to choose professions that are lucrative. They are not coming here to set up humble eateries.

Does that mean that our only link to a country's food comes from the poorest immigrants? A restaurant is often the cheapest business an immigrant can set up, one that requires no official degree or institutional schooling. But what does that say about our relationship to food? Does our education in global food depend on global tragedies?

Many of the immigrants I've met came to America because they were escaping war, famine, and persecution. In exchange for safety and work and a new chance at life, they rewarded us with myriad cuisines that we would otherwise never have had access to. Nigerian food, Uyghir food, Burmese food—the list goes on and on. While I'm glad they're here, a prevailing tragedy hangs over their existence. Do we need global tragedies to continue our exploration into world cuisines? Is that a sustainable system? I wonder if there is some other way we can honor and learn the cuisines of faraway nations without the tragic circumstances that bring them to our shores. If there is a way to create a true evolution in German food or any other country's cuisine, we will have to do it without waiting for another victim of war to bring the knowledge here to America.

ON THE LAST NIGHT OF OUR TRIP, Dianne and I venture out to Dorf Haus, a supper club just outside Sauk City, Wisconsin. The name comes from a religious congregation founded by German immigrants in 1852 here in the middle of prairie farmland and small, isolated towns. The menu is burgers, steaks, and seafood. There are a few German specialties sprinkled throughout. Dorf Haus features live oompah music on the weekends. The place is full at 5:30 p.m. The hostess tells me it will be an hour wait for a table. I look at my restless daughter doing pirouettes at the bar and know we can't wait that long. I place an order to go: schnitzels and sauerbraten, pancakes and sauerkraut. My wife is chatting up a couple at the bar. They look furtively at me.

The hostess hands me a small Styrofoam box and tells me to fill it up at the salad bar. I look over at the communal salad station and politely tell her no, thank you.

"But it comes with the dinner. It's free," she explains to me slowly.

"I know, but I'm okay."

"Well, I can't discount your dinner."

"I wouldn't want you to. I'm fine."

"Just take it. You might want it later."

"Really, I'm okay."

She looks at me in frustration. It doesn't make sense to her. My order comes out in plastic bags, and we take it to our car. I explain the interaction to my wife. She tells me it makes sense. They don't want to owe anything to anyone. Also, Germans never refuse anything that is free.

"Well, that's just ridiculous," I tell her. Dianne is looking through the bags of food. She pulls out a small Styrofoam box filled with iceberg lettuce, cabbage, and sliced raw carrots.

The hostess gave me the salad anyway. "Germans are stubborn, too!" My wife giggles. This is the same fight we have all the time. We are both stubborn as rocks.

The sun is setting over barren farmland. Our daughter falls asleep in the car. From everything I've read, residents here are struggling, and many of the young people have left for the promise of a better life in big cities. These are good folk, salt of the earth, as they say. They came because of war and persecution. They have cultivated this land. They have cared for it and nurtured it. Now, after more than a century here, they want a better life. Who wouldn't? They are honest, too honest. The hostess's guilt couldn't allow her to overcharge me for meal that included a salad worth barely a dime.

I look at our sleeping daughter dreaming about cows jumping over the moon. I see a Korean girl, but she is half-German, too. She is the union of my wife and me. She is America. I want her to know as much about German food as she already does about Korean food.

My wife is feeding me chunks of schnitzel as I drive. It's bland, so I ask her to put some of the German mustard on it. Nothing beats the sharp German mustards that come in toothpaste tubes. She does. I take a bite. The mustard has twang. It lights up my nose.

"You're not supposed to put this mustard on schnitzel," Dianne scolds me. But she admits that it is good. I remark that it is very un-German of her to stray from the rules.

"And that's why we're meant for each other." She leans into me.

Parenting is hard. Dianne and I have been fighting a lot recently. For no good reason, just because life is what it is. She tells me we should do these road trips more often.

"We will, and we'll cook together more, too," I tell her, which implies that I'll spend more time at home. It grows dark outside, and we hold hands as we drive along the empty highway back to our hotel.

HASENPFEFFER

Hasenpfeffer is a famous German dish of wild hare and juniper berries. It epitomizes the German technique of long sour brining that both flavors and helps tenderize meat. The recipe is simple, but it takes some time to make, so plan ahead. Ideally, the rabbit should marinate for 2 days, but if you are pressed for time, 24 hours will do. The word *Hase* refers to a wild hare, not a farm-raised rabbit, so if you have a friend who hunts and can supply you with one, this will taste even better. If not, a good farm-raised rabbit will work just fine.

MARINADE

2 cups red wine, preferably
   pinot noir, plus more if
   needed

1½ cups apple cider vinegar

1 cup water

¼ cup gin

1½ tablespoons salt

1 tablespoon juniper berries

1 tablespoon whole black
   peppercorns

3 bay leaves

2 teaspoons allspice berries

2 garlic cloves

1 small bunch thyme

1 whole rabbit
   (about 2½ pounds), cut into
   6 pieces: back and front
   legs, legs separated, and
   rib section, split in half
   (ask the butcher to do this
   for you)

BRAISE

¼ cup chopped bacon

2 cups coarsely chopped
   onions

1½ cups halved button
   mushrooms

1 cup chopped peeled turnips

1 cup chopped cabbage

1 to 2 cups chicken stock

½ cup sour cream

Salt and freshly ground
   black pepper

1 tablespoon chopped fresh
   dill

Rice or egg noodles,
   for serving

TO MAKE THE MARINADE: In a large saucepan, combine the red wine, vinegar, water, gin, salt, juniper berries, peppercorns, bay leaves, allspice berries, garlic, and thyme, bring to a boil, and boil for 3 minutes. Transfer the marinade to a large nonreactive container that will hold the rabbit snugly and refrigerate until completely cool.

Put the rabbit pieces in the marinade. Make sure the rabbit is completely submerged in the liquid; if necessary, add a little more red wine. Marinate in the refrigerator for 48 hours, turning it a few times. (If you are in a rush, just marinate it overnight.)

When ready to cook, remove the rabbit from the marinade and pat it dry with paper towels. Strain the marinade and reserve the liquid; discard the solids.

TO MAKE THE BRAISE: In a medium pot, cook the bacon over medium heat until it renders its fat and gets slightly crisped, about 5 minutes. Using a slotted spoon, transfer the bacon to a plate.

Add the onions, mushrooms, and turnips to the fat remaining in the pot and cook for 3 minutes, or until beginning to soften. Add the cabbage and cook for another minute. Add the rabbit, return the bacon to the pot, and cook for 3 to 5 minutes, until the rabbit is lightly browned.

Pour in the reserved marinade and 1 cup of the chicken stock. The rabbit and vegetables should be completely submerged in liquid. If not, add up to another 1 cup chicken stock. Reduce the heat to low, cover the pot, and cook for about 1 hour, checking the rabbit occasionally, until the meat is just falling off the bone.

Transfer the rabbit and vegetables to a serving platter and cover loosely to keep warm. Raise the heat to high and cook the braising liquid until it has reduced by half and thickened slightly.

Measure out 2 cups of the braising liquid and transfer it to a bowl. Whisk in the sour cream. Season with salt and pepper.

Pour the sauce over the rabbit and vegetables. Garnish with the dill. Serve with rice or egg noodles.

ROAST BUTTERNUT SQUASH SCHNITZEL WITH SQUASH KRAUT IN A MUSTARD CREAM SAUCE

Schnitzel is such a simple idea: meat pounded thin, breaded, and fried. It can be made with pork or chicken—or even beef, as they do in Texas in the form of the chicken-fried steak. Here is an unusual vegetarian version. I treat the butternut squash as one would a prized meat. The schnitzel is eaten with a kraut made out of the butternut squash, too. It takes 5 days to make the kraut, but it gives the dish a beautiful punch, so plan ahead.

1 butternut squash

2 tablespoons unsalted butter

Salt and freshly ground black
  pepper

MUSTARD CREAM SAUCE

¼ cup white wine

2 tablespoons chopped shallots

Pinch of salt

¼ cup chicken stock

¼ cup heavy cream

1 tablespoon spicy German
  mustard

½ teaspoon grated fresh
  horseradish

Pinch of freshly ground
  black pepper

½ tablespoon cold unsalted
  butter

1 cup all-purpose flour

2 large eggs

2 tablespoons milk

2 tablespoons water

1 cup bread crumbs

Vegetable oil, for panfrying

Butternut Squash Kraut
  (recipe follows)

Preheat the oven to 325°F.

Cut off the neck of the butternut squash. Trim and discard the stem. Reserve the bulb for the Butternut Squash Kraut (recipe follows).

Put the squash neck on a square of aluminum foil. Add the butter and sprinkle with ½ teaspoon salt. Wrap it tightly in the foil. Bake for about 45 minutes—the squash should yield when you press it but hold its shape, not collapse. Remove from the oven, unwrap, and let cool.

Cut the squash into ¾-inch-thick rounds. Remove the skin. Press down on each round with your palm to flatten it. Re-form each piece into a round. Put on a plate and refrigerate for 15 minutes.

MEANWHILE, TO MAKE THE MUSTARD CREAM SAUCE: In a small saucepan, bring the wine to a boil. Add the shallots and salt, reduce the heat, and simmer for 4 minutes, or until most of the liquid has evaporated. Add the stock and cream and simmer until reduced to about ½ cup, about 5 minutes. Add the mustard, horseradish, and pepper and simmer for another 2 minutes to allow the flavors to blend. Add the butter to the pan and swirl it around to melt. Set aside.

Put the flour in a shallow bowl. In another shallow bowl, beat the eggs with the milk and water. Put the bread crumbs in a third bowl.

Remove the squash from the refrigerator. Dredge each piece in flour, dip in the egg wash, letting the excess drip off, coat with bread crumbs, and place on a plate. You may need to reshape them again after coating in bread crumbs so they are flat and even.

Heat about 3 tablespoons vegetable oil in a large skillet over medium heat until hot. Working in batches, fry the breaded squash, turning once, until golden brown on both sides, about 2 minutes per side. Drain on paper towels and season with salt and pepper.

Arrange the schnitzel on serving plates. Serve with the butternut kraut and drizzle the mustard cream sauce over the top.

BUTTERNUT SQUASH KRAUT | Butternut squash makes a nutty, crunchy kraut that is both vibrant and earthy. MAKES 2 CUPS

1 butternut squash bulb (reserved from the Roast Butternut Squash Schnitzel recipe, page 267)	1 tablespoon sea salt
	1 teaspoon caraway seeds
¼ cup thinly sliced onion	1 garlic clove, grated (use a Microplane)
	⅛ teaspoon ground allspice

Halve the squash lengthwise and remove and discard the seeds and membranes. Peel the squash. Grate it into fine shreds on a box grater.

In a medium bowl, combine the squash with the onion, sea salt, caraway seeds, garlic, and allspice. Mix with your hands, squeezing and kneading the mixture, for about 8 minutes.

Place the squash, with all its juices, into a glass jar that holds it snugly. If needed, add ½ cup water so that the kraut is fully submerged in liquid. Cover the top with several layers of cheesecloth and secure it with a rubber band. Let stand at room temperature for 48 hours.

Transfer the kraut to the refrigerator and let stand for 3 days more. The kraut is now ready to eat, but you can refrigerate it for up to a month; replace the cheesecloth with a tight-fitting lid.

CHAPTER 15

THE PALACE
OF
PASTRAMI

WOULD YOU BELIEVE ME IF I TOLD YOU THE BEST Jewish deli in America is in Indianapolis, that somewhere between Katz's Deli in New York City's Lower East Side and the chandeliered cafeteria of Langer's Deli in Los Angeles is a palace of pastrami that has been upholding a tradition of kosher cured meats for more than a hundred years? I, too, was incredulous when I first heard about Shapiro's Delicatessen. When I think about the pillars of Jewish culture, Indiana doesn't immediately come to mind. And what does it really mean to be the best, anyway? I can't claim I've done a formal side-by-side taste test of the matzo ball soup at Shapiro's against the versions at Canter's or Barney Greengrass. Truth be told, I don't know if anyone does herring better than Russ and Daughters. And the kreplach at Zingerman's can't be beat. But what if I told you there was a kosher deli in the middle of the Hoosier State that arose out of a cultural utopia of diversity and stayed true to its family roots over the next four generations, untouched by rampant tourism and gentrification, untarnished by the culinary whims of the passing decades? Well, that's Shapiro's.

Shapiro's Delicatessen is split into two sections. One is for take-out meats, and the other is a cavernous cafeteria-style deli that can seat up to three hundred people. The line gets long, so the best time to go is around 11:30 a.m., just before the lunch crowd descends. You begin your dining experience by grabbing a plastic tray and silverware at the start of the buffet line. You pick up your dessert and salad first, from a refrigerated display case. This is confusing if you're new to Shapiro's, but after a few trips, you realize the ingenuity of it. Think how much more fun ordering would be if every restaurant asked you to order dessert first. Imagine contemplating a strawberry cheesecake or banana pudding before considering the appetizers. All the desserts are served on unbreakable plastic plates, each one individually wrapped in a layer of protective plastic wrap, as if your grandmother were behind the line packaging it herself.

As you move down the line, you look up to see a menu board of sandwiches. One of the more peculiar inventions of the modern deli world is the naming of sandwiches after famous people. How am I supposed to know what comes in a "Woody Allen," and do I really want to think about *him* as I'm diving into a corned beef on rye with creamy coleslaw? At Shapiro's, the menu is pragmatic: the items are simple and clearly labeled. A corned beef sandwich is called just that. In fact, the menu board reads like that from any other pedestrian deli, but once you smell the pastrami for your sandwich as it's being sliced before your eyes, you understand you are someplace special.

While you wait for your sandwich meat to be sliced, you can choose from a steam table of sides. There's everything from German potato salad to noodles with sour cream to latkes (potato pancakes). I've learned to get two desserts: if the line is long, I can chow down on a plate of cinnamon rugelach while patiently waiting for my sandwich to be assembled. At the end of the line, you get a cup for your fountain drink and then pay at the register. It's quick, cheap, and easy.

Brian Shapiro is the fourth generation of the Shapiro family to run the restaurant. His office is behind the take-out section. It includes large windows so he can peek out and see the activity in the deli. His wife, Sally, runs the website and media side of the business. Despite having a few offshoot locations, this Southside cafeteria, the original, is their flagship. One afternoon, I find Sally behind the counter using a large camera to take a photo of a corned beef sandwich on a white cutting board. She has a small frame, and her camera is as big as her torso. The sandwich stands tall and proud on a plain Shapiro's plate. There is no hand-stitched linen napkin carefully made to look randomly placed under the plate; nor is a vintage fork effortlessly balanced on the plate's rim, as though someone were about to dive into lunch but realized she'd forgotten to pour herself a glass of rosé.

I immediately disturb Sally's concentration. "Can you tell me the history of Shapiro's again?" I ask her. One can find this story on the deli's menu and website, but I like hearing it from Sally. She has a jovial way of recounting the familiar milestones while sprinkling in small anecdotes that you won't find in the brochures.

SHAPIRO'S KOSHER-STYLE FOODS DELICATESSEN has been open since 1905. Its founders, Louis and Rebecca Shapiro, fled Odessa to avoid the anti-Jewish pogroms that swept through Russia. When he first arrived, Louis worked in the scrap metal business, then a mostly Jewish industry and booming because of an innovation in steel processing that made it practical to work with used steel. You didn't need much to get started—just a wagon and the willingness to work long hours.

But Louis hated it. Back in Odessa, he had sold food and flowers at a market, so he started to sell provisions from a pushcart: coffee and tea at first, then flour and sugar. He expanded into meats and produce. Louis and Rebecca stored everything he sold in a little apartment they had at 808 Meridian Street. One day, the floor caved in under the weight of their inventory. They then decided to buy the store below them and turn it into a grocery and bakery. Business was good. Even during the Great Depression, the grocery continued to profit. After Prohibition ended, Louis Shapiro began to sell beer at ten cents a bottle. Customers would have a few beers and ask if there was anything to eat. They'd complain, "You sell bread and you sell meat. Why don't you just make me a sandwich?" So he did. Rebecca started to sell the dishes she made, mostly soups and potato salads. Soon, they added a few tables and chairs. The neighborhood was transforming from a mostly residential one to an industrial one. The grocery business was declining, but the restaurant business was buzzing, so the family focused on growing the cafeteria.

Louis retired in 1940, citing old age and back problems. He left the store to his sons, Abe, Izzy, and Max. Max has been integral to Shapiro's growth over the last twenty years. While Izzy was officially the boss and Abe spent most of his time in the kitchen, supervising the recipes, Max manned the front of the house. He worked there past the age of eighty, and even today, many longtime customers still remember him. "You would never go more than a minute without Max filling your water or asking how the food was" is how one customer remembers him.

Before officially retiring, Max convinced Mort Shapiro, his cousin, and Mort's son Brian to join him in running the business. That was in 1984. Max died in October of that same year, knowing that Shapiro's was in good hands. When Mort Shapiro died, in 1999, his son Brian became the sole proprietor and the fourth generation of Shapiros to run the business.

"YOU SEE ALL THESE PICTURES?" Brian points to the vintage photos that hang on the walls. "They aren't just for show. My DNA is in these photos. I still remember my great-uncle Max. I am the last of the generation who actually saw how hard he worked."

Brian has a full head of curly gray hair. He is in his sixties, and his face shows the decades of exhaustion that come from running a restaurant this big. He agrees to sit with me as I eat lunch and interview him. He asks me what newspaper I write for. I tell him it's for a book, and he seems irritated. He is on the phone with his veterinarian. One of his dogs is sick, and he's worried about his medicine. While he's on hold with the doctor, he looks down at my tray of food.

"You gonna eat all that?" he whispers toward me incredulously.

I like to eat a lot at Shapiro's. My lunch spans two plastic trays: matzo ball soup, a Reuben sandwich, a chopped liver sandwich, a smoked tongue sandwich, cabbage rolls, deviled eggs, boiled greens, and banana pudding.

I take a few bites of each plate while Brian finishes his call. The chopped liver sandwich looks gray and emotionless, but it is the perfect temperature of chilled but not too cold. The tiny speckles of fat are unctuous, and the liver tastes fresh and luxurious. I don't need teeth to enjoy this sandwich; it literally melts in my mouth. The smoked tongue is the opposite: it is toothsome and briny, the smoke just a whisper, and the texture of the fatty tongue, sliced thin and layered two inches high, is pure decadence. The cabbage rolls are sweet, and their texture is as tender as a child's tears. And the pastrami is some of the best I've ever had. Dare I say, at the risk of getting hate mail for the rest of my life, better than Katz's?

I ask Brian what makes the food taste so good.

"We make everything from scratch. We do it the old way, everything cut by hand. We make so much chicken stock every day; it goes into everything—and schmaltz, a lot of it," he adds, referring to the rendered chicken fat used for frying or spreading on bread.

He stands up to adjust a framed photo on the wall. It is of Mort.

"The older generations, they had the immigrant touch. They did things with their hands. They weren't afraid to work hard. I feel a duty to them."

"How has it lasted so long?" I inquire.

"Are you a chef? You own a restaurant?" He is onto me.

"Yes," I tell him.

"All the chefs these days are artists, and that's fine, but then you have a restaurant linked to an individual, not a tradition. There will never be a restaurant that lasts one hundred years anymore. Chefs change their food depending on the trends. We don't."

"So there is no chef here?"

"We don't call them chefs. It is family recipes that are made by everyone. It speaks to the culture of a group, not an individual. If we persist in making food that is an individual expression, our restaurants will only last as long as the artist's whim or the public's attention span. This . . ." He gestures to the room. "This can go on forever." Brian gets up to fix a flickering light in the dessert case.

I GREW UP EATING PASTRAMI and corned beef from Katz's, pierogis from the Second Avenue Deli, and potato knishes from the Yonah Schimmel Knish Bakery. I always knew I was eating Jewish food. Maybe it was because I went to the old places that were not shy about displaying the Star of David on their menus. Maybe it was that the people who served the food sprinkled it with a Yiddish New York City accent and a side order of admonition and guilt. "Do you even know how long it takes to make this pastrami salmon?" I remember being scolded at Russ and Daughters once, when I ordered my lunch in a hurried fashion.

Nowadays, pastrami sandwiches and Reubens and bagels can be found anywhere; they are no longer the exclusive property of Jews. They have evolved into that gray category of food that is both lauded for being part of a long-standing tradition yet consumed daily without much thought about its cultural identity. It is both Jewish and not Jewish at the same time.

"Does it bother you when this food gets taken over by stores that sell it as American sandwiches, not Jewish food?" I ask Brian.

"No, that's just reality. And what's Jewish food, anyway? We prefer to say it's kosher. The food we serve is from eastern Europe; it has its roots in German food. Stuffed cabbage is Hungarian. Israeli food is more grain based, and it comes from Sephardic Jews. It's still Jewish food, but totally different."

"You don't think your business will suffer when it's no longer perceived as authentic Jewish?"

"Whenever Arby's starts running commercials about their Reuben sandwiches, our sales go up. Tell me who is out there still using real brisket with the deckles attached. Mine is better. For as long as I am here, it will remain that way."

Brian shakes my hand and tells me he has to hurry off. I press him one last time for a reaction.

"Don't you want to preserve some of the Jewish proprietorship of this food before it gets completely swept away?"

"It already has. Only the strict Jews care if it is kosher or not. Everyone else just comes in here wanting a good sandwich. But it's always been that way. You're looking for a nostalgia that just doesn't exist. The Southside has always been home to a lot of people, not just Jews. And they've been coming here for generations."

On my way out, I order two pounds of pastrami to go. It will not last long in my fridge. I don't have the heart to tell Brian I'm going to layer it with kimchi and gravy for a poutine.

I NOSE MY CAR SLOWLY through what is left of Southside, or Babe Denny, as it's now called. Shapiro's is the anchor of a Southside neighborhood that was home to African Americans, Italians, and Jewish immigrants. It was once a neighborhood of small businesses and merchants who coexisted in a thriving community that is still remembered today, a community that, unfortunately, does not exist anymore. What is left are a few factories, vacant lots, and crumbling one-family houses. Most of the homes on the north side of the interstate are empty. The absentee owners are holding out for a developer to buy the properties. There is talk of turning this neighborhood into the next booming corridor of Indianapolis, with the familiar mix of condos, retail shops, and food halls. Looming high above these crumbling homes is Lucas Oil Stadium, where the Indianapolis Colts play to a packed crowd on Sundays in the fall.

For generations, this neighborhood was a melting pot of displaced Appalachians looking for factory work, African Americans fleeing the

South, and Jews, Italians, Irish, and Greeks from Europe. Indianapolis was centrally located and offered many opportunities for immigrants who found New York City too crowded. During the Great Migration, more than two million African Americans moved away from the Jim Crow South to the industrialized North. Between the boll weevil infestation and the Great Mississippi Flood of 1927, the northern cities offered hope and the promise of a new life. Indianapolis, a northern city, was a resting point before heading to Chicago. Many decided to stay. At a time in America when racial tensions were boiling over, the Southside enjoyed relative peace. Jews and African Americans alike remember it as a golden era of cooperation and mutual respect.

I drive past a small home where an older African American man is raising an American flag on his front porch. Through the doorway, I can see a sparse living room with fraying upholstery and a few framed pictures on the wall. The man's aging hip forces him to lean awkwardly to one side as he lifts the flag. I park my car and speak to him. His name is Perrie Morris.

"This used to be a great neighborhood," he tells me proudly. "Everyone had fruit trees and mulberry trees out here. Where you see that empty lot was all houses, friends and relatives of mine. We all lived here. Kids be playing out on the streets. The Jews and Italians and blacks—we all lived together, and it was a nice place to live."

"Why did you all get along so well?"

"We gave each other's kids jobs. We did trade with one another. There was no real need to be nasty. If we did well, we all did well together."

"And then what happened?"

"That all changed when they built the highway. That hill over there, I used to roll down them hills when I was a kid. "He points to an embankment that leads to an overpass where cars are speeding by on I-70. The interstate highway was built in the early 1970s, abruptly splitting this blossoming neighborhood in half. People who owned homes in the path of the highway were paid off through a process of eminent domain. Many took the money and moved north. Renters were evicted. Children were suddenly cut off from their schools. Residents were separated from their churches. Streets were widened. It became difficult to walk from place to place. The neighborhood now is just a series of on-ramps to I-70. There are only a few streets where you can cross under the highway by foot, via unlit concrete underpasses that shake violently from the vibration of the cars overhead. The silt and runoff flow down and flood the street with dirt. The earth sloping down the embankment is overgrown with wild grass, thistle, and honeysuckle.

There is little evidence that a utopian society once existed here. The highway dominates the landscape. A few old factories remain, along with a small, empty playground and an old Baptist church. And then there is Shapiro's, standing proudly at the corner of Meridian and McCarty Streets. It still draws big crowds every day. I always meet someone new at Shapiro's, and usually they have a story to tell about the Southside.

Leo is an older Jewish man whom I had lunch with on a recent visit. I asked him why he thought this neighborhood was so integrated and peaceful at a time when the rest of the country was going through deep racial discord.

"Everyone owned small businesses," he told me. "At Passo's, you could sit down and get a fountain soda and sit next to a black man without anyone making a row. There were fruit markets everywhere, shoe repair stores, watch repair shops, hat shops, flower stalls. We all traded and bartered with each other. We needed each other to survive."

"Why can't we re-create another Southside today?"

"It's so different now. Back then, you could see how people made their money. You lived and worked side by side with them. Today, I walk around downtown and I see hordes of people in offices just typing away on their computers. What the hell do they do all day long? I don't get it."

Part of me laughs at his quaint misunderstanding of the modern economy. The other part of me grieves with him. In ten years, this neighborhood will be fancy hotels and high-rise condos. For now, though, it still holds the ghosts of the old neighborhood. I can find people who regale me with stories of the old Southside, and I'm determined to find every last one of them as they walk through the glass doors of Shapiro's.

Shapiro's exists not simply because it serves good food, but also because it reminds us of who we were and who we still can be. It gives us a reason to talk to the person sitting next to us. You don't have to be Jewish to appreciate the food, and you don't have to be from Indianapolis to understand the importance of the Southside. Like an ancient civilization that was abruptly ended too soon, Indianapolis's Southside is a place that should be remembered and studied because it can teach us about how to live with one another with humility, grace, and respect.

THE BROWNSTOWN SPEEDWAY is a quarter-mile oval dirt racetrack tucked into Jackson County, in between a lake and a series of small farms. Every Saturday night in the summer, people come from all over Indiana to race late models, modifieds, superstocks, pure stocks, and Hornets. The speedway is more than sixty years old, and it looks it. The wooden bleachers bow in the middle, and the wire fence that separates the cars from the crowd does not look like it could hold back a hungry dog, let alone a speeding car weighing 2,200 pounds.

It's a week before the Indianapolis 500, the most celebrated car race in the world. Everyone is in the city for the buildup to the event. I'm at Shapiro's getting a pastrami sandwich to enjoy later at Brownstown. The food at Brownstown amounts to a concession stand offering the usual fare of hot dogs, burgers, fries, and chicken fingers, none of it remarkable. The truck selling T-shirts is upholstered in Confederate flags and hot rod stickers. People bring coolers full of beer and Mountain Dew. I bring a sandwich from Shapiro's.

Brownstown Speedway is a family-friendly environment, and I've taken my daughter there a few times to watch the speeding cars. The sound is deafening as the cars accelerate out of their turns. Dirt track racing isn't for everyone. You either love it or you don't. My four-year-old daughter loves it. I press the palms of my hands over her ears to muffle the noise. Her head pivots back and forth as she follows the colorful cars racing up and down the track. She throws her fists in the air when the checkered flag comes out waving. It's exhilarating.

I'm aware of the fact that I'm almost always the only person of color here, but it has never kept me away. I have never felt race was an obstacle. I've generally never felt unwelcome. I've always been comfortable in situations unfamiliar to me. Indeed, I thrive in them. I've met some really nice folks here at Brownstown, and they've always gone out of their way to make sure I feel welcome without ever making too big a deal of my ethnicity. But I've always wondered what it would take for a dark-skinned person to walk into a place like this and not feel completely awkward at first.

AS I'M WAITING ON LINE at Shapiro's, I notice a tall African American man wearing a car racing jacket. He is getting the same thing as I am, and we strike up a conversation as we wait for our pastrami sandwiches. I tell him I'm on my way to Brownstown Speedway tonight. He knows the place well, he tells me. But he doesn't go very often. He lives here in Indianapolis and promotes African American racing as a side gig.

"I always thought racing was a white man's sport," I say to him, surprised at my gumption.

He laughs and nods, as if to acknowledge both the truth and the ignorance of what I've just said. "Sanctioned racing, yes. But go out on Saturday nights on the Southside and you'll see brothers drag-racing all kinds of souped-up cars and bikes."

He asks me if I've ever heard of Charlie Wiggins. I tell him no.

"Charlie Wiggins was the best mechanic in all of Indianapolis at one time," he says. "He built machines so fast, drivers from the Indy 500 wanted him on their teams. But he was never allowed because he was black."

I'm scribbling notes on my pad so I can research Wiggins later.

"They started the Gold and Glory Sweepstakes because of him. It was the first African American motor race in America. Charlie won it three times." He slows down his words to allow me to absorb them. "Before there was Jackie Robinson, there was Charlie Wiggins. And he had his shop right here in the Southside."

We get our sandwiches and head to the cashier. I follow him to his table as he continues his tale.

CHARLIE WIGGINS was born in 1897 in Evansville, Indiana, the son of a coal miner. He worked at a shoe shine stand outside a car repair shop. After the death of his mother, he got a job as an apprentice at the repair shop. Wiggins was a protégé in every sense of the word, and he quickly rose to become chief mechanic, which made him the first African American mechanic in Evansville. Word spread about his technical skills, and in 1922, he and his wife, Roberta, moved to Indianapolis, the mecca for auto mechanics. They opened up their own garage in the Southside, and Wiggins was soon acknowledged by racing aficionados as the best mechanic in the city. In his spare time, Wiggins assembled parts from auto junkyards to develop his own car, known as "the Wiggins Special." He tried to enter his car into the Indy 500 but was blocked by the American Automobile Association because of his race. Wiggins then began to assemble a group of African American drivers to start his own racing group. It caught the attention of William Rucker, a wealthy African American businessman who happened to live in Indianapolis. Rucker started the Gold and Glory Sweepstakes, an annual one-hundred-mile race for African American drivers on a one-mile oval dirt track at the Indiana State Fairgrounds.

There were fifty-nine cars entered in the Gold and Glory in 1925, and only twenty would qualify for the main event. Charlie's car, the Wiggins

Special, was one. Built completely by hand by Wiggins himself, it was the only car in the race to benefit from Wiggins's discovery: a way to make a fuel-efficient engine that ran on a combination of motor oil and airplane fuel. Wiggins painted the number twenty-three on the side of his vehicle, next to a painted image of Felix the Cat. The other drivers quickly nicknamed his car "the Black Cat."

His car performed beautifully in the race. While other drivers needed pit stops to refuel, Charlie's engine went the distance without stopping once. Charlie won by more than two full laps. That night, there was a grand party for him at Trinity Hall. Wiggins was the pride of Southside. There were posters all over the neighborhood with his picture on them. Over the next decade, he would win the race two more times. Then, in 1936, he was involved in a thirteen-car wreck and lost one of his legs. Aside from being a personal tragedy, it was devastating to the Gold and Glory Sweepstakes, which folded soon after.

Charlie Wiggins built his own prosthetic leg out of wood and continued to build and repair cars, but he would never race again. He became a champion of African American race-car drivers long before Willy T. Ribbs became the first official African American driver to compete in the Indy 500, in 1991. Charlie Wiggins died in Indianapolis in 1979 at the age of eighty-two.

"THEY GONNA TRY and bring back the Gold and Glory Sweepstakes, just one time, to celebrate the history," my lunch companion tells me. "Right here in Indy."

If they do, I'll be there.

I jump in my car and tear down the highway to get to Brownstown. I cross the Muscatatuck River and turn onto the back roads to take a shortcut. I get there just in time to meet some of the racers before the qualifiers. I'm excited to talk to Justin Shaw, one of the most talented young drivers in the sport. He drives the number-two car, a late-model

Chevrolet with a 604 crate engine that boasts 400 horsepower. On a quarter-mile track, he can hit top speeds of eighty miles per hour. When these cars hit the turn at those speeds on a dirt track, they pretty much slide out through the entire turn.

"It looks like we're drifting, but we are really in control and steering the car back to straight," Justin tells me.

Justin works by day and races on the weekends. Most of the racers here do the same. Justin is the grandson of the legendary mechanic and driver C. J. Rayburn, who is credited with inventing the modern dirt race-car chassis. Justin grew up in a mechanic shop in Whiteland, Indiana, immersed in and surrounded by racing cars. Even star stock-car racer Tony Stewart came around the house when Justin was a kid.

There was never a question of *if* Justin was going to race, only a matter of *when*. He started racing at sixteen. He has a winning record, and there are some high expectations, but he takes it all in stride. He is poised and quietly confident. He shows me the detail work that goes into making a car like this. It is a work of beauty. His car is painted black with pink trim because his daughter likes those colors.

Justin politely tells me he has to go. The races are about to start. I scamper back to the bleachers and find a seat next to group of men from Kentucky. Bobby is a racing enthusiast, and he's got the racing gear and the cooler full of beer to prove it. He offers me a Miller Lite. The green light goes off, and the cars roar down the dirt track. Bobby tells me to watch how the tires spin out. He shows me how the outside car tries to sneak up on the lead car. There are no rearview mirrors on the cars, and the drivers can't turn their heads too much, so they can see only as far back as their right shoulder.

The engines seem to be moaning in anger. The vibrations go right down my spine. I sit back and unzip my backpack. The qualifying races are short and thrilling. I take out my pastrami sandwich. My Dr. Brown's Black Cherry soda is still cold. I offer Bobby half my pastrami sandwich in exchange for another beer. He gladly accepts the barter.

"Damn, that's a good sandwich," he yells to me through the engine roars.

"It's from Shapiro's, in Indy," I yell back.

"I heard 'bout that place. Never been, though."

"They been making pastrami for four generations. It's a family business."

"Family's everything, man."

We spend the rest of the evening occasionally yelling at each other about food and cars. It is dark by the time the races are over. Everyone is packing up their empty beer cans and heading to the parking lot. My eardrums are ringing, and there is a powdery layer of silt attached to my cheeks. Below each floodlight is a hive of bugs in frenzied flight. June bugs are making lazy patterns through the crowd. The katydids are singing loudly, happy not to compete with the scream of engines. Justin qualified, but he didn't win the final race. He was gracious in defeat, though. He has to be; he is racing royalty here.

"He'll get another chance," Bobby tells me before he heads off. "Boy's got racing in his blood."

BEEF TONGUE PASTRAMI

Don't be alarmed by the thought of eating tongue. It is a delicacy that has been eaten by many cultures throughout history. It is a decadent piece of meat that is easy to cook and meltingly tender. To start, you need to find a good butcher who can source whole fresh, not frozen, beef tongue. After that, the tongue needs an entire week to brine. This is a large cut of meat, so I offer you two different recipes to make with it—a simple sandwich and a composed first course. You can also slice the tongue thin and make tongue tacos (which are popular in Mexico) or cube some tongue and add it to a stir-fry. Once the tongue is brined and cooked, it can be frozen for up to a month.

MAKES ABOUT 3½ POUNDS SLICED BEEF TONGUE

BRINE

1½ pounds (2¼ cups) kosher salt

¾ pound (1½ cups) brown sugar

1½ tablespoons whole black peppercorns

1 tablespoon red pepper flakes

5 garlic cloves

2 bay leaves

1 teaspoon juniper berries

1 gallon water

1 whole beef tongue (4 to 5 pounds)

BRAISE

8 cups chicken stock

1 cup white wine

½ cup chopped onion

2 celery stalks, coarsely chopped

1 carrot, coarsely chopped

2 garlic cloves

2 bay leaves

SPICE RUB

2 tablespoons ground coriander

2 tablespoons freshly ground black pepper

1 tablespoon smoked hot paprika

TO MAKE THE BRINE: In a large pot, combine the salt, brown sugar, peppercorns, red pepper flakes, garlic, bay leaves, juniper berries, and water. Bring to a boil, stirring to dissolve the salt and sugar. Let cool, then refrigerate until cold, about 3 hours.

Pour the brine into a nonreactive container large enough to hold the tongue and submerge the tongue in the brine. You will need a plate or other weight to keep the tongue submerged. Refrigerate for 5 days; check on the tongue every day to make sure there is no mold growing on the top of the liquid. There is no need to turn it.

TO BRAISE THE TONGUE: Preheat the oven to 300°F.

Remove the tongue from the brine and rinse it under cold water, removing any peppercorns or other remaining seasoning; discard the brine. Put the tongue in a roasting pan and add the chicken stock, white wine, onion, celery, carrot, garlic, and bay leaves. Cover with aluminum foil and braise in the oven for 3 hours, or until the tongue is tender and easily pierced with a fork. Let cool in the braising liquid for 1 hour at room temperature.

MEANWHILE, TO MAKE THE SPICE RUB: In a small bowl, combine the coriander, black pepper, and smoked paprika.

The skin of the tongue must be peeled before serving. It is best to do this while the tongue is still warm. Remove it from the braising liquid and transfer it to a cutting board. Peel off and discard the tough outer layer of skin. Trim any remaining fat or gristle off the base of the tongue. Return the tongue to the braising liquid and let cool completely in the fridge.

Remove the tongue from the braising liquid and transfer to a platter. Keep the braising liquid for another use (it makes a great base for a hearty soup). Pat dry with paper towels. Rub the spice rub all over the tongue, coating it thoroughly.

Wrap in plastic wrap and transfer to the fridge. Keep it like this for at least 1 day. The pastrami is now ready to use. It can be sliced thin or thick. The pastrami will keep in the refrigerator for at least a week.

BEEF TONGUE SANDWICH ON EVERYTHING-SPICE SALLY LUNN BREAD

Sally Lunn is an easy-to-make brioche-like bread that was originally from England but became popular throughout the American South in colonial times. Light and yeasty, it makes perfect sandwich bread. Traditionally it is baked in loaf pans, but for this recipe, I form the dough into baguette-shaped rolls that can be stuffed with the beef tongue, then sliced into bite-size portions for a delicious appetizer. The "everything spice"—a traditional topping for New York City bagels—is an homage to Jewish delis everywhere.

SERVES 6

BREAD

¾ teaspoon active dry yeast

¼ cup warm water
    (about 112°F)

½ cup whole milk

4 tablespoons unsalted butter,
    melted and cooled to tepid

2 large eggs

3 cups all-purpose flour,
    plus more for dusting

2 tablespoons sugar

1 tablespoon kosher salt

EVERYTHING SPICE

1½ teaspoons sesame seeds

1½ teaspoons poppy seeds

1½ teaspoons fennel seeds

¾ teaspoon dried onion flakes

¾ teaspoon dried garlic flakes

½ teaspoon kosher salt

2 tablespoons finely chopped
    scallions

3 tablespoons prepared
    horseradish

1 cup mayonnaise, preferably
    Duke's

1½ pounds Beef Tongue
    Pastrami (page 286),
    thinly sliced

TO MAKE THE DOUGH: In a small bowl, combine the yeast and warm water and let stand for 10 minutes, or until foamy.

Add the milk and melted butter to the yeast mixture, stirring to combine. Whisk in the eggs until thoroughly combined.

Sift the flour into a large bowl, then stir in the sugar and salt. Add the yeast mixture and stir until a wet dough forms. Transfer the dough to a clean, oiled bowl, cover with plastic wrap, and let rise in a warm spot for 1 hour, until doubled.

Transfer the dough to a lightly floured work surface. Cut the dough in half and transfer to a baking sheet dusted with flour. Shape each piece into a baguette-shaped loaf, about 2 inches wide by 7 inches long, leaving space between the loaves. Let the dough rise again in a warm spot for 45 minutes. It will almost double in size.

TO MAKE THE EVERYTHING SPICE: While the dough rises, in a small bowl, combine the sesame seeds, poppy seeds, fennel seeds, onion flakes, garlic flakes, and salt. Set aside.

Position a rack in the center of the oven and preheat the oven to 325°F.

Brush the tops of the risen loaves with a little water, then sprinkle the everything spice evenly over the tops of the loaves.

Bake the loaves for 15 to 18 minutes, until lightly browned with a crusty outer layer. Increase the oven temperature to 375°F and bake for another 4 to 5 minutes, until the crust is golden. Remove the bread from the oven and let cool for about 15 minutes.

In a small bowl, combine the scallions, horseradish, and mayonnaise, mixing with a fork.

Slice open the warm loaves and slather the horseradish mayonnaise on both cut sides. Stuff the loaves with the beef tongue and close the sandwiches. Cut crosswise into 1-inch-wide slices and serve immediately.

BEEF TONGUE ON JOHNNYCAKES
WITH THOUSAND ISLAND DRESSING

Unlike the tongue sandwiches on page 288, for this more elegant
first course, it is important not to slice the tongue too thin; about
½ inch thick is ideal. The slices of tongue are seared on both sides in
a hot pan until caramelized on the outside but still very tender on the
inside. Johnnycake is a variation of cornbread, somewhere between
a flatbread and a pancake, that is popular in the American South. The
tangy Thousand Island dressing pairs beautifully with the rich meat.
Use any extra dressing for potato salads and chicken salads and as a
fun dip for French fries, too.

SERVES 6 AS A FIRST COURSE

DRESSING

1 cup mayonnaise, preferably
 Duke's

1 tablespoon ketchup

1 tablespoon gochujang
 (Korean chile paste)

1 tablespoon grated onion

1 tablespoon chopped fresh
 flat-leaf parsley

1 tablespoon minced dill
 pickle, plus 1 tablespoon
 pickle juice from the jar

1 tablespoon fresh lemon juice

1 tablespoon sugar

1 teaspoon grated fresh
 horseradish

1 teaspoon Worcestershire
 sauce

½ teaspoon cayenne pepper

Salt and freshly ground black
 pepper

JOHNNYCAKES

1¼ cups cornmeal

¼ cup all-purpose flour

1½ tablespoons ground
 caraway

½ teaspoon baking powder

¼ teaspoon baking soda

½ teaspoon salt

1¼ cups buttermilk

1 large egg

2 tablespoons unsalted butter,
 melted and cooled to tepid

Vegetable oil, for cooking

12 ounces Beef Tongue
 Pastrami (page 286),
 cut into ½-inch-thick
 slices

Chopped fresh parsley or
 chives, for garnish

TO MAKE THE DRESSING: In a medium bowl, combine the mayonnaise,
ketchup, gochujang, onion, parsley, pickle and pickle juice, lemon juice,
sugar, horseradish, Worcestershire sauce, cayenne pepper, and a pinch

each of salt and black pepper. Whisk until well blended, then cover and refrigerate until ready to use.

TO MAKE THE JOHNNYCAKES: In a medium bowl, combine the cornmeal, flour, caraway, baking powder, baking soda, and salt and whisk together with a fork.

In another medium bowl, combine the buttermilk, egg, and melted butter and whisk until smooth. Add to the dry ingredients and whisk together until a batter forms.

Heat a large skillet over medium heat and add about 1 tablespoon oil to the pan. Spoon about 2 tablespoons of the batter into the skillet for each johnnycake, leaving space between them. Cook as many as can fit in your skillet at one time. Cook for 3 minutes, until golden and crisp on the bottom. Flip and cook on the other side for 1 minute, until browned. Transfer to a paper towel–lined ovenproof plate and keep warm in a 180°F oven while you make the rest of the johnnycakes. If you have extra cakes, let them cool to room temperature and freeze them for a later date.

Heat a large sauté pan over medium heat and add about 1 tablespoon oil to it. Add the tongue slices and sear on both sides for 2 minutes, or until caramelized and warm in the middle.

Place a johnnycake on each plate and arrange a slice of tongue on top. Spoon a little dressing over the tongue. Garnish with chopped parsley and eat right away.

CHAPTER 16

A TALE OF TWO CORNBREADS

I N WEST LOUISVILLE, THERE IS A SOUL FOOD RESTAURANT called Hosanna's Kitchen, run by Janice. Hosanna's is a small, white, one-story house that does not look at all like a restaurant. Until recently, there was no sign. Janice recounts the story to me one afternoon while I'm eating her fried chicken. The sign was a gift from a bus driver whose route stopped in front of her restaurant. He had been driving this same route for years and never knew that the little white house was a restaurant. One afternoon, a passenger got on the bus with a bagful of food, and the bus driver asked him where all those good aromas were coming from. When the passenger pointed to the white house, the bus driver parked the bus and took a look inside. Janice sent him back to work with pork chops and spaghetti. He was so thankful that he asked his wife, who worked at a sign company, to make up a sign for the building. He put the sign up on a day when the restaurant was closed, to surprise Janice. I ask Janice how a bus driver wouldn't know about her restaurant after all these years.

"Well," she says, "I guess 'cause he's white."

Hosanna's Kitchen serves some of the best soul food in Louisville. Actually, Hosanna's Kitchen serves some of the best food in Louisville, period. Yet it is a restaurant that very few people who live outside the West Louisville community have been to. I hate that some restaurants are categorized by race or class. The prices at Hosanna's are below ten dollars for every item on the menu, so that makes it an affordable restaurant. But there is nothing in the plates of food Janice serves that is cheap or poor. Her food is thick with gravy, rich with love, and bountiful with flavor. A meal here can show you that a wealth of flavors can come from the humblest of restaurants.

I ask Janice who "Hosanna" is. She tells me she has no idea. The name just sounded good when she opened the restaurant. Janice is the kind of person who "dances by her own rules," as she likes to say. She likes whom she likes, and she refuses to serve anyone she doesn't. She didn't like me at first. She thought I was suspicious. I asked too many questions. It was only after I visited with a mutual friend who was able to vouch for me that she warmed up to me. That was years ago. Nowadays, Janice always has time to come out from the kitchen to talk with me.

Inside her restaurant are two tables, an old TV in one corner, and a Magic Marker board with messages from people who've stopped by over the years. Next to the order window is a wall covered in business cards— everything from taxi companies to DJ services to tax help. Hosanna's is more than a restaurant; it is where a community connects, whether to watch TV or talk politics or catch up with the neighborhood gossip. Over the course of a lazy lunch, I see people come in and ask how this person is doing, if that person's mamma is still in the hospital. Who needs Facebook when you have Hosanna's?

Janice has lived in Louisville her entire life. She started cooking as a child, helping her mother make dinner. Her father was a career waiter and her mother a domestic, so the world of food was always at the periphery. When I ask her how she learned to cook, she says she can't recall. It was just something she picked up along the way, she tells me. Her mother and older sister were, in fact, better cooks. After her mother passed away, Janice found out from a relative that, as a young woman, her mother had dreamed of owning her own restaurant.

At twenty-four, Janice started selling food out of her home: fried chicken, fried fish, pork neck and sauerkraut, and sides of sweet potato, collards, and creamed peas. People liked her cooking, and business was good. Then, one day, someone tipped off the Health Department, and they shut her down. She's pretty sure she knows who it was, but she doesn't want to stir up trouble. She isn't angry. She grins slightly, like a woman who has seen a lot in her life. Now sixty-seven, she runs her business with her daughter, Antoinette, who is in her late twenties. She is large and feisty and proudly wears blond curls on her head.

Janice is not flashy. She keeps her hair short, like a man's. She wears the same navy blue T-shirt every time I see her. She never uses an apron. She lets me into her kitchen when she's not busy. Everything is cooked in the four dented pots and two large skillets hanging above her stove. She talks in poetic lyrics, never full sentences. Sometimes, I jot down the things she says and make poems out of them. I once asked her to define what soul food is. She had this reply, which I transcribe here word for word, though the line breaks are mine:

Always greens, always mac'n'cheese
Always bunch o' fried things
Beans and starches
The fat you not supposed to have
Grease, a lot
More heavy on the salt
And you ain't gonna find as much sugar
But in the cornbread and tea
And Kool-Aid is a flavor

Janice was born in 1950. She grew up on Walnut Street, in downtown Louisville, which was more integrated back then. She remembers growing up with white kids in her neighborhood, though everyone was poor. When Martin Luther King Jr. was murdered, a lot of people burned their local businesses. The city tore down the buildings under a policy of urban renewal but also created a system of urban segregation. Everything was different after that, she tells me. Janice worked for General Electric and then as a private nurse. She watched the civil rights movement play out on the sidewalks in front of her home. Today, she lives less than a mile away from the street she grew up on. She has fond memories of that neighborhood and of her neighbors, both black and white.

I wonder out loud if that is where she learned to cook with sauerkraut, which is not typically an ingredient you see in a soul food restaurant. She tells me all the black folks ate sauerkraut when she was a kid. Pork neck and sauerkraut was a pretty common dish at the dinner table. She makes it occasionally at the restaurant. It's not on the menu when I visit, but I know that if I ask her for it, she'll tell me to come in next week and it'll be ready. It is one of my favorite things to eat. Rich, unctuous pork falling off neck bones and swimming in a briny liquid with strands of softened sauerkraut that disintegrate in my mouth. There are chilly autumn nights when I fall asleep dreaming about it.

Her restaurant is closed on the day I show up with a bag of neck bones and sauerkraut so Janice can show me how she makes it. She is surprised by my request. All I do is boil it, she keeps telling me. Her kitchen is small and cluttered. She doesn't even have a steam table. She heats everything to order.

"I don't deal with people getting all fussy with the food. I don't like people pointing at shit and telling me what to scoop up. You feel me?"

I tell her I do. It's more work this way, and she has little room to cook, but she prefers it. The food tastes better. She cares little if her customers have to wait.

"Sometimes they curse me out, and then they always ease back in here 'cause they like my food."

I like Janice. I like the way she deals with people. Her manner is not always nice but it's always honest.

She tells me to hurry up with the neck bones. She hasn't got all day. I unwrap the bag with the pork neck pieces, and she instructs me to rinse them under cold water.

She starts with a pot of boiling water, then adds the neck bones and waits until the water comes to a boil again. She lets it boil for about ten minutes. She then changes it out, adding fresh water. She adds salt and lemon pepper, measuring it out with the palm of her hand. She adds a little garlic powder, quite a lot of onion powder, and a few bay leaves. When the water comes to a boil again, she places a lid over the pot and turns the heat to low. That's it, she says. She'll add the sauerkraut in about thirty minutes and then let it all go until the meat breaks off when you stick a fork in it.

I'm surprised at how simple the recipe is. I'm not sure what I was expecting. It just seems almost too easy for a dish that comes out so meltingly tender and flavorful. I ask her again if that is really all there is to it.

"That's it. No magic here. Just food."

We sit down at a table and talk while waiting for the pork to braise. Janice used to be married, but they divorced after they had Antoinette. She is still friends with her ex, but she didn't like being married. She has always felt more comfortable being alone than sharing a house with a companion.

"God made me a square peg and then put me in a round world."

It is a profoundly sad thing to say out loud, but Janice rattles it off as if she were telling me the weather. I ask her if she has friends. Her customers, she tells me. I ask her what she does on her days off. When she's not working, she doesn't cook. She likes to eat chicken wings and stromboli. She does her own thing, she says, but won't tell me what that is. Being here four days a week, she is surrounded by customers who all want a piece of her, so she likes to be alone on her days off.

"Most people like me because I am blunt. They come here, and there's comfort in knowing the truth. I got no reason to lie to you. I got a lot of people talking to me more than my own child does. When the week's done, I'm tired of people."

There's so much overlap in the things she says and the things I feel. I know my life and Janice's are so different in so many ways, but there is something universal in running a restaurant.

"I get tired of people, too," I tell her. "Sometimes a carrot is all the company I need." This makes her laugh.

We commiserate over stories of bad customers, a topic that restaurant people never tire of. Then we talk about the neighborhood and about how life in West Louisville has changed. On the television, the news is on; a crime reporter is talking about a shooting not far from here. I ask Janice if things are better or worse now than when she was a kid.

"Economically we are doing better; spiritually we are worse." She turns the channel to a game show.

When the pork smells done, we look inside the pot. Janice takes a fork and pierces the meat. It is good, she tells me. She makes me a plate and tells me to sit down. She's not eating.

She tells me I have to eat it with cornbread. She makes a quick batter and spoons it onto a skillet. She calls it cornbread, but it is more of a corn pancake. It is light and fluffy, but with a gritty texture that tells you this is homemade food. It comes out hot and steaming. She tops it with a little pat of butter, and it immediately melts into a pool of gold that seeps into the corn cake. This is the way she likes it. It's fast, and she can make it all day long without getting tired.

I have had cornbread a thousand different ways. Soul food restaurants usually serve it on the sweet side. Some people, such as Ronni Lundy, will strangle you if you put sugar in your cornbread. Chain restaurants serve corn muffins and call them cornbread. High-end restaurants use stone-ground meal from places such as Anson Mills. Community restaurants use the cheapest cornmeal they can find on sale at the grocery store. There is a natural assumption that the cheap stuff is bad, but I have been to the Kroger in the West End and watched as bags of dirt-cheap cornmeal flew off the shelves. Cheap or not, when it's sold this fast, it's fresh. The supermarket brand may not be from heirloom corn, but the lingering smell of sweetness tells me it has not been long since the corn was milled.

Janice's cornbread is a reflection of her. It is efficient, tasty, and in a generous enough portion to take up the entire plastic plate. The taste is sweet but not too much. It is salty, and smells of cheap butter and a little pork fat. It's not flashy. It doesn't seem like anything special while I'm eating it, but the next day, I can't stop thinking about it.

I devour my food in seconds. The corn pancake is perfect for sopping up the liquid on the plate. Janice has disappeared for a long time. When she reappears, she tells me she's gotta go. Her demeanor has changed. It's her day off, and I've taken up enough of her time, she tells me.

"Okay, Janice. I'll see you next week, then." I give her a hug that she doesn't return.

She tells me to stop hanging out with old people. She gives me advice about how to raise my daughter. I help her lock up and then watch her walk briskly down the street to wherever she's going. I watch her all the way to the corner to see if she'll turn around to look at me. She doesn't.

EXACTLY EIGHT AND A HALF MILES east of Hosanna's, Shirley Mae runs her namesake café and bar in Smoketown. This Louisville neighborhood was named for the old factories that used to make bricks. The factories were so busy that the smokestacks filled the sky with a permanent thick, dark smoke. The neighborhood has gone through its ups and downs over the years, but recently the city has shown a renewed interest in making it safer and more livable.

When she's not in the kitchen, Shirley Mae can be found sitting in the small vestibule of her restaurant, smoking Marlboros and drinking Coke. She wears a hairnet over her silver hair. She has a strength in her hands, the kind that comes only from a lifetime of picking and counting. When she lights a cigarette, her fingers tremble ever so slightly. Everybody greets her as they walk in to get their food.

Shirley Mae is older than Janice by half a generation. She grew up an only child on a farm in College Grove, Tennessee, and a lot of the farmwork rested on her. She carried in wood for the stove. She fed the hogs and chickens. She picked the greens from the fields. The most lucrative crop they grew was tobacco. Shirley Mae would follow along after her father in the field, picking the small tobacco leaves he missed. They would lay the leaves out in a barn to dry. Every two weeks, they would take them to the tobacco house in the city to sell them. It was good money, she recalls.

I never go to Shirley Mae's unless I know I've got a lot time. She makes her hot water cornbread to order, and it can take twenty minutes sometimes. She boils water in a small pot. In a bowl, she spoons out cornmeal with a little bit of sugar. She slowly drizzles the hot water into the cornmeal and works the wet meal with her hands until she gets a dough that feels right. Then she breaks it into small nuggets and fries each one in a cast-iron skillet with a deep pool of hot oil. She watches each piece of cornbread carefully, and flips them with a spoon. When they are ready, she takes them out and lets them drain for a few seconds before loading them onto a paper tray.

"It's important not to fuck with them too much," she tells me. Shirley Mae curses a lot. If I ask her a question she doesn't like, she looks at me like I'm crazy, lights a cigarette, and shakes her head, all the while probably asking herself what the fuck I'm talking about.

The cornbread comes out with a golden-brown crust that is sweet and chewy. You have to let it rest a moment or you'll burn the roof of your mouth. When her cornbread nuggets break open, they let off a violent puff of steam. The bread inside is crumbly and dense. I have tried to make hot water cornbread just like hers but I can never mimic the perfect texture she gets right every time.

"Originally, I was making old-fashioned corn muffins. Then one day, early on, these two drunks come in and they order pig's feet and slaw. They was eating one of my muffins, and I overheard one of them say, 'This sure would be good if we had some hot water cornbread.' And the other guy said, 'I bet she don't even know how to make it.' Now, this pissed me the fuck off. I went back, made the hot water cornbread, and just slid it right in front of them. They both looked shocked. They ended up fighting over the last piece. I been making it ever since."

It is getting dark. Outside, motorcycles are racing down Clay Street. A bar across the way opens its doors and plays music out into the night. Every few minutes, someone walks by and asks Shirley Mae if she's got anything left to sell. Shirley Mae closes her place by 9:00 every night. She's closed, she says, but she tells them to check with her daughter inside.

She stubs out a cigarette and takes a deep breath. "This is the same food that my mamma cooked for me. I learned just by watching her. She only cooked in a skillet. So I do the same. She cooked by feel. She had me do a lot of shit in the kitchen. I worked my ass off. But I had a happy childhood; they taught me love. I loved being with my mom and dad. I was always with one or the other of them."

As a child, she went to a one-room schoolhouse with about forty kids. The bathroom was an outhouse, and the only heat source was a potbelly stove. Annie May Storm was her one teacher all through childhood, until Shirley Mae's family moved to Nashville when she was in high school. She smiles as she tells me about her life on the farm. But it was a hard life, she insists, and she's glad to be living in a city now.

An argument breaks out in the kitchen. Shirley Mae's daughter is fed up with people asking for food after closing time. The dispute takes a long time to die down. Everyone is told to get the hell out of the restaurant.

It feels like this might be a nightly incident. Shirley Mae is just too nice ever to say no to a customer. And they love her food. Everyone comes by and gives her a hug and a kiss and tells her how good her food is.

"My husband was Templeton Simpson," she tells me. "We had five kids together. There was nothing else to do. Back then, you only had three channels, and on Saturday nights, the TV would go off at eleven p.m. What else were you supposed to do after dark but enjoy yourself? He's gone now. I miss him from time to time, but I got my work to keep me busy."

Shirley Mae has had this restaurant for almost thirty years. It's a remarkable accomplishment. Her food is simple—too simple, the way she describes it. I ask what's in her turnip greens, and she looks at me bewildered. Turnips greens, she says. The recipe for her pig's feet is pig's feet, salt, and water. But everything tastes more complex than she describes it. Shirley Mae's gift is coaxing out the flavors that are intrinsic in the ingredients. She doesn't see the need to "fuck around" with aromatics and spices. The different flavors of the different muscles, cartilage, skin, and fat of the pig's feet are complex enough without adding anything else.

"All this time I been cooking and I never learned to measure things," she says. "I don't even know what a teaspoon is. How I measure is with my hand. I only know how to measure from here to here." She traces the length of her left palm with her right index finger.

Nowhere in her restaurant is there a reference to soul food. She doesn't call it that.

"I don't call what I do 'black food' or 'soul food.' It's just food. I don't mess with that other shit. When I make turnip greens, I boil up turnips greens. Why do I want ham in that? Why do I want garlic or other shit in there? And I certainly don't want anyone telling me what to call my food."

I ask her if she's been to Janice's restaurant. Not in years, she tells me. She's too busy with her own life. I suspect Janice would say the same thing if I asked her about Shirley Mae. These two ladies, upholding traditions for decades, have never been honored by magazines or given awards or other accolades, yet they are two of the most important chefs in Louisville.

I've been eating at their restaurants for years now, well before the world got hip to Southern food and cornbread. When I first arrived in Louisville, you couldn't find upscale restaurants that served fried chicken or collards or cornbread. You had to go to Shirley Mae's or Hosanna's Kitchen or Big Momma's Soul Food Kitchen or Jay's Cafeteria. Nowadays, you can't throw a stone without hitting a cornbread skillet. And the newspapers are clamoring for the recipes. I hate it that these women, the true guardians of this tradition, are getting overlooked. They are the ones who kept this food alive while the culinary world was busy fawning over European or California cuisine. For Janice and Shirley Mae, food was never about a trend or a concept. It was, and is, their heritage. And because of women like them, we now have an actual flavor profile we can reference when we talk about dishes such as pork neck and turnip greens. It's a living thing, not just words in a historical text. My first taste of pork neck was at Hosanna's; my first taste of collards was at Jay's Cafeteria; my first rib tips were at a tiny barbecue joint called Finley's, which no longer exists. I owe my career to these restaurants. And to this day, I've had no better cornbread than at Shirley Mae's.

IT IS LOGICAL for me to compare the cuisine of these two women and conclude that what they're doing is the same. They're cooking soul food. But I would be wrong in assuming this. I learned from Janice and Shirley Mae that each cornbread recipe is unique. I also learned that two African American women cooking food in Louisville aren't necessarily cooking the same food. Each has a distinct story. Shirley Mae grew up on a rural farm in Tennessee, and Janice in downtown Louisville during the civil rights movement. Janice talks freely about herself within the tradition of soul food, while Shirley Mae rejects the term. Their lives have never intertwined, and their food is as personal and as individual as they are.

There is a tendency to speak of them in the same breath, but nothing could be further from the truth. If I can't see those distinctions, that just means I have more work to do, more questions to ask, more respect to give.

When I was a young cook in New York City, one of the things that always angered me was the assumption by other cooks that when it was my turn to open a restaurant, it would be an Asian restaurant, because of my race. My ethnicity, in their minds, was something that would define my career toward a path that was both logical and without controversy. So I did the opposite. I've always been that way. When my parents urged me to go to church, I grew my hair long and smoked pot. When my high school teachers told me I should be good at math because I was Asian, I flunked on purpose and excelled in literature. When I was lectured by my father to get a job in law or medicine, I became a cook. And when my mom admonished me to marry a good Korean girl—well, that didn't work out as she wanted, either.

I was thirty years old when I moved to Louisville, Kentucky. I smoked, I drank, I had no money and no plan. I remember my mom, in a fit of exasperation and tears, asking me why I always did the opposite of what she asked. It made me feel terrible. On the surface, it seemed that my life had been one rebellious choice after another. She implored me not to ruin my life just to make a point. I had left New York City and moved to a place I knew nothing about.

Yet I realized then that I wasn't pulling away from her; I was just following my heart. I have loved reading ever since I was a little kid. I loved Johnny Cash when the other kids on my street were listening to Michael Jackson. And I've always sucked at math. Poetry has always come naturally to me. I've loved my wife from the first night I tried to steal a kiss from her in the parking lot of a bar in Louisville. And ever since I sat in the laundry room of my mom's tenement apartment building in Brooklyn reading old *Gourmet* magazines while the other kids were reading comic books, I've always wanted to be a cook.

It has taken me a lifetime to convince my mom that I wasn't trying to make her miserable on purpose; I was just pursuing my dreams, which, unfortunately, looked very different from her idea of who I would become as a Korean man in America. To this day, I've pushed back against the assumptions of what a Korean man in America is supposed to be: an accountant, a model citizen, a meek human being. These are not negative stereotypes, and mostly they're not believed out of malice. Yet they represent a crass oversimplification of a person whose identity is formed out of many years of experiences and choices.

I'm guilty of the same thing. I looked at Janice and Shirley Mae and assumed they were cooking the same things—because they were black, because they were women, because they cooked in Louisville. And though there are similarities between them, the differences are much more significant. Those differences define who they are and how they've made the choices they've made in their cuisine. Their two approaches to cornbread are not simply a variation in technique. They represent a rift in their upbringing: one rural and the other urban. I never would have made that distinction if I had not talked to them at length. I would simply have assumed that they made different cornbreads for reasons that were random. It took me a long time to understand that their choices in their cornbread recipes tell an intimate story of their past.

There was nothing terribly difficult or noble about my coming to this realization. I just took the time to get to know Janice and Shirley Mae. They made me realize that recipes can be an incredibly personal expression. A simple conversation about the origin of a recipe can lead to an entire afternoon talking about one's childhood in Tennessee. There is nothing terribly difficult about making cornbread, either. I could give you Shirley Mae's recipe in one paragraph. But you'd be missing the point. In fact, I'm not giving you Shirley Mae's or Janice's recipes—partly because they don't translate easily into words. Each of them cooks from memory, and neither can stand following recipes. They would think it silly for me to even try to figure out the measurements. But don't despair. You should try to figure out your own recipe. You've come this far with me, and I hope by now you understand that the best cooking is not about perfection, but rather the flawed process of how we aim for a desired flavor.

If you want to make cornbread, all you need is cornmeal, salt, a pinch of sugar, and some butter. You can use hot water, milk, or even a little oil if you want. Don't put eggs in it, though. And don't add too much refined flour. Mess around with the proportions, and you'll come up with a mixture you like. That's how I make cornbread at home. It comes out a little different each time, but that's the fun of it.

I've been experimenting with cornbread for almost two decades, and I've only recently discovered a recipe I like, which I'm happy to share here. It's a recipe I came up with while fooling around in the kitchen one day after I'd come back from having lunch with Janice. I was trying to re-create her pancake, and I forgot to add the leavening to a batch of dry ingredients. The result came out flat and crispy. In other words, it came out "wrong," but I liked it. And I've been making it ever since. It's not really cornbread. It's more of a lace cookie. It's unpredictable and sensitive to the weather. When it's good, it's amazing, and when it's not, it tastes like rubber. I like it because it's me. It is neither a bread nor a crispy cracker. It's something in between, something hard to define. It is me. Rice flour is not traditional in cornbread, but I'm sure by now you understand that I don't know what "traditional" even means.

LACY CORNBREAD WITH RHUBARB JAM

Lacy cornbread gets its name from the holes that form when the wet cornmeal batter hits the hot fat in the skillet. It is a satisfying way to cook cornbread, though the result is more of a crisp or a cracker than it is bread. It is important to get the proportion of cornmeal to water just right so you get the holes and the lacy result. You may have to adjust the proportions, depending on the type of cornmeal you use. And the cooking technique is a bit tricky, so you will most likely not get it right on the first try. But once you do, this will become an easy recipe to make.

I like to snack on lacy cornbread with rhubarb jam served on the side. But these cornbread crisps are versatile. Top them with thinly sliced ham or pimento cheese, or any dip that you like.

MAKES ABOUT 12 CRISPS

½ cup yellow cornmeal, sifted
2 tablespoons rice flour
¼ teaspoon salt
¾ cup water

1 cup rendered pork lard (you may need additional fat to cool the oil while frying)
Rhubarb Jam (recipe follows), for serving

In a medium bowl, combine the cornmeal, rice flour, salt, and water, stirring to blend. Set aside for 10 minutes to hydrate the cornmeal. Stir again before frying.

Set a cup of water next to the stove and have a teaspoon handy. Heat ¼ cup of the pork lard in a large skillet over medium-high heat until hot but not smoking. Slowly pour about 1 tablespoon of the batter into the pan and then pour 1 teaspoon water directly into the center of the batter. The batter should immediately begin to sizzle and form a lacy pattern. Cook for 3 minutes. Once the edges of the lace begin to turn golden brown, flip the crisp and cook for another minute. Drain on paper towels. Repeat with the remaining batter, adding more fat to the pan as necessary.

Serve very soon after cooking, with the rhubarb jam.

RHUBARB JAM | When rhubarb is in season in early summer, I make enough of this jam to get me through the fall. I love the fruity, tart, and earthy flavor of rhubarb. I add a little black pepper to give the jam a bit of spice to complement the sweetness. MAKES ABOUT 2 CUPS

2 pounds rhubarb, trimmed and diced	1 teaspoon kosher salt
1 pound fresh strawberries, hulled and diced	½ teaspoon freshly ground black pepper
1 cup fresh orange juice	2 teaspoons vanilla extract
2½ cups sugar	Juice of 1 lemon

In a medium pot, combine the rhubarb, strawberries, orange juice, sugar, salt, pepper, vanilla, and lemon juice and bring to a slow simmer over low heat, stirring constantly. Cook for 20 to 25 minutes, stirring frequently, until the fruit has broken down.

Stir the jam vigorously with a wooden spoon to break up any remaining chunks. Transfer the jam to a medium bowl and let cool to room temperature.

Pour the jam into a jar, cover, and refrigerate overnight before using. The jam will keep in the fridge for at least a month.

EPILOGUE

I'VE TRIED IN THIS BOOK TO GIVE A VOICE TO THE PEOPLE who seldom get one. I've tried to investigate cultures I didn't know a lot about. I've tried to cook food I was previously unfamiliar with. Maybe cooking the food of others is appropriation; maybe it is learning. Often I ended up with more confusion and more questions than answers. A question such as "What is Nigerian food?" never has a simple answer. In fact, even Nigerians will debate the answer endlessly. In the face of so many uncertainties, how can any of us be authorities on anything? It is disheartening at times, but it is also the reason I still yearn to learn and discover new cultures and foods I know are out there.

I believe in the power of stories. The people I met during the process of writing this book entrusted me with their stories. And I've tried to be respectful of their words as well as their craft. I've tried my best to show that their traditions are a part of an intricate lineage of American food that will only continue to grow more exciting as we all make our own connections to the foods that surround us. Our food reflects who we are as a people. And if my small journey is any indication of where we are as a culinary nation, then we are living through an incredible time in a beautiful place.

You have your own story and your own history and your own connections to make. There is good food to be discovered everywhere. All it takes are an adventurous palate and an inquisitive mind. You can link both to the foods that sit in your memories. It is amazing how the thread of connections leads somewhere, once you reach out and start pulling on it. Exploring these connections can take you to unexpected places and teach you stories that challenge your imagination. It can link two things together that you might not have thought belonged together—like buttermilk and graffiti. It is an adventure worth taking. It is a road worth exploring. It is a dish worth tasting.

ACKNOWLEDGMENTS

This book was a new adventure for me in many ways. I could not have done any of it without the brilliant minds who surround me.

Dean Crawford, you are a true mentor and teacher and friend.

Judy Pray, thank you for allowing me to roam and travel and write.

Allison McGeehon, you are tireless in your mission to make me look good.

Lia Ronnen, I am so grateful to be a part of the Artisan family.

Kim Witherspoon, it was your wise words that made me take this plunge.

Ken Goodman, really, man, you take the best photos and eat the most fried chicken.

Dimity Jones, for all your astute recipe notes and lovely pictures.

To all my restaurant folks who held it all together while I pursued my writing—thank you from the bottom of my heart.

To everyone I came across in the writing of this book, these pages belong to you. Thank you for making me laugh and cry. Thank you for sharing your time and stories and emotions and recipes. Thank you for admonishing me, yelling at me, teaching me, guiding me, and trusting me with your sacred wisdom.